A Short History of Charleston

To Ida Tanenbaum Rosen,
a schoolteacher in the public schools
of South Carolina and a lover of
books who taught me the value of both;
and to Annie and Sol Rosen,
planters (in their way) and merchants
in early 20th-century Charleston:
Charlestonians, all!

. . . and I am grateful in countless ways to my wife Susan, for her editorial assistance; to my daughters Annie and Alexandra and my son William; my family — Morris, Richard, and Debra; my old friend Tom Cole; my law firm, for the time; J. Arthur Brown; A. J. Tamsberg, Esq.; Robert Stockton, for reading the manuscript; Jay Fraser, Marjorie Peale, Robbins Brackett, Joyce Chaplin, Ruth Williams Cupp, Bill Wallace, and Martha Severens, for their assistance; Charlie Brown, for his knowledge; Sol Breibart, formerly of Rivers High School; Willie Lee Rose, Paul Gaston, William Harbaugh, Bernard Mayo, Richard Ellis, William Abbott, and Norman Graebner, of the University of Virginia history department, 1965–1969.

A Short History of Charleston

Robert N. Rosen

University of South Carolina Press

Edited by M. Rita Howe and Tom Cole
Design by Carolyn Brand
Maps by Tom Dolan

Second Edition

First edition published by Lexikos, San Francisco, July 1982
Second edition published by Peninsula Press, Charleston, 1992
First University of South Carolina Press edition published 1997 by arrangement with the author

Published in Columbia, South Carolina, by the
University of South Carolina Press

Manufactured in the United States of America

01 00 99 98   5 4 3 2

Library of Congress Cataloging-in-Publication Data

Rosen, Robert N., 1947–
    A short history of Charleston / Robert N. Rosen. —2nd ed.
        p.   cm.
    Originally published: 2nd ed. Charleston : Peninsula Press, c1992.
    Includes bibliographical references and index.
    ISBN 1–57003–197–5
    1. Charleston (S.C.)—History. I. Title.
F279.C457R67   1997
975.7'91—dc21   97–7228

Contents

Prologue

The beauty of Charleston mesmerizes people and makes it difficult for them to visualize the morality play that is Charleston's history. There is good and evil in that history, for the city is not innocent. Is Sullivan's Island the Ellis Island of black America? Or is it the scene of Edgar Allan Poe's "The Gold Bug"? Or is it just a nice oceanfront suburb? Is the Old Exchange Building a fancy architectural jewel designed to house 18th-century assemblies? Or is it the ghoulish prison of the Revolution, the place where the martyr Isaac Hayne spent his last night? Or is it the place where George Washington greeted his fellow citizens? And there is no question that slaves were sold for generations next to the very balcony from which the Declaration of Independence was read.

It is the tragic and ironic aspects of Charleston's history that give it such power. It resembles the classic Greek tragedy — its aristocratic and noble leaders were plagued by fatal flaws, by hubris, by pride, by something. They foresaw the decline of the aristocracy. As early as 1833 Hugh Legaré wrote: "We are (I am quite sure) the last of the race of South Carolina." Perhaps the drama was played out in the Civil War, which, as Sidney Andrews said, left "a city of ruins." For it is, after all, the fall of the noble hero that is the essence of Greek tragedy.

When Henry James visited Charleston in 1905, some forty years after the Civil War had ended, he also was captivated by the antique quality of life; by "the Battery of the long, curved seafront, of the waterside public garden furnished with sad old historic guns"; by Fort Sumter and the start of the Civil War. "The Forts, faintly blue on the twinkling sea," he wrote, "looked like vague marine flowers; innocence, pleasantness ruled the prospect." James, a northerner, was reacting to the start of the Civil War — the firing on the flag at Sumter. But Fort Sumter is so far from the Battery. "The Flag would have been, from the Battery," he concluded, "such a mere speck in space. . . ."

There is more. Charleston's history has a power even beyond the supposed climax, defeat in the Civil War. Her people are so complicated that the "blacks and whites all mix'd together" produced a greatness after the war—a great literature, art, and music in the twentieth century. The matrix that was Charleston "after the fall" produced Porgy and Bess, *"the Charleston," the jazz of the Jenkins Orphanage Band, the preservation movement, and the Spoleto Festival U.S.A.*

In an article that appeared in Venture *magazine in May 1969, Maggie Davis suggested that Charleston's history is difficult to explain because Charleston "has never had the kind of history we like to boast about in our textbooks." Charleston's history, she went on to say, "is not only bloodstained and wicked but continuingly unrepentant." There is just no way to explain all of the contradictions. Unlike American history, generally, it does not always have a happy ending. C. Vann Woodward, the dean of southern historians, has suggested that the South has known defeat and felt history. History is not something that happened to other people.*

The point is that Charleston remains unrepentant and proud. The city defies history, defies time, and continues to defy America. Charlestonians of all races, creeds, and colors reflect the uniqueness of their city. Charleston Blacksmith: The Work of Philip Simmons, *by John M. Vlach, tells the story of one special Charlestonian. "The old work was good," acknowledged blacksmith Philip Simmons, a black man, in 1980. He was referring to Charleston's wrought iron gates, and he observed that the scrolls "were curved nice and round. If you see it curve like that it's either 200 years old or I have done it." This is the perspective from which we approach the history of the city of Charleston.*

Good King Charles's City (1670–1720)

1

In April of 1670 a group of colonists in two English ships, the *Carolina* and a nameless sloop, entered what is now Charleston Harbor and proceeded up what is now the Ashley River. The Spanish had called it St. George's Bay. The Indians did not name the rivers, but called the entire area "Kayawah," for the tribe that inhabited it. The English ships sailed past a large, gleaming white oyster bank to their right. It was later named Oyster Point and, still later, White Point Gardens. They proceeded up the river past marshes, trees, and creeks, past the present site of the two Ashley River Bridges, and landed on the first high land on the western bank of the Ashley River, which they named Albemarle Point, now Charles Towne Landing. They were five miles from the sea, just south of an Indian village. They named the settlement Charles Town in honor of King Charles II of England.

Perhaps no other city in American history was more aptly named. Charles II, the Merry Monarch, was the son of Charles I, the hapless king beheaded by the Puritans, the Parliament, and Oliver Cromwell in 1649. Charles II fought bravely for the English crown, but was forced into a penurious and humiliating exile. In 1661, he returned to England as a king. Puritanism was in decline. Restoration England, the merry old England of bawdy theaters, wenches, witty playwrights, horse racing, formal gardens and easy virtue was in its ascendancy. And it was in "Good King Charles's Golden Days" that the city that bears his name was born. Charles was to turn forty in May 1670, just one month after the founding of Charles Town.

The character of Charleston was indelibly stamped with the character of Charles II and his reign. The aristocratic city that developed in the 18th and 19th centuries reflected Restoration England just as 18th and 19th century

Named for Charles II, King of England, the city was known as "Charles Town" during the rule of the Lord Proprietors (1670-1720), as "Charlestown" under the Royal Government and during the Revolution (1720-1783), and as "Charleston" after it was incorporated in 1783.

Opposite page
Charles II: A King fit for Charleston, and vice versa.

Boston reflected Puritan England. In fact, the early Charlestonians, like the early Bostonians, came to the New World on their own "errand into the wilderness": to recreate the luxurious, cosmopolitan, pleasure-filled world of Restoration England. Charleston was the namesake of one of the most hedonistic of English monarchs, and its unspoken mission was to build a miniature aristocratic London in the midst of a recreated English countryside inhabited by a landed gentry.

Charles's life is a treasure chest of symbols in Charleston's history. He was born on May 29, 1630, "at noon with Venus the star of love and fortune shining high over the horizon." His grandfather was French. Charles was one-quarter Italian, and he was very dark, in fact, abnormally dark, in complexion. His mother was reputed to have said that she had given birth to a black baby, and Charles, because of his skin coloring, was called a variety of names, including "the Black Boy."

Charles's astonishing appetite for women was a hallmark of his reign. He had countless mistresses before and after his marriage and fathered at least 14 illegitimate children. It was said of Charles that he was "the father of his people, or at least, a great many of them."

Four of his mistresses were actresses, the most famous being Nelly Gwynn. Nell was small in stature, with plump cheeks and dimples. Her greatest attributes were her small feet, perfect legs, and great wit. When, at a time of anti-Catholic hysteria, an angry mob approached her carriage, believing another of Charles's mistresses (Louise de Kérouälle, a Catholic) was inside, Nell yelled, "Good people, this is the Protestant whore!"

Charles loved the theater almost as much as he loved the actresses. He attended plays regularly, and he was a patron and friend to writers and poets. It should come as no surprise, then, to learn that more theaters were built in colonial Charleston than elsewhere in America. Good King Charles also loved horse racing. Under his reign it became the true "sport of kings." Banned by the Puritans, the races were revived with a vengeance by Charles. The Newmarket races became a great tradition in the 1660s and 1670s. Charlestonians were later to name a racecourse "Newmarket," and the South Carolina Jockey Club was the city's most venerable institution until after the Civil War. What was true of racing was also true of music, the arts, formal gardens, and raising dogs. All were cultivated in Restoration England, and all came to early Charles Town — together with an overindulgence in drinking.

The place names of the Carolina Low Country — Berkeley, Clarendon, Colleton, Albemarle, Monck, Ashley, Cooper — are a living monument to

The famous enlightenment philosopher John Locke. Locke was the secretary to Lord Anthony Ashley Cooper and the author of *The Fundamental Constitutions of Carolina* which attempted to create an elaborate feudal society in early South Carolina.

Restoration England. They are the names of friends, counselors, or supporters (from time to time) of Charles II. Ironically, the name most common to Charleston's history, that of Anthony Ashley Cooper, Earl of Shaftesbury, belonged to a man not always loyal to the King. As a Lord Proprietor, he was unable to devote much time to Carolina during the middle years of Charles's reign because he was busily engaged in undermining his sovereign lord and was imprisoned in the Tower of London for a time. Charles did not have much use for Shaftesbury by 1677. "Few men," said Clarendon, "knew Lord Ashley better than the King himself did, and had a worse opinion of his integrity."

Yet Charles forgave most of those who plotted against him, including many who had been involved in the execution of his father. He was kindly, tolerant, pleasant, and a good king — a man who enjoyed worldly pleasures to the utmost.

On June 23, 1666, Robert Sandford took possession of the whole country of Carolina "for his Majesty Charles the Second, King of England, and to the use of the Proprietors." The Lord Proprietors owned and governed the colony, which was also named in honor of Charles II, but that name was really a matter of convenience since the French had already named the area "Carolina" in honor of Charles IX of France!

The Early Years: In 1669 three ships, the *Carolina*, the *Port Royal,* and the *Albemarle*, left England filled with colonists from England and Ireland bound for Carolina. Only the *Carolina* completed the voyage; the other two ships were damaged or lost in hurricanes but the passengers survived.

When they arrived in the new colony of Carolina in early 1670, the colonists followed in the path of Robert Sandford, an explorer sent earlier by the Lord Proprietors. Sandford had originally landed in what is now the North Edisto River, and the official ceremony by which England claimed Carolina had already taken place either on Seabrook Island or Wadmalaw Island. Sandford had befriended the Kiawah Indians and had visited with their chief (Cacique) in a town near the site of present-day Rockville. He described it as "divers fields of maiz with many little houses . . . ," and he also saw the Indians' circular house of state. It was the Cacique of the Kiawahs who urged the English to settle on their lands. Originally the settlers planned to go to Port Royal near Beaufort, and the *Carolina* and a sloop that replaced one of the lost ships first went to Port Royal. At the insistence of the Cacique, however, the sloop left Port Royal to view the site at Albemarle Point. When it returned the colonists discussed whether to locate Charles Town at Port Royal or on the Ashley River. "The Governor adhearing for Kayawah & most of us being of a temper to follow though wee knew noe reason for it." So, for no ascertainable reason with no overall plan, at the insistence of an unknown

Although historians credit the Cacique with noble intentions, his tribe was weaker than those inland and he befriended the English for strategic reasons. A statue of him stands at Charles Towne Landing.

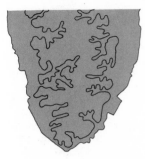

Charleston's original water line at high tide.

Indian, the colonists moved to the lands of the Kiawah, on the Ashley River, to establish Charles Town and Carolina.

Life in the wilderness at Charles Town was not as difficult as it had been in Virginia and New England. By the 1670s, North America and the West Indies had been settled by the English: Virginia since 1607, Massachusetts since 1620, and Barbados since 1625. But the early years, from 1670 until the 1720s, still proved trying.

The first settlement was a fort. The greatest threat was not from Indians but from the Spanish who had colonized Florida. Even a casual visitor to the original site can see that the high land afforded the colonists a view of the river so that Spanish ships could be spotted long before they got within shooting distance of the town. The original settlement was not situated directly on the Ashley River, but up a large creek, Old Towne Creek. The first Charlestonians lived "more like souldiers in a garrison than planters." They slept within fortified walls at night and went out to work the fields during the day. They planted on ten-acre plots and grew oranges, lemons, limes, pomegranates, figs, wheat, potatoes, flax, and tobacco. There were also Barbadians among the earliest settlers, and they attempted to produce staple money crops — sugar, silk, tobacco, and cotton — but with no success. More Barbadians arrived in 1671. (Charles Towne Landing, a state park, has recreated this period with remarkable accuracy.)

On August 25, 1671, a parliament was held. And by 1672 Charles Town consisted of 30 houses and 200 people. The Church of England was the established church, but there was no minister. Governor Sayle wrote to Lord Ashley Cooper complaining of the "want of a Godly and orthodox minist'r."

The permanent site of Charles Town was established by a decision of the Grand Council: "we let you know that Oyster Point is the place we do appoint for the port town of which you are to take notice and call it Charles Town."

The early settlers explored the area through the early 1670s to ascertain whether another site for the town would be more desirable, and at least as early as February 1672 they had decided to move the town from Albemarle Point to Oyster Point. On December 17, 1679, the Grand Council decided that Charles Town would be moved to Oyster Point, and, in the spring of 1680, the town was moved back down the Ashley River to a site just north of the large, gleaming, white oyster bank that the original settlers had passed on their journey up the river in 1670. By 1682, there were 100 houses at the new site.

Planning the City: As early as August of 1670 the Proprietors exhibited an interest in the planning of the town. The original plan was based on the checkerboard design proposed by Hooke and Wren for London after the great fire of 1666. The town was to be bounded by present-day Meeting Street (on the west), Broad Street (on the north), Water Street (on the south), and the Cooper River (on the east). The land to the south was variously called Coming's Point (for John Coming who had owned it) or White Point ("no doubt from the whiteness of the oyster shells upon it"). The early city was bounded on three sides by water: on the east by the Cooper River; on the north and south, by large creeks; and, on the west, by a wall.

Of the early American cities, it was only in Charles Town and Philadelphia that the colonists laid out streets before any buildings were built. In Charles Town a site was reserved at the outset for a church — the corner of Broad and Meeting Streets. Originally the Church of England was located there. It was called the English Church or St. Philip's (St. Michael's stands there now), and was built of black cypress. Charles Town and the neck of land between the Ashley and Cooper Rivers made up one parish, "St. Philip's in Charles Town."

In 1682, the town was described by a visitor as "regularly laid out into large and capacious streets, which to buildings is a great ornament and beauty. In it they have reserved convenient places for a church Town House and other public structures, an artillery ground for the exercise of their militia, and wharves for the convenience of their trade and shipping." The population of Charles Town increased. It was estimated to be 1,000 to 1,200 in 1690. At the same time, the population of New York, then called New Amsterdam, was 3,900; Boston's was 7,000; Newport's was 2,600; Philadelphia's was 4,000. Charles Town was, therefore, the fifth largest city in America by 1690.

Other churches were soon built. A second one — the Circular Church — was probably built between 1680 and 1690. It was also known as the Presbyterian Church or the White Meeting, which is how Meeting Street got its name. It was organized by Presbyterians from Scotland and Ireland, Congregationalists from England and New England, and French Protestants or Huguenots (who were Presbyterian in their form of church government). Between 1687 and 1693, a French Huguenot church was built on the site of the present Huguenot church at 136 Church Street (across from the Dock Street Theater). In 1700, a Baptist church was built on the site of the present First Baptist Church at 61 Church Street.

The town had not expanded greatly by 1700. It still consisted only of the land between the Cooper River and Meeting Street. In 1698 no street had a name, but, by 1701, the streets had been given names, many of which survive to this day. The main street was present-day Church Street. Other streets

Lord Ashley instructed governor Sir John Yeamans, to lay out Charles Town "into regular streets, for be the buildings never so mean and thin at first, yet as the town increases in riches and people, the void places will be filled up and the buildings will grow more beautiful."

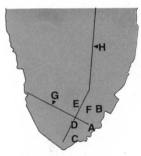

A. Court of Guard (now Exchange Building)
B. Craven's Bastion (Market St. at East Bay)
C. Granville's Bastion (Masonic Temple)
D. Colleton Bastion
E. Carteret Bastion (Cumberland St.)
F. First English Church (St. Philip's; site now St. Michael's)
G. Broad St.
H. Meeting St.

A. Charles Town
B. Charles Towne Landing
C. The Neck
D. Ashley River
E. Cooper River
F. Sullivan's Is.
G. Long Is. (Isle of Palms)

Sullivan's Island was named for the first man to land in 1670. Florence Sullivan was not perhaps an admirable founder. Described by contemporaries as an "ill-natured buggerer of children," he was sent to the island to man the signal gun.

included Queen, Broad, Elliot, and Tradd. East Bay Street was simply called the Bay. Charles Town was a fortified city-state containing six bastions or battlements. Three bastions stood on the Cooper River: Craven's Bastion at the end of what is today Market Street (this was the northeast corner of Charles Town in 1700); Blake's Bastion where the Exchange Building stands today; and Granville's Bastion, at the site of the present-day Masonic Temple, where the High Battery begins. Water Street was a creek, and a fortified wall ran along its northern bank and around the entire town. At Broad and Meeting Streets was a half-moon (later called Johnson's Raveline) and a drawbridge. Where Meeting and Cumberland Streets now intersect stood Carteret's Bastion. Charles Town — in many ways a medieval fortified city — was alive and well on the coast of Carolina in 1700.

Charles Town in 1700 was a trading center, a market town where the products of the interior were brought for sale. The harbor soon was dotted with wharves and sailing ships of every description. Grand private homes had already been built, some complete with drawbridges and wharves. The road out of Charles Town was called the Broad Way and was, by all accounts, beautiful "with oderiferous and fragrant woods, and pleasantly green all year." The countryside was dotted with numerous farms and plantations, and Charleston Neck (the neck of land between the Ashley and Cooper Rivers) was settled with plantations.

In 1698, a post office and a public library were established. The public library, probably the first in America, was established by the Reverend Thomas Bray, the Bishop of London's commissary in Maryland. The Proprietors and citizens of Charles Town contributed to the library, which was located in the rectory of the minister of Charles Town. The legislature provided, through various acts, for its upkeep. All inhabitants could borrow any book.

Those Who Came: Huguenots, or French Protestants, were rapidly assimilated into Charles Town society. By the late 1690s they were granted full rights of citizenship and the right to own land so long as they pledged allegiance to the King. (All Christians were granted freedom of conscience — except "Papists.") The Huguenots were not poor; they had, after all, paid for their voyage to the New World. They began life in Carolina by growing wheat and barley and burning tar for market. One of the first Charleston Huguenots, the mother of Gabriel Manigault and later one of the wealthiest Charlestonians, wrote home: "Since leaving France we had experienced every kind of difficulties — disease, pestilence, famine, poverty, hard labor, I have been for six months together without tasting bread." From these humble, hard-working French Protestants came such great Charleston names as Legaré, Guérard, Gaillard, Laurens, Manigault, Mouzon, Prioleau, and Ravenel.

The Irish, too, were early settlers in Charles Town. An Irishman, Richard Kyrle, was governor in 1684. James Moore, another Irishman, was governor in 1700. The original Lynches, Rutledges, and Barnwells were Irish.

It is perhaps a little difficult to appreciate fully the relationship between Barbados and early Charles Town. In a sense, Charles Town was an outpost of Barbados, a colony of a colony, well into the 1700s. Some historians claim that Carolina existed to take in Barbadians because that island had reached capacity. In 1674 there were 50,000 whites and 80,000 blacks living on Barbados, including some Scots and Irish, a few Dutch and French, and a few Portuguese Jews.

Certainly, Charles Town reflected its Barbadian heritage. In 18th-century Barbados, one found a Bay Street, a Broad Street, and a St. Michael's Church. Barbadian parishes included St. Andrew's, St. James, St. John, and Christ Church — all familiar names of local Low Country parishes. Charleston's famous "single house," complete with piazza, was a typical West Indian and Barbadian house. The first slave code was copied from that of Barbados, and the judicial system was copied from a Barbadian act. The original form of government and its military organization were Barbadian. The colonial government adopted the Barbadian method of election, that is, by parish.

Threats to Safety: Pirates of various descriptions inhabited coastal South Carolina before Charles Town was founded. They roamed the South Atlantic and the Caribbean, free to loot because the fledgling governments of the area were unable to stop them.

In its infancy, Charles Town was constantly menaced by pirates. In 1717, the British government cracked down on piracy and quickly drove the pirates from the Bahamas and surrounding areas. Many of them fled to coastal Carolina. One famous pirate who appeared off Charles Town at this time was Edward Thatch (or Teach), more popularly known as "Blackbeard." In June 1718 Blackbeard's fleet of four ships and 400 men seized eight or nine ships and a number of prominent Charlestonians including Samuel Wragg, a mem-

In September of 1699, according to Mrs. St. Julian Ravenel's *Charleston,* a "tremendous hurricane struck the town. The water rose to the second story of the houses, wharves were swept away, vessels driven ashore, etc., but few lives were lost in the town."

Blackbeard: The prototypical pirate held prominent Charlestonians hostage.

Colonel William Rhett: "A man of violent temper but of great courage and ability" who captured Stede Bonnet. The oldest house in Charleston is the Rhett House, 54 Hasell Street

Stede Bonnet, terrified of hanging, begged Governor Johnson and Colonel Rhett for pity. He offered to separate "all my Limbs from my Body, only reserving the use of my Tongue to call continually on, and to pray to the Lord . . . ."

ber of the colonial Council and his four-year-old son, William. Blackbeard sent one of his captives to Governor Johnson at Charles Town with the message that unless certain medicines were sent within two days, the governor would receive the heads of Wragg and the other captive Charlestonians. The demand was met. Wragg and the others were saved, and Charles Town determined to put an end to this menace. (Blackbeard escaped from Carolina, but was killed shortly thereafter by a military band sent out by Governor Spotswood of Virginia.)

One of the most famous pirates to prey on Charles Town was Stede Bonnet, the "Gentleman Pirate." Bonnet was no ordinary pirate. He had served in the army of Barbados where he reached the rank of major. He came from a good family, attained some wealth, and became a pirate because, as one historian said "his mind was disordered." He was, in fact, with Blackbeard when Samuel Wragg and other hostages were taken.

In August and September of 1718, when news arrived in Charles Town that Bonnet's pirates were at Cape Fear, North Carolina, Colonel William Rhett set forth to capture them. After a fierce battle in which both the pirate ships and Rhett's ships hit ground and remained stationary with guns blasting at each other until the tide changed, Rhett was victorious. Eighteen South Carolinians were killed, but Bonnet was captured and placed under house arrest with only two sentries guarding him. Dressed as a woman, he escaped and hid on Sullivan's Island for a time before he was recaptured.

Bonnet and his crew were tried by a jury in Charles Town. Without counsel to represent him (as was the practice at that time), Bonnet was interrogated by a ruthless, though learned judge, Nicholas Trott, Chief Justice of the colony. Bonnet's defense was that he had never intended to be a pirate but that he was overpowered by his crew. He was convicted, nevertheless, and sentenced to hang.

Public sympathy somewhat favored Bonnet because of his desperate pleas, his gentlemanly nature, and his conduct during the trial. Colonel Rhett was so moved he offered to accompany Bonnet to England to place his case before the King. Governor Johnson, however, did not waver. He set the execution date for December 10, 1718, and on that date Bonnet was hanged at White Point. It is said that Bonnet was in such fright of the hanging "that he was scarce sensible when he came to the place of execution."

Numerous other pirates were hanged that year — 49 in all. An expedition headed by Governor Johnson led to the killing of another famed pirate, Richard Worley, and the execution of his 23-man crew. The skull and crossbones once flew over the seas just outside Charles Town, but the bones of the pirates that flew her lie buried somewhere downtown. According to the historian Isabella Leland, in *Charleston: Crossroads of History*, they were buried below the low water mark in the marsh: "Their bones may rest today beneath some downtown mansion, as the city long since grew beyond the old low water marks, and tradition gives the location as near modern Meeting and Water Streets."

A. Massachusetts (1620)
B. Virginia (1607)
C. Carolina (1670)
D. Charles Town
E. Port Royal
F. Present-day South Carolina (separated from North Carolina, 1713)

Early Charles Town, constructed as a fort, was also plagued by war. "Settled in the very caps of the Spaniards," it became a military objective of the Spanish from its first days. In August 1686 there were 150 Spaniards, Indians, and mulattoes outside the city preparing to attack. Because the militia organized and a great storm came up, the invaders withdrew. Later, in 1706, Charles Town was the object of a joint French and Spanish attack during Queen Anne's War (1702-1713). The invasion, plotted in Havana, failed; the Spanish threat, however, remained.

Indians, too, threatened early Charles Town. There was war with the Westoe Indians in 1673 and with the Stono Indians shortly thereafter. The worst Indian war was the Yemassee War of 1715-1717. It was caused by the usurpation of the Yemassee lands, various abuses inflicted on the Yemassees by unscrupulous traders, and the misuse of Yemassee women. Fifteen Indian nations, including the Creeks, were involved. The war dragged on for two years and at one time a force of six or seven hundred Indians were within striking distance of the town. Governor Craven raised an army, declared martial law, sent to England for supplies, and fought the Indians all over the colony.

One result of the war was the crystallization in the minds of Charlestonians that the Lord Proprietors were both unwilling to send aid and unable to protect the colony. Resentment against the Proprietors, which had been growing for some time, increased dramatically, and in 1717 agents of the colony presented their case before Parliament.

The names South Carolina and North Carolina came into use in the late 1600s, but "Carolina" was one colony until 1713 when a separate governor was appointed for North Carolina.

The Lord Proprietors, who had failed to protect the colonists against the Indians and Spaniards, made matters worse by vetoing a dozen laws, some of them quite important, that would have given the colonial Commons the right to choose the colonial treasurer (the public receiver), encouraged immigration by whites, regulated Indian trade, and distributed lands seized in the Yemassee War.

In what can only be described as a revolution against the Proprietors, angry Carolinians met in Charles Town on the night of November 17, 1719, and formed a revolutionary Assembly. This Assembly refused to recognize the vetoes. It sought, at first, to continue Governor Johnson (a proprietary appointee) in office, but he refused to serve. Then James Moore was elected governor. South Carolina sought to become a royal colony instead of a proprietary one.

The revolution in South Carolina was assisted by powerful forces in England. The Board of Trade and Plantations in England and the collector of the King's customs favored the abolition of proprietary colonies in general. Maryland, for example, once the proprietary colony of Lord Baltimore, became a royal colony in 1690.

The result of all this agitation was that South Carolina became a royal colony when General Sir Francis Nicholson arrived in May 1721 and became provisional royal governor.

In 1717 the fortifications around Charles Town were removed to allow for expansion. Until that time, few houses had been built outside of the walled city, but afterward the city began to spread northward across a creek located at present-day Market Street and westward past present-day Meeting Street. A few buildings still standing in Charleston date from this period. The old magazine located on Cumberland Street was the magazine of Carteret Bastion, and is the oldest structure still standing in Charleston. Colonel Rhett erected his family mansion on Hasell Street about 1712, and it still stands at 54 Hasell Street — the oldest residence in Charleston.

The streets of early Charles Town were, like the streets of all English and colonial American towns, filthy and unpaved. In 1698 the Assembly declared that the inhabitants should put "broken oyster shells" on the streets in front of their homes. Houses of this period were mainly constructed of wood, the most common materials being cypress and mahogany. In 1698 Charles Town experienced its first serious fire, and in 1713 a hurricane wreaked havoc in the town. The Assembly decreed that, thereafter, houses be built of brick, but the law was largely ignored.

The economy of earliest Charles Town was a trading one. Protected by English mercantile laws, the first Charlestonians exported deerskins and furs to England and shipped port, corn, naval stores, and lumber to Barbados and the West Indies. By 1710 Charlestonians were trading with the Dutch in South America and with Antigua, Nevis, and the Bahamas. Through the port of Charles Town were sent slaves and hoops, pitch, tar, beef, rice, candles, butter and peas. From the West Indies and the "Caribees" came rum, sugar, molasses, cotton, and salt. Early fortunes were made in trade and commerce as well as planting.

"Cards, dice, the bottle and horses engross prodigious portions of time and attention: the gentlemen (planters and merchants) are mostly men of the turf and gamesters," snorted the Puritan Yankee, Josiah Quincy, about Charles Town in 1773.

A Short History of Charleston

Charleston's proud reputation as a free and open — some would say decadent — city dates from the earliest days of its existence. Alone among the major colonial cities, Charles Town did not exclude undesirable strangers from its city limits. As early as 1702 women of "ill fame" openly approached men on the streets at night. Gambling was common, but at the same time, it was illegal not to attend church on Sunday, and all gaming was forbidden on the Sabbath. Authorities were constantly inspecting the streets to enforce the laws.

Unfortunately, not much is known about Charles Town's earliest inns and taverns. But if Charles Town was at all like its sister towns, taverns flourished. French cooking and Madeira wine, for example, were served by the innkeeper, Peter Poinsett. At any rate, the foremost historian of colonial cities, Carl Bridenbaugh, flatly states that "Charles Town was probably the least religious of all the towns." This may have been because of the variety of religions represented. In 1702 Charles Town was 42 percent Anglican, 45 percent Calvinist (including the Huguenots), 10 percent Baptist, 2.5 percent Quaker, and Jews were allowed to worship freely under the Fundamental Constitution. Religious preferences were as diverse as the people.

By the end of the proprietary period, Charles Town was no longer just a little fort. It was a true city with a population in the thousands, handsome buildings, and expanding country plantations. Since it could relax its military guard somewhat, there was time to concentrate on building the ideal city of Restoration England. Ashley Cooper, Lord Shaftesbury, had died in exile in 1683, believing, so it is said, that men's souls become a part of the stars after their death and give the stars life. Charles II died in 1685, but his spirit and the spirit of his age were alive and well across the Atlantic Ocean.

The Colonial City (1720–1765)

2

Before there was an Old South, there was a colonial South. And before there was a Charleston in the tradition of the Old South, there was the Charlestown of colonial times. It was the only large city south of Philadelphia, and the economic, social, and political center of the Low Country — a region that eventually extended from the Georgia Sea Islands on the south, to the Pee Dee River on the north, and inland more than 60 miles. Charlestown's influence in the 18th century spread beyond the Carolinas to Alabama, Georgia and Florida. Indeed, as Carl Bridenbaugh has written in *Myths and Realities*, "Savannah, St. Augustine, Pensacola and Mobile prospered as entrepôts for their particular areas and for certain commodities, but always their commercial life was connected with and subsidiary to that of the Low Country metropolis. No wonder that as provincial planters looked out at the world through the Charles Town window their little rivers appeared to be the sources of a great sea."

How did the vulnerable Charles Town, the only fortified city in English America, become Charlestown, fourth largest, most beautiful, and wealthiest city in colonial America? The answer lies in the shipping trade. Rice, indigo, and slavery ("black ivory") were the major ingredients in the original Low Country recipe, and it was on that simple but powerful economy that colonial Charlestown was built.

The first great fortunes of Charlestown were amassed by merchants, not planters. While the South of a later era looked down its nose at trade, early Charlestown reveled in it. The heyday of colonial Charlestown as a great trading port lasted from the 1730s to the 1820s. In his brilliant work, *Charleston in the Age of the Pinckneys*, George C. Rogers, Jr., described Charleston's golden age, which "coincided with the last century of the age of sailing vessels.

Charlestonians had a pleasantry that the Ashley and Cooper Rivers came together to form the Atlantic Ocean. Charlestown *was* the center of its own universe: the major city of the southern half of North America outside of Mexico, one of the leading American ports, home of the richest and most cosmopolitan people in all America.

Opposite page
A view of Charles Town from the Cooper River: busy harbor, St. Philip's Church on the right.

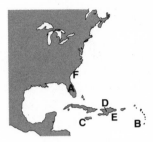

A. Spanish Florida
B. Barbados
C. Jamaica
D. Hispaniola
E. Santo Domingo
F. Charlestown

As long as the age of sail lasted, Charleston was on the main Atlantic highway, which circumnavigated the Bermuda High. Vessels leaving England, or leaving any European port for North America, generally sailed southwestardly to the Azores to catch the trade winds and then with full sail made for the West Indies, Barbados standing out front like a doorman to welcome all to the New World. They next made their way through the West Indies to the Gulf Stream. From the Florida Keys to Cape Hatteras they hugged the American coast before veering off to England and northern Europe. It was a great circle, and Charleston was on its western edge."

The building of a great port, as well as the docks, wharves, and industry to support it, was the foremost activity in colonial Charlestown. There were at least two wharves as early as 1704. By 1739 at least eight wharves jutted out into the Cooper River. All the wharves, or "bridges" as they were called, were located on the Cooper River between Granville's Bastion (the site of the present day Masonic Temple at the beginning of High Battery) and Dock Street (Queen Street since 1739). The "Middle Bridge" was the largest. It boasted eleven warehouses and a market. There were no lighthouses, so mariners aimed for St. Philip's steeple. "Notwithstanding we have few ships of our own," Governor Glen wrote in 1751, "Cooper River appears sometimes a kind of floating market, and we have Numbers of Canoes, Boats and Pettygues that Ply incessantly bringing down the Country Produce to Town and returning." The "floating market" was, of course, serviced by suppliers of all kinds: artisans, coopers shipyards, insurance companies, ropemakers, tavernkeepers, and retail shops.

There were even docks on the Ashley River in 1773, and South Bay Street at the southernmost tip of the city accommodated them. The street known earlier simply as Bay Street was renamed East Bay, and although South Bay has disappeared, the "East" in East Bay remains.

The port of Charlestown was trading heavily with English cities by 1742. As a matter of fact, trade with England was six times greater than that with other American ports. There was regular passenger and shipping service between Charlestown and New York after 1728, but little direct trade with Boston.

The bustling port was only the visible symbol of the trading and merchandising ability of colonial Charlestonians. "Merchandise and trade," wrote Edward McCrady, "were the foundation stones of most, if not all, the great fortunes, in South Carolina." The earliest Indian traders bartered beads, cloth, and hatchets for deerskins and other pelts. It was these items that constituted Charlestown's earliest and largest exports. Deerskins and beaver skins remained a major export well into the 18th century. Early merchants sold Indian captives as slaves in the West Indies, and bought blacks, first in the West Indies and then in Africa. They traded naval stores — lumber, pitch, tar staves, turpentine — for sugar and rum. And, once rice and indigo were cultivated, the traders exchanged these for the manufactured goods of England. "The proceeds of this trade," wrote McCrady, "went into lands and negroes."

The colonial merchants included Charlestonians of nearly every background. They were not aristocrats, but sons of English, French, Irish, or Barbadian middle-class or yeoman farmers. They were self-made men who, like all pioneers, built their fortunes on hard work and ingenuity. The earliest was Isaac Mazyck, a Huguenot from Liège, Belgium, and France, who traded with the West Indies as early as 1688. The wealthiest merchant and probably the wealthiest man in America was Gabriel Manigault, another Huguenot. Joseph Wragg became wealthy trading in slaves. The Indian trade, the fur trade, and foreign trade combined to make Samuel Eveleigh, Samuel Wragg, Arthur Middleton, and Madam Sarah Rhett wealthy. James Crokatt, a native of Scotland, began as an Indian trader, built his own wharf (Crokatt's Bridge), amassed a fortune, and returned to England. Other great colonial merchants were Miles Brewton, Robert Pringle, John Edwards, John Beswicke, and John Nickleson. Andrew Rutledge, a brother of John, Hugh, and Edward, was the largest retail merchant in the Carolinas.

Charlestown merchants spread out all over the region. The Kershaw brothers established a store at a place called Pine Tree, which later became Camden, South Carolina. Charlestown merchants established stores at Cainhoy, Moncks Corner, Rantowle's on the Stono River, and Jacksonborough on the Edisto River.

The great merchants eventually became great planters, for the ideal both in 18th century England and America was the English country gentleman. Ownership of a vast estate and a great country house with leisure time to pursue hunting, riding, and the cultivation of the mind — this was the ideal of the age, the legacy of Charles II. Early Charlestonians, like the Englishmen they were (or, in the case of the French Huguenots, the Irish, or the Scots, like the Englishmen they would become) dreamed of living the life of a country squire.

Plantations Develop: The transition from an overwhelmingly merchant to an overwhelmingly planter economy in Carolina and the resulting changes in the city of Charlestown can be attributed to the tremendous growth in the size of the rice crop. How rice came to be cultivated in Carolina is not clear. The Proprietors sent over a bushel to try out, apparently without success. And Jean Watt wrote in 1726 that "it was by a woman that Rice was transplanted into Carolina." Yet others believe that it came from Africa on slave ships. Some historians credit Dr. Henry Woodward with introducing rice to Carolina. Dr. Woodward, an original settler and friend of the Cacique of the Kiawah, received seed rice from Madagascar, and he and others experimented with its cultivation.

Whatever the source, African slavery was the engine that fueled the production of rice. As Peter Wood wrote in *Black Majority,* "One fact which can be clearly documented . . . is that during precisely those two decades after 1695 when rice production took permanent hold in South Carolina the African portion of the population drew equal to, and then surpassed, the European portion."

The European settlers of Carolina had little knowledge of how to cultivate rice. It had not been grown in England or northern Europe, and England consumed comparatively little rice before 1700. Black slaves probably taught the white planters how to cultivate it since Africans had been cultivating it for centuries. In the Congo-Angola region, rice was so abundant that it sold for little or nothing. It was so prevalent on the "Windward Coast" in present-day Ghana that the area became known as the Rice Coast. Eighteenth-century Englishmen noted that rice "forms the chief part of the African's sustenance," and that Africans were quite familiar with the cultivation of rice fields. The planters obviously knew the value of slaves who knew how to cultivate rice because advertisements for slaves often indicated their origin. (One advertisement, for example, read: "from the Windward Rice Coast.") The cleaning and husking of rice, another major problem, was, once again, probably resolved by African slaves. The mortar-and-pestle technique used in colonial Carolina was known to and used by native Africans at that time.

No matter who knew how to do what, the rice planters of Carolina grew rich, so rich that they became the wealthiest people in the American colonies. And rice became one of the staple crops shipped through the port of Charlestown.

The cultivation of indigo seemed to fit naturally with the cultivation of rice. Indigo was the source of the blue dye so much in demand in the English textile industry that, after 1748, Parliament granted a bounty to encourage production. Indigo was already a popular crop in the West Indies before it was introduced into Carolina by Eliza Lucas, whose father was Governor of

"Opinions differ about the manner in which rice hath been naturalized in Carolina," one 18th-century observer wrote. "But — whether the province may have acquired it by a shipwreck, or whether it may have been carried there with slaves, or whether it be sent from England, it is certain that the soil is favorable to it." And indigo, because it needed no work in the winter months, was compatible with the cultivation of rice and became the second staple crop of Carolina.

Antigua, and who later became the wife of Chief Justice Charles Pinckney and the mother of General Charles Cotesworth Pinckney and General Thomas Pinckney, heroes of the Revolution. It was Lucas' father who encouraged her interest in botany and sent her not only indigo but a man to instruct her on how to cultivate it and extract the dye. After numerous failures, she succeeded in producing it on her plantation at Wappoo, across from Charlestown.

Part of Carolina's success with indigo was the purity and quality of its product, for which an experienced London merchant, Moses Lindo, the "Surveyor and Inspector General of Indigo" in Charlestown after 1762, was responsible.

Plantations in colonial Carolina were numerous and varied. On Edisto Island in 1732, for example, plantations varied from 27 acres to 1,610 acres. The average number of slaves on each was 120. Some plantations consisted of thousands of acres complete with rice swamps, indigo fields, and woods that produced naval stores and lumber. According to Governor Glen in 1751, a white overseer (a manager hired to run a plantation for the owners) could manage 30 slaves. Unlike cotton, rice and indigo were best cultivated in small units.

Most of the great plantations of the Low Country date from the colonial era: Accabee on the Ashley River, Laurens' Mepkin on the Cooper River, Charles Pinckney's Snee Farm in Christ Church parish, Middleton Place, Drayton Hall, Garden's Otranto on Goose Creek, Manigaults' The Oaks, Edward Fenwick's Fenwick Hall on John's Island, and hundreds of others located on the rivers, streams, and creeks fanning out from the Ashley and the Cooper. These natural waterways provided a ready and inexpensive transportation system by which rice, indigo, and other produce were floated to Charlestown.

The planters did not just come to town; they lived in town. The old Charleston saying that "Carolina is in the spring a paradise, in the summer a hell, and in the autumn a hospital" was basically true. The great planters left their plantations for Charlestown in May to escape yellow fever and malaria. They repaired to their Charlestown houses during the season until November or December when they could return. This gave Charlestown a unique character in that the country planters became the elite of the city. Most of them built "town houses" in the city to escape "the country fevers" (mainly malaria and smallpox) and the terrible heat of the summer. They could also escape the doldrums of rural life, for Charlestown offered theater, music, dance, polite society, good food, and intellectual stimulation. For many, the town house became their real home.

By 1750, Henry Laurens said simply that the planters were "full of

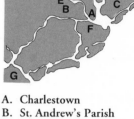

A. Charlestown
B. St. Andrew's Parish
C. Christ Church Parish
D. Middleton Pl.
E. Drayton Hall
F. James Is.
G. Edisto Is.

Former plantations Otranto and Snee Farm are now the names of suburban developments. Middleton Place and Drayton Hall, on the Ashley River Road (State Highway 61), have been carefully preserved, but developers and the state highway department have all but destroyed the once beautiful colonial highway, one of the oldest in America. Fenwick Hall on John's Island is now an alcohol rehabilitation facility — an ironic memorial to Charleston's colonial way of life.

money," and they were. They developed a style of life at Charlestown that was the delight of 18th-century America. J. Hector St. John de Crèvecouer, a native of France who became an American citizen, traveled through the colonies in the 1780s. Of Charlestown, he wrote: "Charles-Town is, in the north, what Lima is in the south, both are Capitals of the richest provinces of their respective hemispheres: you may therefore conjecture, that both cities must exhibit the appearances necessarily resulting from riches . . . Here the produce of this extensive territory concentres . . . The inhabitants are the gayest in America; it is called the centre of our beau monde. . . ."

Charlestown's wealthy planters and merchants built the grandest homes in America during the colonial era. Miles Brewton began construction of his home on lower King Street in 1767. It was designed by Ezra White, architect and builder from London. Josiah Quincy dined with Miles Brewton and found ""the grandest hall I ever beheld, azure blue satin window curtains, rich blue paper with gilt, mashee borders, most elegant pictures, excessive grand and costly looking glasses . . . At Mr. Brewton's sideboard was very magnificent plate: a very exquisitely wrought Goblet, most excellent workmanship and singularly beautiful. A very fine bird kept familiarly playing over the room, under our chairs and the table, picking up the crumbs, etc., and perching on the window, sideboard and chairs: vastly pretty!" This mansion, which still stands at 27 King Street, has been called the finest town house ever erected in the colonies.

Great mansions were built outside of the old walls of the original fortified city. Colonel Rhett's home was eventually surrounded by Ansonborough, laid out in 1746. Church Street was extended southward over a creek. The housing boom continued throughout the century. From 1768 to 1773, more than 300 houses were constructed on the Bay, on the banks of the Ashley River, in White Point, and in Ansonborough, Charlestown's fashionable first suburb.

Further Growth: The city grew in all directions: north, south, east, and west. It grew east by adding numerous large wharves, all of which have disappeared over time. Undoubtedly some lie under landfills that expanded into the Cooper River. The streets themselves are now called "wharves," like North Adgers Wharf.

The building of wharves continued up the peninsula during the late 1700s until wharves lined the entire Cooper River waterfront to present-day Calhoun Street. Christopher Gadsden built perhaps the largest wharf in colo-

Legend has it that when the Miles Brewton House was used by the British as a headquarters during the Revolution, its owner Rebecca Motte stayed in the house and hid her daughters in the attic. The British officers were not supposed to know they were there, but, on his departure, the British commander is said to have casually looked up at the ceiling and remarked how unfortunate it was he was unable to meet the rest of the family.

Opposite page
Built in 1769: The Miles Brewton House, 27 King Street, was the headquarters for two occupying armies.

nial America on the Cooper River, between present-day Laurens Street and Calhoun Street (where the Port Authority terminals and Dockside are now located.) Beginning in 1767 at North End, Gadsden's "Stupendous Work" jutted 840 feet into the river and had docking facilities for up to 12 ships. Gadsden dock was only a part of his enterprise. His housing development next to the docks, known as Gadsden's Middlesex (now demolished) was alluring because of its close proximity to the shops on the wharves that conveniently sold firewood, lumber, bricks, lime, and building materials.

One way to keep fish fresh was to keep them *alive* in watertight compartments in the ships that transported them to Charlestown. An enterprising Philadelphian did just that in 1767 when he sold fish at Wragg's Wharf from a boat called a "Smack."

Also along the North Bay (yes, there was a North Bay Street, too, at one time!) were ferryboats such as Andrew Hibben's to take one into Hobcaws across the Cooper River. "We were rowed," one New Englander who took the trip wrote, "by six negroes, four of whom had *nothing on* but their kind of breeches, scarce sufficient for a covering."

A visit to 18th-century Charlestown would have had to include a walk down the Bay where, looking toward the harbor, nearly a hundred vessels would have been at anchor. If it were after hurricane season, from November to March, there would have been every kind of sailing vessel: brigantines, sloops, schooners, scows, flatboats, canoes, pettiaugers, and more. There would have been ships bringing immigrants; ships bringing slaves; ships bringing Spanish gold, rum, and manufactured goods from England; ships carrying out tons of rice and indigo, lumber and naval supplies.

Looking inland on Bay Street one would have seen commerce, commerce, and more commerce. Bay Street was the trading center of colonial Charlestown. In its environs could be purchased almost anything available in any 18th century city in the world: food, hardware, furniture, clothes, shoes, imported and manufactured goods, and slaves. In the 1730s and 1740s the seat of government was behind the Half Moon Bastion ("the Council Chamber above & a Guard House below"). This building jutted out into Bay Street, which probably explains why the present Exchange Building, built in 1771, juts out into the street. An earlier Exchange Building of the 1730s (now gone) was built along Bay Street itself, where present East Bay intersects with Tradd.

Charles Town's colonial houses were built in a distinctive architectural style derived from England, Barbados, and the West Indies. Some of the earliest houses seem Dutch because the French Huguenots absorbed Dutch culture during their stay in Holland. The Charleston "single house" (one room wide) and Charleston "double house" (two rooms wide) were built in great numbers throughout the colonial era.

Further up Bay Street, past Craven's Bastion (present site of Market Street and East Bay), a creek separated the city from what is now Ansonborough. The creek was wide enough to require a bridge, called Governor's Bridge. Bay Street itself was full of two- and three-story buildings, many built to provide stores at the ground level and residences above. Buildings were close together because this was valuable land, close to wharves and ships and to the customers of both.

A Short History of Charleston

Traveling down from Bay Street to Broad Street on sandy streets, carefully avoiding horses, carts, garbage, carriages, and boys throwing rocks at tied cocks, one would have encountered the New Exchange Building (now the "Old Exchange") just completed in 1771 (and restored in 1981). The planter-dominated Assembly built it for two reasons: first, to provide a merchant's exchange, and, second, to provide a large assembly room for dancing. Proceeding down Broad Street past Union Street (now State Street) to the right, one would soon have reached Church Street. To the right down Church Street was the Church of England, St. Philip's Church, built in 1723 and described by one observer as "spacious and executed in a very handsome taste, exceeding everything of that kind which we have in America." Houses and buildings lined Broad and Church, many of which had "a genteel Appearance, though generally incumbered with Balconies or Piazzas . . . the Apartments are contriv'd for Coolness, a very necessary Consideration."

The intersection of Broad and Meeting was not called the "Corners of Four Laws" by Charlestonians. That name was given by Ripley's "Believe it or Not." The Post Office Building houses the Federal Court, representing federal law; the State Courthouse, state law; City Hall, municipal law; and St. Michael's, God's law.

At the intersection of Broad and Meeting Streets, right in the middle of the street, one would have come across the first statue erected in America, a statue of the great English statesman William Pitt, erected in 1766 at a cost of 7,000 pounds. Pitt championed the cause of the American colonists and the grateful citizens of Charlestown erected this "large colossal statue" — which is now housed at the Charleston Museum. St. Michael's stood on the southeast corner looking just as it does today. A market on the northeast corner (where City Hall now stands) has been variously described as "The New Market" or Beef Market. (Bull has been dispensed from that location since the 1730s.) One would have found a new State House on the northwest corner (where the present County Courthouse is located) and the Guard House or Watch stood on the southwest corner (where the Post Office Building now stands).

What Charlestonians and visitors now call "the Four Corners of the Law" was originally designed to be a great public square, indeed the grand square of the colonial capital. In 1751, the General Assembly passed an act to create a commission to oversee construction of the new State House and to build St. Michael's Church. The great hurricane of 1752 hurried things along also because the site, at the corner of Broad and Meeting, was a pond which added to the flooding during the storm. On June 22, 1753, the Royal Governor, the King's Council, and the Commons House of Assembly observed the 27th anniversary of King George II's accession to the throne of Great Britain. The highlight of the ceremony was the laying of a cornerstone of the new State House. Three years later in 1756 the building, designed to imitate the shire halls and assize courts of England, was completed. It housed the cham-

St. Michael's Church looking north on Meeting Street.

Lord Anson commanded a number of ships which, at various times, protected the Carolina coast. Later he circumnavigated the earth. He was made a baron after his great victory over the Spanish in 1747. The first five streets of Ansonborough were Anson and George (named for the developer); Centurion (the Admiral's ship, now Society Street); Scarborough (another ship, now merged into Anson); and Squirrel (yet another ship, now merged with Meeting).

bers of the Council, the Commons House of Assembly, the Speaker's Chambers and the courts.

Meeting Street was not the most desirable of colonial locations at certain points, given the location of the Market and the Watch, and so it is not surprising that one writer to the *Gazette* described his passage through Meeting Street in terms of "a low set of Wood Tenements, with Walls little thicker than a Sheet of Brown Paper, pent up on all Sides by Wooden Structures." This is where many tradesmen lived, and they found the rents high and the accommodations terrible.

As early as the 1730s Broad Street extended to the marsh that lined the Ashley River. Houses were built, and other streets — Friends Street, Archdales Street, Lambolls Street, King Street — were laid out. In 1739 all streets ended at the city line, which ran across the peninsula a little north of Pinckneys Street (near present-day Market).

The city expanded both north and south. To the north, the city's first suburb was Ansonborough, named in honor of Lord George Anson, a British admiral who resided in Charles Town from 1724 to 1735. According to local legend, the founding of Ansonborough followed Lord Anson's winning the land at cards. In any event, Ansonborough was developed after 1746, to the north of Colonel William Rhett's house, and became a discreet but wealthy neighborhood of great houses because it was located on high ground north of the creek at Craven's Bastion. Henry Laurens, Thomas Lynch, and Chief Justice Pinckney lived there. Other areas were developed in the 18th century: Rhett Borough (between Ansonborough and the creek), the Laurens Lands (east of Ansonborough); and the Mazyck Lands west of present-day Legaré Street. Boundary Street (now Calhoun) was laid out in 1769.

The city expanded south as well. Broughton's Battery had been built to guard the harbor. In 1739 it was located on the southernmost tip of the peninsula. Church Street was extended from this battery southward in such a way as to avoid the mouths of the inlets and creeks cutting into the lower peninsula. For that reason, Church Street bends at the point that used to be Vanderhorst Creek. A bridge was built over that creek to connect lower and upper Church Street. Soon thereafter new houses were built as Meeting Street was also extended across Vanderhorst Creek. Houses began to cover old Oyster Point, especially later in the century when wharves were, for the first time, constructed on the Ashley River (where White Point Gardens is today).

The largest area to be developed in the 18th century was Harleston Village. Located south of Boundary (Calhoun) Street, west of King Street and

the Free School and Glebe Lands (now the College of Charleston), and north of Beaufain Street, Harleston Village remains a monument to 18th- and 19th-century suburban Charlestown development. Early homeowners there, like those in Gadsden's Middlesex and Ansonborough, sought to escape the noise, hustle and bustle, congestion, and odors of the commercial district centered in Bay Street, Broad Street, Queen Street, and environs. The street names once again reflected the revolutionary fervor of the age: Wentworth was named for

Peter Manigault and friends in 1754: The wealthy Huguenot is holding a flask at left. Colonel Howarth holds a wig on the end of a stick.

Lord Rockingham, the British foe of the detested Stamp Act. Beaufain was named in honor of the collector of customs, Hector Berenger de Beaufain. Pitt was named for William Pitt; Rutledge for John Rutledge; Gadsden, for the fiery radical, Christopher Gadsden. Montague and Bull were named in honor of the governor and lieutenant governor at the time.

The Ruling Elite: In time and over the generations the planter class developed into a genuine aristocracy, creating a way of life that surpassed the wildest hopes or dreams of the earliest settlers. "The people of Charleston live rapidly, not willingly letting go untasted any of the pleasures of life. Few of them, therefore, reach a great age," a traveler, Dr. Johann B. Schoepf, noted, adding that "luxury in Carolina has made the greatest advance, and their manner of life, dress, equipages, furniture, everything, denotes a higher degree of taste and love of show, and less frugality than in the northern provinces." Josiah Quincy, Jr. found in 1773 that "state, magnificence, and ostentation, the natural attendants of riches, are conspicuous among this people." They loved to see and to be seen, and the urban setting was more conducive to show than the plantation.

The Charlestown planters loved to eat — or, rather, to *dine*. Their food came from the forest, from the rivers, from the ocean, from the plantation. They dined on fish, venison, oysters, and shrimp; on "plumb marmalade," "mince pyes," "oyster soop," "rich plumb cake iced," "syllabubs," "white custards in glasses," "tarts and cheese cakes"; as well as on terrapin soup, okra soup, rice soup, and a variety of rice breads. They imported wine from all over the world, but especially liked Port and Madeira. And they drank a lot of punch made with lemons and limes, which were considered rather exotic since they had to be imported.

Dinner was at three o'clock in the afternoon, an 18th-century tradition that comported with the plantation day and the hot weather. The other important meal was breakfast — with plenty of grits.

It is hard to say with certainty which form of entertainment the planters enjoyed most, or how they found the time to take it all in. There were numerous taverns and clubs in colonial Charlestown. There was horse racing, dancing, music, theater, billiards, cockfighting, bearbaiting, hunting, fishing, and, of course, wenching. A more hedonistic, pleasure-oriented society never lived on the North American continent.

Horse racing was even more popular than cockfighting in colonial

A Charleston innkeeper named Eldridge constructed a "cockpit" in 1732 and charged ten shillings to watch and bet. Cockfighting was a popular "half-time" diversion between horse races. A barbaric sport, to be sure, but it did not seem to offend the morals of the times.

The ladies of old Charlestown played cards too. Sophia Hume, an early evangelical preacher, told her female listeners in 1747 that "Religion and Cards" did not mix and asked them to hold their cards until they said their prayers.

Charlestown, perhaps because the ladies could also attend. In 1735 a race track, the York Course, was established about one mile from the city. Later, races were held every month. The New Market Track was established at Goose Creek (about 15 miles from the city) in 1743. The "Charleston Races," much admired throughout the colonies, were established by the Yorkshireman Thomas Nightingale in 1754. These races took place in another New Market Course on the neck north of Charlestown. The Carolina Jockey Club was founded in 1758 and offered purses up to 1,000 pounds. Later in the century, the South Carolina Jockey Club, organized by the great horse breeder Edward Fenwick and revolutionary heroes General Charles Cotesworth Pinckney and General William Moultrie, among others, built the even more elegant Washington Racecourse (now Hampton Park).

Race days were big social events that women and men could attend together. "Race week" each February was the social event of the season. It was yet another opportunity for dinners, balls, assemblies, parties, and the show of wealth, new fashions, handsome coaches, and well-dressed servants. The odds were published in the local newspaper, the *South Carolina Gazette,* and great sums were won — and lost — at the Charlestown races.

The planters gambled frequently. Private clubs abounded, mainly for card playing and drinking. One Charlestown lady complained: "There is not one night in the week in which they are not engaged with some club or other at the *tavern,* where they *injure their fortunes* by GAMING in various ways, and *impair their healths* by the intemperate use of spirituous liquors, and keeping late hours." Among the clubs were Fryday-Night Club ("the more elderly and substantial gentlemen"), the Whisk Club, the Amiable, the Fancy Society, Meddlers Laughing Club, the Beef-Steak Club, the Fort Jolly Volunteers, and the Brooms (who naturally advertised "a special Sweep").

And what about the women of colonial Charlestown, or at least the white women? The great ladies of the plantations and townhouses lived a number of lives. By many accounts, the ladies were "generally of a middling stature, genteel and slender," and they had "fair complexions, without the help of art." Others acknowledged "that the ladies in the province considerably outshine the men." Their dress was certainly beautiful and far superior to the women of Virginia or the North. As one Charlestonian put it: "the girls for fashion sake go to town." The "gaiety" of dress rivaled the "Court-end of London." They excelled in the social arts of dancing, music, art appreciation, and the preparation of great dinners. Cooking was always a fine art in Charlestown, and a lady was expected to keep her own recipe books, know how to supervise servants,

Contrary to popular belief, widows were not always stoic and forlorn. Some, "by forward carriages do snap up the young men." This aggressiveness of well-to-do widows (of whom there were a number, given the life-style of the planter!) caused a "Melancholy Disposition of Mind" in the eligible young girls of Charlestown according to one writer.

and entertain lavishly.

Others found the ladies of colonial Charlestown to be "generally of sallow complexion and without that bloom" of other American ladies. In *White over Black,* Winthrop D. Jordan wrote of the white women of Charlestown that: "Some visitors to the city were struck by their desiccated formality, which seems now to betray the strains imposed by the prevailing pattern of miscegenation. . . . The dissipation of the white gentleman was as much a tragedy for his white lady as for him. A biracial environment warped her affective life in two directions at once, for she was made to feel that sensual involvement with the opposite sex burned bright and hot with unquenchable passion and at the same time that any such involvement was utterly repulsive."

So began the great southern tradition of placing women on a pedestal. They could not be reached by those below, and they could not step down. Timothy Ford, in his travels, noted that, while the men were "as agreeable as any I have ever seen," the women of Charlestown "carry formality and scrupulosity to a considerable extreme. . . . The maxims of the country have taught them and custom has forced them to almost consider a sociability on their part with gentlemen as an unbecoming forwardness."

No doubt the great wealth of colonial Charlestown's women added to their beauty. Marriages were often the result of astute business and political judgments. Sarah Rhett was described by the *South Carolina Gazette* as "a beautiful and accomplish'd young Lady, with a large Fortune." Susannah Seabrook was "a young lady endowed with all agreeable Accomplishments, and a fortune of 15,000 pounds." In describing the great 18th-century Charleston matches (Charles Pinckney and Eliza Lucas; George Roupell and Elizabeth Prioleau, for example), the papers always noted that the lady was beautiful "with a large Fortune."

There were other women in Charlestown, but not much is known about them. We do know that some worked alongside their husbands and that some ran taverns and inns, cooked, and gave lessons of every sort from dancing and singing to needlework and embroidery. And there were a number of female teachers in Charlestown who taught French, English, geography, history, and "many instructing amusements."

"He who should presume to shew any displeasure against such a thing as simple fornication, would for his pains be accounted a simple blockhead; since not one in twenty can be persuaded, that there is either sin; or shame in cohabiting with his slave." So wrote Edward Long of 18th century Jamaica. The white planters of Charlestown were, like their West Indian counterparts, openly involved sexually with black women. In 1743 the Grand Jury of Charlestown condemned *"the too common practice of criminal conversation with Negro and other slave wenches in this province."*

The Pervasive Institution: It was the institution of slavery, above all else, that molded Charlestown's elite. Absolute and unquestioned rule over the lives of other human beings, a rule that included, as a practical matter, life-and-death decisions, gave to the planter class a justified feeling of absolute power. Each planter was king of all he owned. His friends and neighbors were the government and the courts. In all the history of America it is doubtful that a more absolutely powerful class or group ever ruled a city, colony, or state. And Charlestown *was* the colony. As the distinguished southern historian U. B. Phillips phrased it, the Low Country "focused in Charleston to such a degree as to make the whole district in some sense a city-state." Their power unchecked by a working class (they owned the working class, the slaves), or a middle class (it was small, ineffectual, and dependent on the planters), or by strong religious institutions (there was an easy tolerance and much division), the planters held absolute sway over their domain.

The last of the planters' great pastimes, womanizing, is a topic about which most historians of Charlestown have been rather silent. While Josiah Quincy's view of Charlestown society in 1773 is often quoted by historians of the city, one line is frequently omitted: "The enjoyment of a negro or mulatto woman," he wrote, "is spoken of as quite a common thing; no reluctance, delicacy or shame is made about the matter." Charlestown planters were quite open about their sexual liaisons with black women. Unlike the rest of colonial America (but like their cousins in the West Indies), the men of Charlestown's ruling class were not reluctant to take advantage of their female slave population.

Winthrop Jordan, again in his classic *White over Black,* wrote that "while permanent unions between persons of the two races normally were quiet or secretive affairs elsewhere on the continent, in South Carolina and particularly in Charlestown they were not... Charleston was the only English city on the continent where it was at all possible to jest publicly concerning miscegenation ... Only in Charlestown was it possible to debate publicly, 'Is sex with Negroes right?' In other colonies the topic was not looked upon as being open."

The *South Carolina Gazette,* published in Charlestown, occasionally carried a series of cute poems and letters on the subject of interracial sex. One letter to the editor, supposedly from ladies newly arrived from Bermuda, advised that, if Charlestown bachelors and widowers "are in a Strait for Women, to wait for the next Shipping from the Coast of Guinny. Those African Ladies are of a strong robust Constitution; not easily jaded out, able to serve them by Night as well as Day. . . ." Another writer replied the next week that "our Country-Women are full as capable for service either night or day as any African Ladies," and he hoped "they'll have the Preference before the Black Ladies in the Esteem of the Widowers and Batchelors at C-town."

"The inhabitants may well be divided into opulent and lordly planters, poor and spiritless whites and vile slaves," the Bostonian, Josiah Quincy, wrote of Charlestown in 1773. Crèvecouer divided everyone differently: in the 1780's the "three principal classes of inhabitants are, lawyers, planters, and merchants; this is the province which has afforded to the first the richest spoils, for nothing can exceed their wealth, their power, and their influence . . . ."

Middleton Plantation.

The Charleston ruling elite, in short, was able to do as it pleased, defying many of the standards of its time, because slavery made it an elite without opposition. Over time the planters, the great merchants, and the elite of colonial Charlestown developed a way of life distinguished not only by great wealth but also by the elevation of pleasure and pleasure seeking to the greatest of social goals. "In Charleston we are a set of the busiest, most bustling, hurrying animals imaginable," Dr. Alexander Garden wrote, "and yet we really do not do much, but we must appear to be doing. And this kind of important hurry appears among all ranks, unless among the gentleman planters, who are absolutely above every occupation but eating, drinking, lolling, smoking and sleeping, which five modes of action constitute the essence of their life and existence." Garden, a physician and botanist (for whom the gardenia was named) knew the planters well. Another traveler noted that the planter's "life is whil'd away in idleness, or consumed in dissipation." Crôvecoeur blamed it on the heat: "The climate renders excesses of all kinds very dangerous, particularly those of the table; and yet, insensible or fearless of danger, they live on, and enjoy a short and a merry life: the rays of their sun seem to urge them irresistibly to dissipation and pleasure: on the contrary, the women, from being abstemious, reach to a longer period of life, and seldom die without having had several husbands." In short, as Richard Hofstadter has written, "By comparison with Charles Town's elite, old Boston's uppercrust looked poor and flimsy, and the hedonistic life of the South Carolina capital put the other seaboard towns in the shade."

Other Townspeople: People other than planters and great merchants populated colonial Charlestown. It is a sad fact of history, however, that usually only the educated, powerful, and wealthy leave diaries, letters, and newspaper accounts, and it is from these sources that our knowledge of history is primarily drawn. Charlestown teemed with working people of all kinds: shipbuilders, tanners, shoemakers, carpenters, silversmiths, cabinetmakers, coopers, shop clerks, drivers, blacksmiths, jewelry makers, tailors, and others. Coopers, for example, made barrels, pipes, kegs and "caskes" for shipping. Caulkers, rope makers, and braziers were needed on the waterfront. There were two milliners' shops, two rum distilleries, three ropewalks, and two sugar houses in early colonial Charlestown.

Because of slavery, skilled craftsmen were in much shorter supply in Charlestown than in other colonial cities. Pelatiah Webster came to

Charlestown in 1767 from Philadelphia and reported that "they have very few mechanic arts of any sort, and [a] very great quantity of mechanic utensils are imported from England and the Northern Colonies." When so much of the labor was performed by slaves, white artisans were not anxious to come to Charlestown, although their services were badly needed. The shipbuilding industry, for example, which would have been a natural industry for Charlestown, never fully developed there as it did in the other ports because of the lack of skilled workers. Yet there were small shipbuilding and repair industries with such names as Rose's Yard, Emery's, Wright's, and Black's, and some ships were built for the coastal trade.

Cabinetmakers and silversmiths were in great demand. In 1760, for instance, there were 28 cabinetmakers; in 1790 the number had grown to 35, and, by 1810, it had reached 81. Thomas Elfe is the most famous, probably because his records survive. Elfe's shop produced more than 1,500 pieces between 1768 and 1776, including bedsteads, bookcases, chairs, card tables, sofas, and desks. Rice was so popular that Charlestown cabinetmakers created the "rice bed," with rice ears and leaves carved on the bedposts.

But the goal of the artisan was to become a planter, and that is exactly what many of them did. Upward mobility was a hallmark of colonial Charlestown. John Paul Grimké, the silversmith, eventually purchased 500 acres on Edisto Island. Artisans such as Benjamin Hawes and George Flagg became great shipping merchants. The planter, Thomas Heyward, had been a hatter; Daniel Cannon, a carpenter. And the best of the cabinetmakers, Thomas Elfe himself, made a small fortune and became a planter.

The great shadow of slavery crossed every class, every occupation, every neighborhood. Mechanics, artisans, and tradespeople adapted to the system and came to depend on slaves for labor, too. "I have seen tradesmen go through the city," a visitor noted, "followed by a negro carrying their tools — barbers who are supported in idleness and ease by their negroes who do the business, and in fact many of the mechanics bear nothing more of their trade than the name."

Physicians were the first professional men to arrive in Charlestown. Dr. William Scrivener and Dr. Henry Woodward came in the early years. Dr. John Lining, a Scot, practiced medicine and conducted scientific research as well. His writings concerning the relationship between weather conditions and diseases were published by the Royal Society of London. Dr. Lining also studied "non-infectious diseases" (the first such studies in the colonies), corresponded with Benjamin Franklin about electricity, and kept detailed meteoro-

In 1772 Governor Nicholson convinced the Assembly to create a formal government for Charlestown. "An Act for the Good Government of Charles Town" was passed renaming the city "Charles City and Port" and modeling the government on New York City's. No record of the act survives, but it apparently provided for a council and a mayor to be elected annually on the King's birthday. This government was petitioned to death in about a year. Anti-government agitation reached its climax here in 1860.

logical observations.

Dr. Lionel Chalmers (for whom Chalmers Street is named) practiced in Charlestown and worked with Dr. Lining on the connection between weather and disease. His publications, published in Charlestown and London, became the most important contribution to general medicine made by an American during this era.

Charlestown's contributions to science were small but interesting. The foremost scientist of the period, Dr. Alexander Garden, corresponded with the great botanists of his age both in Europe and America including the great Linneaus. He was a member of virtually every prestigious scientific society including the Royal Society of London. Garden sent plants and drawings of plants to fellow botanists in America and abroad, and that is why Linnaeus named the gardenia in his honor.

Whether it was a result of the life-style, the climate, slavery, or the lack of any real religious "mission" in settling Charlestown, the ruling planter elite never developed a strong civic consciousness. They created few noted public institutions.

The College of Charleston.

Every effort to establish a college in the colonial period failed. Harvard College was established in Massachusetts in the early years of that colony. Philadelphians and New Yorkers helped establish "Prince Town" (Princeton) in New Jersey in 1746. Philadelphia established its own college in 1755. New Yorkers established King's College (now Columbia University) in 1754. Yale was established in 1716 when Cotton Mather was defeated in his attempt to become president of Harvard. But the richest city in the richest province in colonial America had no college until the College of Charleston opened in 1790. A proposal in 1723 to establish an Anglican college in Charlestown had failed. A proposal for "a public college" in 1764 had also failed. "The Rich," one citizen wrote, "may be indifferent about such an establishment which might deprive their sons of the only advantage of being distinguished among their Countrymen." In 1770, another attempt was made to found a public (as opposed to a church) college. Governor William Bull, John Rutledge, and numerous citizens supported it, but the planter-dominated legislature refused to enact the legislation.

The planters and other wealthy Charlestonians contributed heavily to colleges in Rhode Island, Philadelphia, and New Jersey, and many of their children went to college there. Some of their children attended schools in England. (The number of South Carolinians in the later colonial period who attended the Inns of Court, where lawyers were trained, exceeded the number of students from all of the other colonies combined.) The planters, unconcerned about providing higher education to others and unconcerned about creating their own institutions, sent their children to fine colleges, but established none in Charlestown even though they had the resources to do so.

The city was governed, then, by the colonial government itself, which consisted of a Royal Governor appointed by the King and a Council appointed by the King on the recommendation of the Governor. The Council consisted of the Upper House (from which the later Senate was derived) and a Commons' House of Assembly, that is, a House of Commons or Lower House, which was popularly elected by those allowed to vote. The Commons was often referred to simply as the Assembly.

While New England towns were developing a new form of democratic self-government, the town meeting, and while other colonial cities were becoming municipal corporations complete with various degrees of power, Charlestown was not even a separate entity.

Colonial Charlestown's basic governmental and social needs were met by two institutions: various commissioners who governed the roads, fire fighting, the workhouse, and other such matters; and the vestry of St. Philip's Church, the established Anglican Church, which tended to the needs of the poor.

Fire was Charleston's major urban problem, and numerous blazes wounded the town. The great fire of 1740, the worst in all America to that date, destroyed 334 dwellings and did about 200,000 pounds worth of damage. Other towns took up collections for homeless Charlestonians and Parliament granted 20,000 pounds to help. (A fire insurance company had been started in 1735 to insure against this terrible peril, but ironically, it failed as a result of the great fire of 1740.)

Hampered by medieval English concepts of municipal governments and by the opposition of the planter class and some townspeople to any government at all, the various commissions did the best they could. The streets were generally neglected and unpaved — Broad and Queen Streets were first paved by donations from private citizens.

There was no regular police force and crime was another major problem. The city was protected by an "armed watch" and, ultimately, by the military. The watch patrolled at night and was paid out of import duties and tavern fees. It was always poorly organized and complaints issued regularly from the Grand Jury. The men of the watch were generally of "mean and low character," often bribed, and fond of "beating and abusing negroes sent on errands by their masters with tickets [that is, passes or permission slips], and letting

The colony's military organization served to keep the peace, although it was primarily designed to fight the Indians and Spanish and to suppress slave revolts. The military tradition of South Carolina and Charlestown can be traced to this "military police organization of the white people." Charlestown was one of the several military districts, the chief of which was a colonel. Each district contained subdivisions headed by a captain. Thus, many prominent citizens became colonels and captains when they headed up the militia in their areas. "To this source," writes Edward McCrady, "may be traced the prevalence of military titles in the South." Thus began the tradition of the "Southern Colonel."

others escape that have none," at least according to the Grand Jury. The captain of the watch at its lowest ebb was the Governor's dog keeper.

Since there was no formal City of Charlestown, the city's legislators after 1751 were actually delegates from "St. Philip's and St. Michael's" parishes. All that remains of that important district is today's "St. P. & M." precinct in the Union Heights section of the Neck, between modern Charleston and North Charleston.

The vestry wardens who cared for the poor were aided in their work by numerous charitable and ethnic organizations formed to aid fellow countrymen who had fallen on hard times. These included the South Carolina Society (probably the wealthiest, founded by French Protestants), the Fellowship Society, the Charitable Society (Baptist), the German Friendly Society (1766), the Hebrew Benevolent Society (1784), the St. Andrew's Society (1729), the St. George's Society (1733), the Friendly Sons of St. Patrick (1774), and the Hibernian Society (1801), which succeeded the Friendly Sons of St. Patrick. Many, having once served a useful purpose, have now become exclusive social clubs.

Religious Tolerance: The Churches of Charlestown flourished and grew in the colonial period. Religious tolerance, taken for granted by modern Americans, was a new concept in the 17th and 18th centuries. Certainly the Puritans of Massachusetts had none of it. But Charlestown, from the beginning, was a model of religious tolerance. Even before the colony was settled, John Locke's Fundamental Constitutions had guaranteed "ye liberty" of religion to the Indians ("ye natives . . . utterly strangers to Christianity, whose idollatry, ignorance, or mistakes gives us noe right to expell or use ym. ill"), and even to "yt heathens, Jues, and other dissenters." Thus, while the Anglican Church was established and supported by taxes, no one was forced to belong to it or to refrain from the practice of another religion. There were Methodists, Huguenots, Baptists, Presbyterians, Jews, Quakers, various Dissenters, and those who belonged to no church. Charlestown, unlike Boston or Philadelphia, was not founded by a religious group. It was founded as a business enterprise. Religion was certainly a force, but it was less influential among the tolerant and easy-going Charlestonians than among the Puritans of Boston or the Quakers of Philadelphia.

In 1824, Kahal Kadosh Beth Elohim became America's first Reform Jewish congregation. Because the Nazis destroyed the first Reform synagogues, which were all in Germany, this synagogue stands today as the oldest Reform synagogue in the world — and a lasting tribute to religious liberty in Charleston.

St. Philip's moved to its present location on Church Street near Queen in 1727. (The architecture of the present church dates, however, from 1835.) The establishment of St. Michael's was authorized in 1751 because of the expansion of the city's population. The cornerstone was laid on February 17, 1752, with great ceremony, an official dinner, and toasts to King George II. Nine years in the building, St. Michael's opened for services on February 1, 1761, and has remained virtually unchanged since. The new church contained a pew for the Governor and Council and special pews for the members of the Assembly. Two future presidents of the Continental Congress (Henry Laurens and Henry

Middleton) and one future signer of the Declaration of Independence (Thomas Heyward, Jr.) were members.

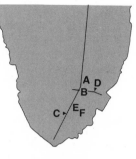

But a majority of Charlestonians were not Anglicans, and other congregations flourished. The Scotch Presbyterians built a frame church (the Scots Kirk) in 1731 on Meeting, south of Tradd Street. Today this is the First (Scots) Presbyterian congregation.

Jews from Spain and Portugal came to Charlestown early, some by way of London. There were Jews in Charlestown as early as 1695, and, by 1749, the congregation of Kahal Kadosh Beth Elohim (the Holy Congregation Beth Elohim, or House of God) was organized. They met first on Union Street, now State Street, but moved shortly thereafter to Hasell Street. The congregation was strictly Orthodox, and its ritual was the same as the Spanish and Portuguese congregations in London and Amsterdam. In 1792 the Jews of Charlestown constructed the largest synagogue in the United States.

A. Ansonborough
B. Wm. Rhett House (1717 Hasell St.)
C. Meeting St.
D. Hasell St.
E. Dock Street Theatre
F. French Huguenot Church

The Quakers met at a meeting house located on King Street. The Lutherans began construction of St. John's Lutheran Church in 1759. Construction of a Unitarian Church was commenced in 1772 after a number of Congregationalists broke with that church. Charleston's Unitarian Church is, thus, the oldest in the South.

Beginning with Jonathan Edwards's sermons in 1734 and continuing through the work of the Reverend George Whitefield, who read Edwards's tracts in Savannah, the religious revival known as the Great Awakening arrived in Charlestown in the person of Whitefield himself. (John Wesley, who read the same Edwards tracts in England, was moved to preach the evangelical message, and Methodism was born.) Reverend Whitefield was the greatest preacher of his day. He preached in Charlestown in 1738 and 1740 and caused quite a stir. One of Whitefield's biographers wrote that Charlestown was "the place of his *greatest success* and of the *greatest* opposition." It was in Charlestown that he confronted the Anglican establishment and began his split from the Anglican Church.

Methodism was firmly entrenched in the city from at least the founding of the Cumberland Methodist Church (1787) and the Bethel Methodist Church (1797). John Wesley himself had preached at St. Philip's in 1737, and Asbury organized the Methodist Church in South Carolina. The Methodists were unpopular for a time, not only because of their "enthusiasm" but because many opposed slavery. The Baptists had been in Charlestown since 1699. In 1751 the Charles Town Baptist Association, the second Baptist Association in America, was established. It consisted of four churches in and near Charlestown.

Despite its many religions, Charlestown remained an Anglican stronghold. "As to the State of Religion in this Province," Dr. Garden wrote after the decline

St. Phillip's church as it appeared from 1725 to 1835.

of the Whitefield movement in 1743, "it is bad enough — Rome and the Devil have contriv'd to crucify her between two Thieves, Infedelity *[sic]* and Enthusiasm. The formers, alas! too much still prevails; but as to the latter, Thanks to God it is greatly subsided, even to the Point of vanishing away." The word "enthusiasm" was a derogatory word used in the 18th century to connote irrational thought or behavior, and it was often associated (unfairly at times) with evangelical preachers. It would be quite erroneous to conclude, however, that the evangelical sects did not prosper in normally tolerant Charlestown.

The Anglican Church may have lost more than it gained by being "established." The planter class and elite, eager for the pleasures of this world, found little time for religious study. "Not a single native took Episcopal orders before the Revolution," writes Carl Bridenbaugh in a final note on Anglican Charlestown.

Social Life: The tavern, inn, or, "punch house" was, in Charlestown as all over colonial America, the most important of social institutions. Despite the protests of some (including the Grand Jury from time to time) Charlestown maintained in excess of one hundred taverns during the colonial era. The most famous was Dillon's on Broad Street. It was always stocked with wine, liquors, and "good Larder in season." But there were others, including the Sign of the Bacchus, Henry Gignilliat's, and the Georgia Coffee House.

Taverns provided more than just drinks. They provided food and entertainment. In 1738, for example, one traveling show boasted of an "Ourangnogang (or Man of the Woods), Tho' this . . . a female of that Species." A slackwire act appeared later, starring "Mr. Sturges from London," and "A White Negro Girl" with gray eyes and white hair amused yet another Charlestown tavern audience.

"The importation of liquors at Charles Town in 1743," wrote Carl Bridenbaugh, "staggers the imagination — 1,500 dozen empty bottles, among other items, to be used for 'six months' supply' of 1,219 hogsheads, 188 tierces, and 58 barrels of rum."

Colonial Charlestonians loved music. The St. Cecilia Society, which is still in existence, was founded in the early 18th century for the purpose of bringing to Charlestown the best concert music available. In the early years the concerts were held at Dillon's Inn and later at Williams' Coffee House. The society's balls became major social events in time. The society was open to anyone who could purchase a subscription, but the subscription was relatively expensive. The music, though, was good. Even young Mr. Quincy approved: "The two bass-viols and French horns were grand. One Abercrombie, a Frenchman just arrived, played a first fiddle, and a solo incomparably better than any I ever heard. . . ." The society was, by all accounts, the first musical group in British America to support a paid orchestra.

The early Charleston theater was as glamorous as its music. As early as 1735 or 1736 Charlestown boasted a theater. The first theaters were located on the southwest corner of Church and Dock Street, now Queen Street, and were thus called the New Theatre in Dock Street. There appear to have been three or four theaters at that location — all called the New Theatre. (Around the year 1800 the Planter's Hotel was built on this site and the present facade of the Dock Street Theatre is the old Planter's Hotel.) By the late colonial period, Charlestown was the undisputed center of drama and theater in the colonies. "In 1773-74, 188 performances were given in Charleston, including eleven of Shakespeare's plays. It was," concludes George C. Rogers, Jr., "the most brilliantly dramatic season in colonial America."

Probably the main reason for the success of drama and theater in early Charlestown was the city's ingrained tolerance. Actors were not exactly respectable people in the 18th century. Statutes in England against vagrants included "rogues, vagabonds, stage-players, and sturdy beggars." The Puritans of both England and New England had no use for theater; nor did the Quakers of Pennsylvania. Yet in Charlestown, theater was so accepted that the Court House was the site of the first dramatic performance in the city (a use to which the Court House has been put ever since.) Charlestown was a haven for traveling actors. The planters were able to pay handsomely for the importation of convivial entertainment.

And import they did. Anthony Aston showed up in Charlestown in 1703 "full of lice" but able to act. *The Orphan or the Unhappy Marriage* was performed in 1735, making it the first recorded performance. The players were almost always professional traveling companies. The best always came to Charlestown and stayed for long periods. The Hallam's Company traveled to Charlestown, for example, in October 1754 and entertained the city for three months with *A Bold Stroke for a Wife, The Mock Doctor,* and *Cato* by Addison, among others. In the 1760s Charlestown saw *Romeo and Juliet* and *King Lear* performed by the American Company. That company, which met only hostility in Rhode Island and New York, came to Charlestown in November 1763 and stayed until the spring of 1766!

Dancing was as popular as music and theater, if not more so. Eighteenth-century Charlestonians loved to dance. Unlike the Virginians who danced at home, Charlestonians liked to go out. Subscription balls were popular at local inns, such as the Long Room at John Gordon's. In 1755, Governor Glen gave "a Supper and a Ball to the Ladies at Mr. Poinsett's." Charlestonians liked dancing so well that they included a ballroom in the new "Custom House and Exchange."

"Pray what is your Assembly about — Dancing?" asked Charlestonian Henry Laurens of a member of the Florida Legislature in 1763. An assembly was a dance *and* a legislative body in 18th-century parlance.

Charlestonians loved to have their portraits painted. Jeremiah Theus, a Swiss, for example, came in 1739 and became "portrait painter in residence" to the planters. The Pinckneys and the Middletons were painted in London. The Izards were among Copley's patrons, and Gainsborough also painted an Izard.

In 1775, the five largest American cities were Philadelphia (40,000, the second largest city in the British Empire after London), New York (25,000), Boston (16,000), Charlestown (12,000), and Newport, Rhode Island (11,000). Savannah, Georgia was a mere village of 3,200 souls, dependent on Charlestown for trade, protection, and leadership.

The cultural life of colonial Charlestown has taken on many aspects of a myth. The city's cultural life was a part of its larger life: the hedonistic, sociable, pleasurable life of the planter and merchant elite. That Charlestown was a cultural center, there is no doubt. It abounded with theater, music, dance, and art. But it was an imported culture, not an indigenous one. Actors and musicians were brought in, and plays and music were not written at home.

While it's true that Charlestown had the first public library in America and that the Charleston Library Society, organized in 1743, eventually housed 2,000 books by 1770 (it was the second subscription library in America), it is also true that Charlestonians did not write or publish books in any serious quantity. Between 1743 and 1760, for example, Newport, which was smaller than Charlestown, published 77 titles (almanacs, books, and pamphlets), New York published 495, and Boston published 1,321. Charlestown published 12. "Among a people so sociably inclined . . . reading was never a favorite recreation, nor was learning highly prized for its own sake," concludes Carl Bridenbaugh in *Myths and Realities.*

Charlestonians did, however, like to read newspapers, and Charlestown had a large number for a city its size: *The South Carolina Gazette,* established in 1732 by Benjamin Franklin's partner Lewis Timothy; the *South Carolina Weekly Gazette,* founded in 1754, and succeeded by the *South Carolina and American General Gazette;* and Charles Crouch's *South Carolina Gazette and Country Journal,* founded in 1765.

End of an Era: By the end of the colonial era, Charlestown had experienced its share of success and failure. The population had grown from 2,500 in 1685 to 6,800 in 1742. At mid-century it was the fourth largest city in America, coming after Boston, Philadelphia, and New York. By 1775 its population had climbed to 12,000.

Charleston differed markedly from other large cities of America, though, because more than half of its population was black slaves, a simple fact with not-so-simple implications. According to Governor William Bull in 1770 there were only 24 free blacks. All of the gaiety of plantation and city life depended on what Thomas Jefferson characterized as "a perpetual exercise of the most boisterous passions, the most unremitting despotism on the one part, and degrading submissions on the other. . . ."

Charlestonians survived terrible hurricanes in 1700, 1713, and 1728, as well as the worst ever to that date in September of 1752 when five hundred houses were lost.

The great hurricane of 1752, a hurricane comparable to Hurricane Hugo in 1989, blew in on September 14, 1752. Ships in the harbor were blown ashore. Buildings on Sullivan's Island washed up the Cooper River. "For about forty miles round Charles Town there was hardly a plantation that did not lose every outhouse upon it, and the roads, for years afterwards, were encumbered with trees blown and broken down." They survived numerous smallpox and yellow fever epidemics. The escape of the planters to the "Carolina Hospital" at Newport, Rhode Island, saved many of them. Charlestown also survived fire after fire, including the great fire of 1740.

Yet Charlestown was built on a powder keg: slavery. She would endure Revolution and Civil War before she came face to face with the "peculiar institution."

* * *

A final note on colonial Charlestown by "Capt. Martin of A Man of War" in 1769:

> Black and white all mix'd together,
> Inconstant, strange, unhealthful weather
> Burning heat and chilling cold
> Dangerous both to young and old
> Boisterous winds and heavy rains
> Fevers and rhumatic pains
> Agues plenty without doubt
> Sores, boils, the prickling heat and gout
> Musquitos on the skin make blotches
> Centipedes and large cock-roaches
> Frightful creatures in the waters
> Porpoises, sharks and alligators
> Houses built on barren land
> No lamps or lights, but streets of sand
> Pleasant walks, if you can find 'em
> Scandalous tongues, if any mind 'em
> The markets dear and little money
> Large potatoes, sweet as honey
> Water bad, past all drinking
> Men and women without thinking
> Every thing at a high price
> But rum, hominy and rice
> Many a widow not unwilling
> Many a beau not worth a shilling
> Many a bargain, if you strike it
> This is Charles-town, how do you like it.

The Battery itself is the product of hurricanes. "Especially, does the Battery, the pride of Charleston, owe its origin to this great gale," Mrs. Ravenel wrote of the hurricane of 1752. The old seawall had been blown away; a new one had to be built. Charles Town actually looked better after the hurricane of 1752 than before.

An account published in London stated: "The Bay Street which fronts Cooper River is really handsome and would delight any stranger which approached it from the sea." The walls of the Battery "yielded to every gale and were totally demolished by the hurricane of 1804," according to Mrs. Ravenel. It was then that the city began using stone, which, as we know, has worked very well ever since.

The Revolutionary City (1765–1800)

3

The American Revolution turned Charlestown upside down and inside out. Colonial Charlestown, its government, and its way of life broke like fragile china. The city was never to be the same.

Before the Revolution, Charlestown was governed by the King, a royal governor, the Council and the Commons or Assembly, St. Philip's vestry, and various commissioners. After the Revolution, Charlestown became the "City of Charleston" and was incorporated as South Carolina's first city. It became part of a new national government, first under the Declaration of Independence, then under the Articles of Confederation and, finally, under the United States Constitution. And native sons had a strong hand in all these forms the new government took. The Revolution opened the door to power for artisans, mechanics, young lawyers, small merchants, and "new men." Revolutionary Charlestown saw it all: political agitation, class conflict, war, mob rule, death, destruction, civil war, military occupation, near starvation, and chaos. Many Charlestonians sacrificed their lives for the new nation in spite of a deep affection for the English way of life.

Perhaps more than anything else, the change was one of mood. The people had come to see themselves as separate from the English, and local institutions had matured. The Commons House of Assembly gained power and prestige. It occupied a new State House built on Broad Street in the 1750s. The Assembly resembled the English House of Commons, complete with ceremonial mace and parliamentary journals. Colonial leadership, as it gained confidence, became more assertive.

Charlestonians were in no mood to be obsequious. They had withstood the terrors of the wilderness and the Indians and had fought the pirates without help from the Proprietors. They had deposed the Lord Proprietors themselves. They had fought the Spanish and helped to secure Georgia and the upcountry. They had fought successfully in the French and Indian War, a war that brought out the differences between the American colonies and Great Britain.

In a sense, the American Revolution was the culmination of the French and Indian War, which had brought about the defeat of the Cherokees, the Spanish, and the French in the New World and left Great Britain in control in North America — a victory that soon caused problems for Great Britain, for the American colonies, and for Charlestown. Who was to pay the huge cost of the French and Indian War and the cost of maintaining British troops in America? Great Britain looked to the colonies, but the colonists felt they had already paid their share of the cost of the war both in terms of men and money.

There were two sides to the question, but South Carolinians already paid a wearying variety of taxes on slaves, real property, and interest-bearing notes, for example. And many Charlestonians paid especially heavy taxes because they owned both property and slaves and because of the nature of their businesses. By the late 1760s, many Charlestonians had begun to feel that Great Britain's policies were overbearing.

The French and Indian War also had a bad effect on the economy. So it is not surprising that Charlestown bitterly opposed the Stamp Act of 1765. The act roused lawyers because tax stamps were required for most legal documents. It roused printers because stamps were required for the sale of newspapers, books, pamphlets, and almanacs. The Stamp Act consolidated the revolutionary movement in the colonies. It united those people suffering economic hardships, those outraged at "taxation without representation," those who resented British arrogance. It brought together ambitious young men on the make, idealistic, budding American nationalists, and those who harbored personal grievances.

Charlestown's mechanics had a lot to be unhappy about, not all of it the work of the King of England. First, they had limited political power. While most could vote and were qualified for election to the Assembly, they were never elected because, in a deferential society, a workingman was supposed to know his place. During the agitation that was to come, one aristocrat said quite bluntly that he would have no truck with mechanics because men who only knew "how to cut up a beast in a market to best advantage, to cobble an old shoe . . . or to build a necessary house" were not intended by nature to "be profound politicians or able statesmen." In the 18th century most people still

The Stamp Act brought together a powerful group of "mechanics" (craftsmen and artisans) and working people. The mechanics, later to be called Sons of Liberty, were the moving force in the revolutionary movement in Charlestown, and Charlestown was the moving force in the colony.

A Short History of Charleston

believed in the medieval idea of the Great Chain of Being, an ordered society (God, the King, the Church, the aristocracy, the common people), the rule of gentlemen. Mechanics also suffered from currency problems. In 1764 Parliament passed a law preventing the colonies from issuing paper money, thereby creating a currency shortage. Add to this hard times, scarcities, competition with slave labor (which the mechanics bitterly resented), and the result was a hard-core group of men ready to take a chance.

Agitator of the Revolution: Christopher Gadsden, in a portrait attributed to Rembrandt Peale.

Gadsden and Fellows: Add to this group the leadership of an eloquent and brilliant intellectual, a wealthy merchant, a military leader, a respected churchman, a man with a fiery temper and incorruptible integrity, and, even without the planters and merchants, the Sons of Liberty became a party to be reckoned with. Such a man was Christopher Gadsden, owner and builder of the great Gadsden Wharf and an early champion of Charleston's mechanics.

Gadsden had been angry at the British since the Cherokee War because he thought the British had mishandled it. He was further incensed by a royal governor's attempt to unseat him in the Commons. Gadsden attacked the British government quite early. "Will it be asserted by any friend to the natural liberties of British subjects," he asked, "that, in order to retain those liberties, a man must never stir out of Britain?" He gathered about him angry mechanics, young lawyers, and young planters, and agitated throughout the Revolutionary period. He attended the Stamp Act Congress in New York, together with John Rutledge and Thomas Lynch.

When, on October 18, 1765 (while the Stamp Act Congress was in session), the *Planter's Adventure* arrived in Charlestown harbor with the hated stamps on board, some "very extraordinary and universal commotions" occurred. The next morning a gallows appeared at Broad and Church complete with an effigy, a sign reading "Liberty and no Stamp Act," and a warning that the effigy not be removed or the guilty party would be "born with a stone about his neck, and cast into the sea." Two thousand protesters paraded as a funeral procession that night in search of the stamps. The home of George Saxby, the stamp officer, was searched, and the windows broken.

Nothing was sacred. Henry Laurens's home in Ansonborough was invaded on October 23 because the mob believed he had the stamps. Even though Laurens was opposed to the Stamp Act, the mob put a cutlass to his throat, searched his home (in vain), and rummaged through his wine cellar wasting much of his wine. From there the mob went to the home of Chief Justice Shinner on King Street. An Irishman of great wit, the Chief Justice rose to the occasion by providing bowls of punch and liquor for the protesters and joining them in toasts of "Damnation to the Stamp Act." When British merchants realized that the tax was hurting their business, they called for its repeal in London. Parliament succumbed, and the Stamp Act was repealed.

The Townshend duties taxed and regulated local coastal shipping for the first time. Henry Laurens was so irritated that he twisted Chief Customs Agent Daniel Moore's nose on the Battery. But more noses than Moore's were out of joint in Charlestown.

Despite repeal, events continued to push the planters closer to rebellion. Planters, after all, needed hard-to-find credit because financing staple crops was expensive. And the next axe to fall, the Townshend Revenue Acts of 1767, made the situation worse. The Acts laid a tax on paper, glass, and other articles of commerce, raising prices and creating what seemed to the Charlestonians a permanent class of British customs officers, "a set of Harpies . . . let loose among ye, to Destroy Your Trade . . . harass ye to Death." The fact that the Townshend Acts also permitted searches without warrants in places where smuggled or untaxed goods might be found was even more ominous.

By June 1767 the planters were coming around to the mechanics' point of view and attending meetings at the Liberty Tree. The strategy was to join the northern colonies in refusing to import or buy British goods. John Mackenzie, a planter, joined with Gadsden and Thomas Lynch ("a man of sense," Governor Bull wrote, but "very obstinate in urging to extremity") in leading the growing radical movement.

Because nonimportation hurt the Charlestown merchants, they became involved in the movement in order to protect their interests. A committee composed of equal numbers of merchants, mechanics, and planters was formed to enforce the nonimportation pact, which, very simply, forbade anyone from importing goods from England. Not everyone agreed. William Wragg, William Henry Drayton, and many others bitterly opposed non-importation; loyalists abounded in Charlestown at the beginning of the 1760s and throughout the war.

All during this period there was, or seemed to be, an increase in what Charlestonians called "placemen," that is, Englishmen appointed in England to serve in the colony in the place of local people. Customs officers were placemen. Charles Pinckney was replaced by a placeman, Peter Leigh, as Chief Justice. Peter Leigh's son, Egerton Leigh, replaced John Rutledge as attorney general. Daniel Moore succeeded Beaufain as collector of customs. Royal judges replaced local ones. Local government gave way to strangers. The meetings at the Liberty Tree grew louder, more numerous, and more radical.

Things went from bad to worse in 1772 when the royal governor decided

The Liberty Tree's exact location has been lost, but its approximate location is marked by a plaque placed by the Sons of the American Revolution in 1906 at 80 Alexander Street (near the Gaillard Municipal Auditorium on Calhoun Street).

A Short History of Charleston

to teach the Assembly a lesson. On the pretext that he could not find suitable accommodations in Charlestown he ordered the Assembly to meet in Beaufort, 75 miles away. Making Charlestonians go anywhere is difficult in any age, but Beaufort was Beaufort and a day's journey to boot. The royal governor evidently believed the leaders of the revolutionary movement would not bother to attend. He was wrong.

The legislature met in record numbers and angrily denounced the governor. Not only had he arbitrarily moved the place of government, but he had also delayed the meeting of the Assembly, kept the members in Beaufort for three days without conducting business, made a condescending speech to the Assembly, and then abruptly ordered the Assembly back to Charlestown.

Parliament repealed the Townshend Acts, but kept the duty on tea, which was probably the worst mistake yet. Having alienated mechanics, lawyers, and printers with the Stamp Act, now Parliament alienated the merchants. Under the Tea Act a government-subsidized monopoly, the East India Company, would have the exclusive right to sell tea without paying duty. The sagging radical movement was rejuvenated. When tea arrived in Charlestown it was resolved not to allow it to land. In Boston they dumped the tea overboard. In Charlestown it ended up in the vaults of the Exchange.

In January 1774, the people of Charlestown established an Executive Committee to keep more tea from landing, but Boston was the center of the storm. The tea party there angered Parliament so much that it passed what came to be called the Intolerable Acts, among them: the Boston Port Act, which closed the port of Boston; the Quartering Act, which allowed the royal governor to commandeer private homes for troops; and other acts restricting the Massachusetts colony. Reaction was swift throughout the colonies and the First Continental Congress met in Philadelphia in September of that same year.

South Carolina sent five delegates — all Charlestonians — to the Continental Congress: Henry Middleton, John Rutledge, Christopher Gadsden, Thomas Lynch, and Edward Rutledge. Henry Middleton and John Rutledge were the unanimous choice of all factions, but support for the other delegates was split between the merchants and the mechanics. The mechanics won the heated contest. South Carolinians joined every other colony in sending aid to beleaguered Boston. The good people of Charleston sent money and barrels of rice.

Government of the colony and the city now fell to an extralegal body, the Provincial Congress, which had representatives from all parts of the province.

When planter Francis Salvador was elected to the Provincial Congress, he became perhaps the first Jew in modern history anywhere in the world to be elected to a popular assembly.

The mechanics were well represented in this body in contrast to the old colonial Commons. Names like Cannon, Lockwood, Timothy, Trezevant, and Berwick began to be heard in the halls of government, along with Pinckney and Manigault.

Charlestonians awaited a peaceful resolution of the conflict. The great majority still did not want separation from Britain. Throughout the controversy, Charlestown's families were divided on the issues. Regarding the Stamp Act, William Bull was for the King; his nephews were for the revolutionaries. William Moultrie became a great revolutionary general; his brother remained royal lieutenant governor of Florida. Daniel Heyward was a Tory; his son, Thomas Heyward, signed the Declaration of Independence. The same divisions could be found in the Drayton, Pinckney, Horry, Manigault, Huger, and Lowndes families. The Reverend John Bullman, Assistant Minister of St. Michael's, preached a sermon on Sunday, August 14, 1774, chiding "every silly clown and illiterate mechanic [who] will take upon him to censure the conduct of his Prince or Governor." A meeting was called to challenge Reverend Bullman, and he was ousted by a vote of 42 to 33. The action was hotly disputed. When Reverend Bullman sailed for England he left with a testimonial signed by 81 members of the Church and 986 pounds as a gift. Charlestonians were still divided on the Revolution. But the conflict was not to be resolved. And in the Revolution, as in the Civil War later, brother was to fight brother.

The signers of the Declaration of Independence risked their lives and fortunes for liberty. But the Charlestown delegates fought Jefferson's first draft, which declared that the King "has waged cruel war against human nature itself, violating its most sacred rights of life and liberty in the persons of a distant people who never offended him . . . carrying them into slavery." The paragraph condemning slavery was deleted from the Declaration. The Declaration was signed on August 2, 1776 by 56 revolutionaries, including four young South Carolinians: Edward Rutledge (age 26), Thomas Heyward, Jr. (29), Thomas Lynch (26), and Arthur Middleton (34).

Came the Revolution: The "embattled farmers" of Lexington and Concord in Massachusetts faced British redcoats, and eight were killed on April 19, 1775. The shot may have been heard around the world, but it took time to reach Charlestown. When the news arrived on May 8, 1775, the mechanics were generally for independence and war. Most of the merchants, planters, and "substantial citizens" of Charlestown, however, were for strong measures short of war. John Rutledge recalled years later that a blacksmith, William Johnson, was "the man who first moved the ball of revolution in Charlestown." Yet others were openly for revolt. "I can only tell you," Peter Timothy wrote, "that the Plebeians are still for War — but the noblesse perfectly pacfic [sic]." By June the revolutionary Secret Committee was tarring and feathering those loyal to the Crown.

Every effort at reconciliation with the English government having failed, the American colonies declared their independence. Independence was adopted in principle on July 2, 1776.

A Short History of Charleston

On the very day the committee assigned to draft the Declaration of Independence reported to Congress, the first attempt by the British to crush the revolt in the South was made in Charlestown harbor. Charlestonians were to provide the new nation with one of its first victories. A fort of palmetto tree logs from Dewees Island was hastily constructed on Sullivan's Island. The commander of the fort was General William Moultrie. North of Sullivan's Island lay Long Island (now called the Isle of Palms). Across the harbor was Fort Johnson and the First Regiment commanded by Gadsden.

Moultrie had 435 men from two units, the Second South Carolina Infantry and the Fourth South Carolina Regiment. The north end of Sullivan's Island was secured by 780 men under Colonel William Thompson of Orangeburg. Thompson and his rangers, dragoons, and 50 "Raccoon Riflemen" (from their coonskin caps) awaited the British from behind two small sand batteries.

The British fleet consisted of 50 ships and 3,000 soldiers under the command of Sir Henry Clinton and Lord Charles Cornwallis. The British strategy was to land the soldiers on Long Island, cross Breach Inlet (separating Long from Sullivan's Island) while the ships bombarded the little fort on Sullivan's Island. But Breach Inlet, then as now, proved to be dangerous and deep.

On June 28 the fleet set about its business. There were 11 ships carrying 270 guns anchored off Fort Sullivan, and the bombardment began. The fort, made of spongy palmetto logs, held. Though the British aim was good, their shots did not do great damage. The British fleet, on the other hand, suffered terribly: the Admiral's flagship, the *Bristol,* suffered most, and all men aboard were wounded. The captains of both the *Bristol* and the *Experiment* were killed. Three British ships ran aground on the shoal on which Fort Sumter now stands, preventing them from attacking the fort on its most vulnerable side. Sir Peter Parker had "the hindpart of his breeches shot away, which laid his posteriors bare." The British lost over 100 men and at least one ship, and they suffered heavy damage to other ships. The Americans lost only 12 men.

At one point in the Battle of Fort Moultrie the new state's blue and white flag was shot away. The cheering British thought the lowering of the flag meant surrender, but a brave little Irishman, Sergeant Jasper, replaced it. His actions, now a legend in South Carolina, are best described by an eyewitness: "The expression of a Sergeant McDaniel, after a cannon ball had taken off his shoulder and scouped out his stomach, is worth recording in the annals of America: 'Fight on, my brave boys; don't let liberty expire with me today!' . . . My old Grenadier, Ser. Jasper upon the shot carrying away the flag-staff,

Soldier of the Revolution: General William Moultrie, victorious over the British in 1776, was later captured and offered a regiment of red-coats. "Good God! Is it possible that such an idea could arise in the breast of a man of honor?" He survived to march into Charleston at the head of American troops.

In remembrance of the palmetto logs that saved the day on Sullivan's Island, the palmetto tree was affixed to the state flag. South Carolina became the Palmetto State. Fort Sullivan became Fort Moultrie in honor of General Moultrie, and Colonel Thompson is remembered by a bridge named Thompson Bridge over Breach Inlet.

A. Ft. Sullivan (Ft. Moultrie)
B. Ft. Johnson
C. Breach Inlet
D. John's Is.
E. Hadrell's Pt.
F. Provost Prison (under Old Exchange)
G. Snee Farm

called out to Col. Moultrie: 'Col. don't let us fight without our flag.' 'What can you do?' replied the Col.; 'the staff is broke.' 'Then, sir,' said he, 'I'll fix it to a halbert, and place it on the merlon of the bastion, next to the enemy;' which he did, through the thickest fire."

Charlestown, having witnessed the first great victory of the American Revolution, was ecstatic, and for three years Charlestown was spared further military involvement. The port was open and trade was booming. Young Charlestonians fought elsewhere. But Charlestown's role in the War for Independence was just beginning. Two events signaled the tragedy to come: an incompetent general, Benjamin Lincoln of Massachusetts, was sent to defend the Carolinas and Georgia, and Savannah had fallen to the British by 1778. It was just a matter of time before Charlestown suffered the same fate.

The British had about 40,000 soldiers to Washington's 27,000. The overall British strategy was to squeeze Washington in a vice between the north and south. After New York was secured, Sir Henry Clinton, the British commander, sailed for Savannah. And, when Savannah fell he moved toward Charlestown. Determined not to make the same mistake twice by trying to capture Charlestown by way of the harbor, Clinton landed on John's Island on February 11, 1780. He easily made his way to James Island and then crossed the Ashley River to the Neck, just north of the city. General Lincoln, bullied into defending an indefensible Charlestown by popular demand, kept his troops in the city instead of placing them in the outlying areas where they could surprise the enemy or at least escape to fight elsewhere. The British commander had almost 8,000 regular troops under his command, 2,000 of whom were Hessian (German) mercenaries. Governor Rutledge and three of his council fled on April 12 to avoid the capture of the state's government.

State of Siege: The siege of Charlestown began on April 13 and lasted one month. One shell hit the statue of William Pitt, taking off his right arm. The women were sent out of the city or sent to the cellars. Bombs, "red-hot balls" and "carcasses" (an iron-frame bomb) descended on the city, bringing fires and death. Finally, the people of Charlestown asked to surrender.

The terms of surrender were that regular Continental troops would become prisoners and that soldiers of the militia and townspeople could return home on parole if they promised not to take up arms against the King again. They did not, however, have to agree to take up arms *for* the King. "Sir," one British officer said to Moultrie, "you have made a gallant defense.

But you had a great many rascals among you . . . who came out at night and gave us information of what was passing in town." The Tories of Charlestown were still active.

The Siege of Charleston during the American Revolution.

    Charlestown was occupied for the remainder of the Revolutionary War. The Tories had their day. Two hundred citizens presented an address to the British conquerors declaring their loyalty. Some entertained the British officers and offered their assistance. Most Charlestonians, however, remained loyal to the Revolution. Despite the terms of the surrender, 33 Charlestonians, including Christopher Gadsden, Edward Rutledge, Thomas Heyward, Jr., Peter Timothy, and David Ramsay, were soon arrested for no reason and imprisoned, first in the Exchange and then in a prison ship in the harbor.

Charles Cotesworth Pinckney. Later as a diplomat, Pinckney was said to have uttered the famous words, "Millions for defense, not a cent for tribute."

Finally they were exiled to St. Augustine, Florida, where the fiery Gadsden refused any parole with the British and consequently spent nearly 11 months in a dungeon. When warned that he would be confined to the dungeon, Gadsden replied: "Prepare it. I will give no parole, so help me God." Other Charlestonians were confined in the "Provost," the "damp dark cellar under the Exchange." Men and women of all classes were rounded up and confined together. Some died. Continental officers were imprisoned at Haddrell's Point in Mt. Pleasant. Moultrie and Charles Cotesworth Pinckney were quartered at Snee Farm.

Soon the British, led by Colonel Banestre Tarleton, later called "Bloody Tarleton," began a reign of terror in the countryside. Because British officers and soldiers could legally take the property of "traitors," it was extremely profitable for them to loot. Silver, china, slaves, or other removable valuables were theirs for the taking. This reign of terror was, however, a major blunder, because it roused the small farmers of the upcountry, and drove most of them into the ranks of the revolutionaries. The Gamecock, Thomas Sumter, and the Swamp Fox, Francis Marion, of St. John's, Berkeley, soon finished what the Moultries and the Gadsdens had begun. South Carolina lost more men in the Revolutionary War than any other state, but it was this sacrifice that was ultimately to break the back of the British Army.

The Revolution was almost as much a civil war in Charlestown as it was a war for independence. Those Charlestonians loyal to the King and those loyal to the Revolution became bitter enemies during the last years of the war. Reverend Samuel Prioleau, writing his wife from St. Augustine, declared: "If anything . . . should happen to me that is to say being hung or shot, which I believe they dare not do, I hope my sons will revenge it when they are able, and never be at peace with Great Britain. We hear that the Prisoners familys [sic] have been insulted. I beg as a particular favour if any has insulted you or any of my family you will let me know who it was, and what was the insult, as I think I stand a chance of being relieved and may meet them in some part of the world."

To make matters worse, Sir Henry Clinton next decided to break his agreement and require all South Carolinians to declare allegiance to the crown or lose their right to sue in court, to travel freely, and to conduct their business. Many honorable patriots were forced to accept Clinton's terms or lose their livelihoods. The British also made very tempting offers to Moultrie, the Pinckneys, and others if they would take command of British troops. Bitterness toward the British and Loyalists reached a new peak.

Despite the danger, Charlestonians throughout the occupation gave as much aid as they could to their men at arms. The women of Charlestown smuggled food and clothing to the soldiers and, as Mrs. St. Julian Ravenel tells it, helped in other ways: "Widows were at great advantage; being responsible for no man's proceedings, they were less severely dealt with than were other women, and with the danger of no man's life or liberty on their hearts, they could give their favourite weapon — the tongue — full play." Nor did the women of Charlestown's aristocracy lose their sense of humor. When Tarleton derided Colonel William Washington as "an ignorant fellow" who "could not write his name," Mrs. Charles Elliott replied, "at least, Colonel, he can make his mark," an allusion to Tarleton's hand, from which Washington had cut three fingers with his sword.

The execution of Isaac Hayne.

The Execution of Isaac Hayne: The cruelty of the British was most forcibly expressed in their treatment of Colonel Isaac Hayne, a prominent planter from St. Paul's parish. Hayne had fought for independence with his fellows in the militia and had been paroled along with the rest after the fall of Charlestown. When Clinton illegally changed the conditions of the parole on June 2, 1780, Hayne was ordered to declare his loyalty to the King and bear arms for the King or face imprisonment. Hayne signed the declaration so that he could be with his dying wife and sick children. He was assured by the British, however, that he would never be forced to bear arms against his countrymen. Later the British demanded that he fight for the Crown. Hayne was indignant and, feeling that the British had broken their word, determined to fight again. Unfortunately, he was captured.

The war in South Carolina was not faring well for the British by the time of Colonel Hayne's capture on July 8, 1781. Sumter and Marion were actively harassing the Tories and the British. Men who had sworn loyalty to the King were rejoining the rebels. Lieutenant Colonel Balfour, Commandant of Charlestown, and Lieutenant Colonel Lord Rawdon, now Supreme Commander in South Carolina, decided to make an example of Hayne. Without a proper trial, they ordered his death as a traitor to the crown.

Charlestonians were infuriated and disgusted. Tories as well as rebels petitioned Balfour and Rawdon. Colonel Hayne's deceased wife's sister, Mrs. Arthur Peronneau, and the little Hayne children begged on their knees at the Brewton House before Rawdon to spare Hayne's life. British officers requested that Rawdon allow Hayne to die like a soldier, like the worthy

The Exchange Building was the city's first city hall and played host to a splendid "dancing assembly" in honor of George Washington in 1791.

adversary he was, instead of suffering the death of a traitor. Rawdon would not budge.

On August 4, 1781, Colonel Hayne, accompanied by a few friends, walked from the Provost jail beneath the Old Exchange Building on East Bay Street to the place of his execution. He did not know how he was to die until he left the town gates at the site of present-day King Street between George and Liberty. He paused when he learned that he was to be hanged. His friends urged him to die with courage, and he replied, "I will try."

Isaac Hayne died with great courage. He mounted the cart, which when pulled away would mean his death, without assistance. He prayed for his soul, shook his friends' hands, and drew a hood over his face. He signaled the hangman that he was ready to die. And so Isaac Hayne gave his life for his country — without fear and "with perfect calmness and dignity."

Cornwallis had left South Carolina a prostrate state when he departed with his troops for points north. But the barbarity of British military policies stirred the people to rise up with even greater vigor. The battles of Eutaw Springs and Cowpens proved the undoing of the British in South Carolina. They were driven back to Charlestown.

Meanwhile, events in New York, France, and a little town in Virginia called Yorktown decided the fate of America. King Louis XVI of France decided to commit the major part of his navy to support the Americans against the British; Admiral de Grasse cooperated with Washington and Rochambeau, and sealed up Cornwallis at Yorktown. Clinton, safe in New York, would not budge. Washington made an unexpected decision to attack Cornwallis at Yorktown rather than Clinton in New York. Cornwallis surrendered on October 19, 1781, as military bands played "The World Turned Upside Down."

Almost one year later, the British troops left Charlestown via Gadsden's Wharf, taking with them the booty of war — silver, plates, church books, and the bells of St. Michael's Church, which a Major Traille of the Royal Artillery claimed as his "perquisite." The evacuation was tense but peaceful. The American army left its camps at Ashley Hall and Middleton Place in St. Andrews Parish, crossed the river at Bee's Ferry, and spent the night. As the British departed, the Americans arrived. General Moultrie describes the scene: "I can never forget the happy day when we marched into Charlestown with the American troops; it was a proud day to me, and I felt myself much elated at seeing the balconies, the doors and windows crowded with the patriotick fair, the aged citizens and others congratulating us on our return home, saying

'God bless you, gentlemen,' — 'You are welcome, gentlemen.' Both citizens and soldiers shed tears of joy."

But Charlestown was in ruins. Its neighboring plantations were devastated. Government was in disarray. The victors sought vengeance against the Tories. The end of the war brought great ferment and change. There was fortunately, if inevitably, a postwar boom in business, trade, and especially building. After all, the town had to be rebuilt. In the political arena, the inevitable clash between the mechanics, the merchants, and the planters had not been avoided, only postponed.

In 1783 and 1784 there were riots of all kinds in Charlestown. Violence was directed mainly at the Tories. Some was directed by the Tories at those loyal to the Revolution. Some involved class riots pitting a "democratic" element against everything aristocratic and British. The worst riot occurred on July 11, 1783. Tarring and feathering were frequent.

The mechanics criticized the planters for their use of slave labor, and for their leniency toward the Tories. The merchant class was now largely made up of new British merchants who became established during the occupation and decided to stay on after the peace was concluded. The status of the merchant in Charlestown society suffered from this period forward. Democratic societies were formed to resist what was seen as an aristocratic takeover of government. Alexander Gillon founded the Marine Anti-Britannic Society to harass the Tories and the British and to encourage trade with other countries.

New Governments Are Born: It is significant that the municipal government of Charlestown was born in the tumultuous year 1783. Charlestown, it will be recalled, had no municipal government throughout the colonial era, that is, there was no mayor or city council. Now the General Assembly acted, apparently because it feared the violence in the streets, to establish a city government. So on August 13, 1783, after a summer of civil disorder, Charlestown was incorporated, and its name was changed to Charleston.

At last the city had a municipal government. The mayor was known as the Intendant. Elected representatives were known as Wardens. Together they formed the City Council of Charleston, which was given wide authority to regulate the "harbour, streets, lanes, public buildings, work-houses, markets, wharves, publichouses, carriages, wagons, carts, drays, pumps, buckets, fire-engines . . . seamen or disorderly people [and] negroes."

The Intendant became known as the Mayor and the Wardens became known as Aldermen in 1836. The 1783 charter remained in effect as legal basis for the city until 1976, when, under a new Home Rule Act, each city in South Carolina received a standardized charter. The Aldermen are now called Members of Council.

John Rutledge: Revolutionary, Governor, Judge, and one of the architects of the United States Constitution. He was appointed Chief Justice of the United States by George Washington.

In the first city election, the voters chose a pro-aristocratic Intendant, Richard Hutson, but the Council reflected all elements of Charleston society (except, of course, blacks). Some mechanics were elected. But riots and violence continued despite the best efforts of the new Council and many mechanic societies, which were concerned lest the city fall into a permanent state of anarchy.

In March 1784 the most famous confrontation of this period occurred. John Rutledge was invited to a dinner to be given by the Sons of Saint Patrick and told a tavernkeeper, Captain William Thompson, he could not attend. Thompson apparently forgot to pass along the message. Rutledge summoned Thompson to explain his behavior. Thompson took offense at Rutledge's questioning, and a great argument ensued. The House of Representatives, at Rutledge's request, investigated the matter and ordered that Thompson be arrested "for a gross insult on" a member of the House! Thompson demanded a hearing and an attorney. He was released, but the incident further deepened the bitter divisions between the mechanics and "common folk" and the aristocracy or "Nabobs," as they were called by their enemies. Thompson complained he was punished because *the great John Rutledge* was individually offended by a *plebian.* Rioting broke out again in July, after a Fourth of July celebration. Soon, however, the city settled down.

The mechanics reached their peak of power in the postrevolutionary period. Over time they were absorbed into the planter class or at least into a class of small farmers who owned a few slaves. The people of the city and the state became resigned to the fact that South Carolina in general and Charlestown in particular would be a democracy, but a democracy generally dominated by an aristocratic ruling class.

Charlestonians of all classes were committed to the future under a new flag and a new government. Henry Laurens, for example, imprisoned in the Tower of London, was released and exchanged for Lord Cornwallis. He then went to France and helped to negotiate the treaty of peace, together with Benjamin Franklin, John Jay, and John Adams. Charlestonians muddled through the Confederation period along with the rest of the country and saw the need for a new form of national government. Four Charlestonians — Pierce Butler, Charles Pinckney, Charles Cotesworth Pinckney, and John Rutledge — went to Philadelphia in 1787 and helped to draft and then have their state ratify the new Constitution of the United States.

Charlestonians strongly favored the new federal government. Trade was the basis of Charleston's economy, and stable international trade required a strong national government. Charlestonians were in the forefront when that government was created. Charles Pinckney and John Rutledge had dinner together at Rutledge's home at 116 Broad Street prior to leaving for Philadelphia. There the two men met and discussed the shape the new Constitution would take. From that meeting emerged "the Pinckney Draught," Charles Pinckney's proposed draft of the new Constitution. "Indeed," as the historian James M. Beck has written, "Pinckney's plan was the future Constitution of the United States in embryo. . . ."

That draft was presented to the convention on May 29, 1787. Undoubtedly John Rutledge, later elected to chair the Committee on Detail (which actually wrote the first draft of the Constitution), had a copy of Pinckney's draft before his committee.

Pinckney proposed many key provisions of the Constitution. He proposed on August 30, 1787, and the Convention adopted, an amendment to Article XX of the Constitution that states "no religious test shall ever be required as a qualification to any office or public trust under the authority of the United States." As all states had a religious test for public office, it was an important precedent. He proposed a limitation on congressional powers to appropriate money and to raise and support armies for a longer term than two years. Indeed some historians view Pinckney as the earliest proponent of a Bill of Rights which the federal Convention did *not* propose.

Pinckney also contributed immensely to the creation of the presidency. The Virginia Plan did not specify the nature of the Executive, and, in fact, Governor Randolph, the proponent of the Virginia Plan, vigorously pressed for a three-person Executive Branch together with a "Council of Revision" to be composed of the executives and a number of federal judges. It was analogous to the British Privy Council. Pinckney's plan and his argument on the floor, however, called for a single executive to be called the "President." The name was Pinckney's suggestion.

Pinckney also proposed that the House of Representatives should exclusively possess the power of impeachment; that the President report on the "state of the union"; that the President commission all officers and that he be the Commander-in-Chief of the Army and Navy. Pinckney's other contributions include the names of the House and Senate; granting the Congress the power to coin money, to establish post offices, to call forth the aid of the militia; provisions forbidding the states from maintaining an armed force in time of peace and forbidding the states from coining money. Pinckney proposed that each house choose its own presiding officers and establish its own

Charles Pinckney in a portrait attributed to Gilbert Stuart. His boasting about his role in drafting the Constitution earned him the nickname "Constitution Charlie." Though Pinckney argued for a pro-slavery Constitution, he was the first to propose a Bill of Rights.

rules. Pinckney first proposed uniform bankruptcy laws.

Pinckney never received the credit he deserved for his contributions. In the first place, he was intensely disliked by James Madison, who kept the best journal of the convention. He was vain and pompous. And his records were all destroyed by fire and he left no credible account himself. A biographer later wrote: "A very strange and melancholy feeling overtakes us as we search the remains of Charles Pinckney. Here is a man upon whom Heaven appears to have showered its gifts . . . and yet, here are his memorials in a few tattered bits of paper. . . ." Modern historians, however, appreciate his role. Christopher Collier wrote, "The Father of the Constitution he was not; but he must be seen as one of the group, with James Madison, James Wilson, Roger Sherman, and others, who did the most in shaping it."

John Rutledge, too, was instrumental in the writing and ratification of the Constitution. He headed the Committee which wrote the final document. In the 1830's Alexis de Tocqueville, a French journalist, came to the United States to study its people and government. His book, *Democracy In America*, became a classic. He researched the origin of the Constitution and was told Thomas Jefferson had written it. De Tocqueville knew Jefferson was in France at the time, so he knew that wasn't possible. After researching the archives and interviewing numerous people, he exclaimed "There is no mystery about it — the authorship of the Constitution is quite clear — a man named John Rutledge wrote it." De Tocqueville came to Charleston to interview Rutledge's family, but it was 50 years later and they knew very little of Rutledge's contribution. It had been forgotten.

Charlestonians also worked for ratification of the Constitution. Those who supported it became known as Federalists. Their opponents, generally older residents of the upcountry, were anti-Federalists. In May 1788 Charleston and the Low Country voted overwhelmingly for ratification. The upcountry voted overwhelmingly against it.

Ratification of the federal Constitution led to a movement in the upcountry for a new state constitution. Charleston had lost her place in 1786 when the capital was removed to the Taylor plantation in the center of the state, and, as David Duncan Wallace writes, "given the nationalistic name Columbia." The convention called in 1790 to rewrite the state constitution voted again on the location of the state capital. By a vote of 109 to 105 the capital remained at the plantation named Columbia (a city-to-be).

Charlestonians did not give up. They sought to have two capitals! (The idea was not unique. Rhode Island had two capitals — Newport and Providence — until 1900; Connecticut had two capitals until 1874.) A compromise was reached in which there would be two state treasurers, certain state offices would function in both Charleston and Columbia, and the Courts of Appeals would convene in both cities. The legislature could, by a two-thirds vote, move the capital. Thus Charleston unwillingly lost its status as the capital of South Carolina.

Charlestonians were active in government affairs from the national to the local level throughout the remainder of the century: William Moultrie, Thomas Pinckney, Charles Pinckney, Arnoldus Vander Horst, and Edward Rutledge served as Governor. John Rutledge became Chief Justice of the United States in 1795, although he was never confirmed by the Senate. Charles Cotesworth Pinckney served as Washington's Minister to France after rejecting an offer to become Secretary of State.

In 1797, Pinckney was sent to France, together with John Marshall and Elbridge Gerry, to negotiate with the French government, which, in the aftermath of the French Revolution, allowed French privateers to prey on American ships. When Tallyrand, the French Foreign Minister, secretly proposed, through envoys named X, Y, and Z, the possibility of a bribe of $250,000 and a $10 million loan in order to negotiate, Pinckney held firm. "No, not a sixpence," he said. Or, as a congressman reported it: "Millions for defense, not a cent for tribute." The XYZ affair caused a great stir in America. Pinckney was welcomed home in grand style. Charlestonians armed themselves for a possible war with France. Castle Pinckney was built in the harbor. Fort Mechanic (built by labor donated by the mechanics) was built on East Battery.

Pinckney's role in the XYZ affair earned him his party's nomination for Vice-President of the United States. He ran as a Federalist with John Adams against Republicans Thomas Jefferson and Aaron Burr, but he lost. Charleston remained a Federalist bastion, and Pinckney was the Federalist nominee for President in 1804 and 1808.

In 1791, President George Washington visited Charleston as part of a southern tour. He arrived at Prioleau's Wharf at the foot of Queen Street on a barge manned by 12 captains of various ships then in port, accompanied by "a flotilla of boats of all sizes filled with ladies and gentlemen." He was welcomed to Charleston by the Governor, the Lieutenant Governor, the Intendant (Mr. Vander Horst), the City Council, and the Society of the Cincinnati, an organization of Revolutionary War officers. The crowd proceeded to the Exchange where Washington stood "bareheaded on the steps and received the cheers and homage of the public." The president was wined and dined in the

Charles Pinckney's mansion — now destroyed — once stood at 16 Meeting Street, now the site of the Calhoun Mansion, a large Victorian home constructed by a descendant of John C. Calhoun after the Civil War.

Columbia was laid out on the Taylor plantation, "The Plains." Colonel Taylor is reputed to have said: "They spoiled a damned fine plantation to make a damned poor town." Charlestonians agreed.

James Hoban, the architect of the White House, met George Washington on his trip to Charleston in 1791. Hoban may have been the architect of the Charleston County Courthouse.

The Charleston County Courthouse as it appeared after the Civil War.

finest Charleston tradition.

Of the Charleston ladies, Washington wrote in his journal: "Went to a concert where were 400 ladies, the number and appearance of wch. exceeded anything I had ever seen . . . . was visited about two o'clock by a great number of the most respectable ladies of Charleston, the first honour of the kind I had ever experienced, as flattering as singular." In Washington's honor, the ladies of Charleston wore ribbons painted with the President's likeness and the words "God bless our President." The Father of His Country won the hearts of all Charlestonians, then left for Savannah.

While in Charleston, Washington was taken on a tour of the city and undoubtedly took an interest in the new courthouse which was almost completed. The President had charge of building the new "Federal City" later named for him and he was searching for competent architects and builders. The State House, erected with such pride only 35 years before, had mysteriously burned in 1788 just before it was to serve as the site of the Ratification Convention for the United States Constitution. Because of the fire, the Ratification Convention was held at the Exchange Building. Since the capitol was being moved to Columbia, the Assembly decided to rebuild the State House, its walls still intact, as a courthouse. James Hoban, a young Irish builder, probably was involved with its rebuilding in some way. Washington, on his return to the Federal City, decided to hire Hoban to build "the President's House," now called the White House. Washington had met Hoban, whom he remembered as a "practical builder," in Charleston; he was introduced to him by the Commissioners appointed to build the Courthouse. Hoban went on to design the White House and its original design was based, so it appears, on the 1792 Charleston Courthouse. The leading historian of the White House, William Seale, in his definitive history, *The President's House,* contends that the Courthouse was probably a "model for the president's house."

A Charleston newspaper put it this way in 1792: "We have received accounts from the Northward, and with much satisfaction, that Mr. James Hoban, of this city, has furnished the best plan, section and elevation for the presidential palace in the federal city of Washington. . . ." Hoban and Charleston should have been proud. He beat out two designs by Thomas Jefferson himself.

Charlestonians continued calling this venerable building the "State House" even after its use changed to a courthouse. They hoped the State would come to its senses and bring the capitol back where it belonged.

The 18th century closed on an optimistic note. Charleston was recovering rapidly from the ravages of the Revolution. The economy was booming. Population was expanding. Native sons had played a great role in the War for Independence and in the creation of the new federal government. The future looked bright. Perhaps the only ominous note at the close of the century was the arrival in Charleston of refugees from Santo Domingo (now Haiti) in the early 1790s. The French refugees added color, gaiety, cultivation, and high fashion to Charleston's life. But the reason for their flight was not lost on Charlestonians: A bloody slave revolt had turned the island into a battleground. Thousands of whites were killed or wounded by black revolutionaries. The lesson was not lost on Charleston's blacks, either. "They write from Charleston (S.C.) that the NEGROES have become very insolent," one northern newspaper reported in 1793, "in so much that the citizens are alarmed, and the militia keep a constant guard."

In 1785 Thomas Jefferson wrote of slavery: "Indeed I tremble for my country when I reflect that God is just: that his justice cannot sleep for ever." Like Mr. Jefferson, Charlestonians of the late 18th century were troubled by slavery, the South's "peculiar institution." Yet for years to come its continued existence as an institution was beyond question.

In a very real sense Charleston and Charlestonians delivered South Carolina to the Federalists. Historians generally agree that the majority of South Carolinians were opposed to the ratification of the United States Constitution.

* * *

A final note on Charleston and the Constitution:

A TOAST TO THE CONSTITUTION
Given by The Honorable Alexander Sanders, Chief Judge of the South Carolina Court of Appeals at Charleston, South Carolina, September 16, 1987, On the Occasion of The Bicentennial of the Signing of the United States Constitution:

Three things of lasting value are uniquely products of the United States of America: Jazz music, Mark Twain and the Constitution. We can take pride in the fact that all three were produced in the South. Jazz music was, of course, invented in New Orleans. Mark Twain was, of course, born on the Mississippi River. And, as everyone knows, the Constitution was carried to Philadelphia by Charles Pinckney of South Carolina with perhaps some assistance from Washington and Madison of Virginia.

At the same time, however, we are constrained to recognize the further fact that all three were exported to the North soon after their creation. Jazz music was sold up the river and has scarcely been heard from since, at least not around here lately. Mark Twain ended up in New England, where he achieved his greatest popularity. And, even sadder to say, the Constitution has not always been uniformly embraced on this side of the Mason-Dixon Line.

So, with these facts in mind, my wish on this occasion for the Constitution, the most enduring charter of freedom the world has ever known, is that it may continue to endure in perpetuity and with it, the United States of America, and to these ends, that we, as patriotic sons and daughters of the South, may always realize the essential truth spoken by that quintessential Yankee, Daniel Webster, when he said, "One country, one Constitution, one destiny."

The Capital of Southern Slavery (1670–1865)

4

The institution of slavery shaped and defined Charleston as much as, if not more than, any other force in its history. The economy and the great wealth of the city rested on slave labor, and Charleston was more committed to the institution than any other southern city. Charleston was unique among colonial cities because its population was half black, and more whites in Charleston owned slaves than in any other city. In 1820 and 1840 three-fourths of all "heads of families" in Charleston owned at least one slave (compared to New Orleans, where two-thirds of the whites owned slaves in 1820, or Savannah, where one-half owned them). "Carolina looks more like a Negro country than like a country settled by white people," Samuel Dyssli wrote in the early colonial era.

On August 23, 1670, five months after the original settlement, the first slave was brought to Charles Town from Virginia. He was described simply as "one lusty negro man." A few weeks later, three other slaves arrived from Bermuda. Others, many others, followed.

Charleston was America's major slaveport. "Here was a thin neck in the hourglass of the Afro-American past," wrote Peter H. Wood in his brilliant work, *Black Majority,* "a place where individual grains from all along the West African coast had been funneled together, only to be fanned out across the American landscape with the passage of time." Newly arrived slaves were initially quarantined at Sullivan's Island so they would not bring disease and sickness into the country. In a sense, Sullivan's Island might, according to Wood, "well be viewed as the Ellis Island of Black Americans."

Slavery in Charles Town was a product of forces at work for a hundred years before the city was founded. Englishmen had come across black people

In 1860 Charleston's slave population was 13,909. New Orleans's was 13,385, Savannah's 7,712, and Richmond's 11,699.

Opposite page
Slave sale: Most slaves were sold on or near East Bay Street. This engraving is from the *Illustrated London News,* 1856.

in West Africa in the 1550s, when, as Winthrop D. Jordan has written, "one of the fairest-skinned nations suddenly came face to face with one of the darkest peoples on earth." The result was not good. The English, unlike the Spanish, had had no experience with darker-skinned people. Blacks were mysterious. Captain Thomas Phillips wrote in 1694 that blacks "in odium of the colour say, the devil is white, and so paint him." Some Englishmen cited Ham's Scriptural curse to prove that blacks were accursed. They were clearly not Christians but savages, and the English relished stories of cannibalism and other barbarities.

Shakespeare, in *Othello*, expressed as early as 1602 the racism that was to plague Charlestonians from their earliest days: "Her name, that was as fresh,/As Dian's visage, is now begrim'd and black/ As mine own face," laments Othello.

To the English, as to the Spanish, slavery came to mean "negro slavery." "The term *negro* itself," Jordan writes, "was incorporated into English from the Hispanic languages in mid-sixteenth century.... This is more striking because a perfectly adequate term, identical in meaning to *negro,* already existed in English," namely, "black." Slavery, as the English adopted it, had many, if not all, of the characteristics that were to distinguish Southern slavery.

The pattern was set in the West Indies where the Lord Proprietors owned slaves before Carolina was even settled. As there was no such thing as slavery in England in the 17th century, the English settlers there took slavery as they found it. Barbadians adopted the practices of the Spanish and the Portuguese, who had utilized slave labor in the New World since the early 1500s. The English made what Jordan has called an "unthinking decision"; they just followed along.

Slavery was brought to Charles Town by men already familiar with its practice. Sir John Colleton was a planter from Barbados, and Sir Anthony Ashley Cooper was part owner of a Barbadian plantation in the 1640s. The Berkeleys were slave traders. Slavery was encouraged by giving new settlers more land if they brought slaves with them. And the Fundamental Constitutions, written before Charles Town was even settled, guaranteed that "Every Freeman of Carolina, shall have absolute power and authority over Negro Slaves, of what opinion or Religion soever." Charlestonians imported the institution of slavery; they did not invent it. As the colonial plantation system expanded, however, slavery grew by leaps and bounds. "Negroes," one Carolinian wrote in the 1730s were "the bait proper for Catching a Carolina Planter, as certain as Beef to catch a Shark."

Eli Whitney's invention of the cotton gin in 1793 further revolutionized the economy of South Carolina. Because removing the seed from the cotton by hand had been a difficult and time-consuming task, it was the gin that made growing cotton profitable. Cotton had been raised by the earliest settlers and had been shipped from Charleston as early as 1785, but it was not until the early 1800s that cotton became a major crop and Charleston a major cotton port. Cotton became king, replacing rice and indigo as the chief staple crop of South Carolina. Cultivation of cotton spread to the upcountry, and with it, spread the institution of slavery.

Slaves in the city were removed from the mass of slaves in the rice and cotton fields. Many were house servants who gradually became better educated than their less fortunate brothers, forming an upper caste among slaves. Some became artisans and craftsmen. During the colonial era most of the carpenters, masons, coopers, sawyers, and blacksmiths were slaves, and some were highly skilled. Skilled slaves competed with white craftsmen. In 1742, the Grand Jury condemned the practice of owners putting their slaves out in the market to compete. The myth that slaves were indolent, lazy, and incompetent cannot withstand historical inspection; many of Charleston's buildings are a monument to their skill.

S lavery in the Fields: Early slaves contributed to the economy in various ways: they cut wood, prepared tar, built boats and houses, and hunted and fished with expertise. They brought skills from Africa that the English in Carolina did not have. They knew, for example, how to "poison" a stream by adding a mixture of quicklime and plant juices to stun the fish so they could be easily gathered. They knew how to fight a shark or kill an alligator. They brought skills in weaving and basket making, and some became great craftsmen. And they fought in early military battles, including the Yemassee War.

With the introduction of rice as a staple crop, slave labor became essential to the economy of Carolina. It was rice that brought large numbers of blacks to Carolina. The irony is that West Coast Africans, unlike the English, were experienced farmers who knew how to cultivate rice; they had sold it to slave traders in Africa. Rice planters in Carolina searched for slaves who knew how to plant and clean rice since their productivity was excellent and profitable. The rice was "fanned" in winnowing baskets of traditional African design and cleaned using a mortar and pestle.

The greatest irony of all was that blacks could survive the "fever and ague" (malaria) because they had become immune in Africa. The sickle-cell trait is a defense against malaria, and it survived among Charleston blacks. White Europeans had no such defense. Thus slaves survived the summer

Gullah is a "pidgin" language, that is, a hodge podge of various tongues. The Gullah word "crawl" is derived, for example, from the Dutch and Portuguese word "Kraal." "Pickaninny," another Gullah word, comes from *pequeño niño*, Spanish for "very little one." Slaves brought many African words into the English language: yam, banana, tote (from "tota" in the Congo), and tabby (a mixture of oyster shells, sand, and cement used in Charles Town to make walls —from "tabax" in Africa).

fevers in the swamps while the whites died by the score.

From the matrix of colonial slavery came a distinctive speech and language spoken by Low Country blacks: Gullah. Dragged from their homeland, forced into ships like cattle to cross the Atlantic Ocean (during the dreaded Middle Passage a large percentage died), unable to communicate with fellow slaves because they spoke different African languages, black Carolinians developed their own language. The origin of the word "Gullah" itself is unknown, but it may have come from "Angola" or from the Gola tribe of the Windward Coast of Africa.

Slavery in the City: During the colonial and antebellum periods most white Charlestonians — three-fourths of all family heads — owned slaves. In 1830, out of a total of 2,873 heads of families, only 379 owned no slaves. There were 401 Charlestonians who owned at least 10 slaves, and 87 had 20 or more. There were more female slaves than male since urban work was predominantly domestic. In 1850 there were 10,901 female slaves and only 8,631 males. The same ratio held true among free blacks.

Slavery in antebellum Charleston, that is, from about 1800 to 1860, had become a settled institution. Domestic chores were entirely performed by slaves, and before dawn the women began the day's cooking and cleaning. "No white woman," Richard C. Wade wrote in *Slavery in the Cities,* " 'however humble in the scale of society,' would touch this domestic work if she could avoid it, for as De Bow [a contemporary writer] observed, she 'considers such services a degree of degradation to which she could not descend.' "

The jobs of urban slaves also could include going to market daily for food (no refrigeration meant daily shopping), running errands, butchering, fishmongering, loading ships, repaving streets, and performing construction work, although most slaves were domestic servants. In a survey taken in 1848, 1,886 men and 3,384 women were listed as domestic servants; 120 as carpenters; 39 as bakers; 36 as tailors and cap makers; 67 as draymen, 50 as pilots and sailors; 35 as porters; 68 as masons and bricklayers; 40 as blacksmiths. The survey also shows 11 fishermen, 16 painters and plasterers, 61 ship's carpenters, 61 coopers, 3 coach makers, 8 cabinetmakers, 2 gun- and locksmiths, 6 shoemakers, 3 bookbinders, 5 printers, and 5 cigar makers. Individuality had some place in the slavery system of antebellum Charleston.

Among the free blacks (of whom there were 1,475 in 1820, and 3,237 by 1860), the predominant occupations were: seamstresses (196 women); tailors (42

There were no white barbers in Charleston in 1848. All the barbers were black — four slaves and 14 free. None of Charleston's six hairdressers were black. The logic of it all is hard to understand now.

A Short History of Charleston

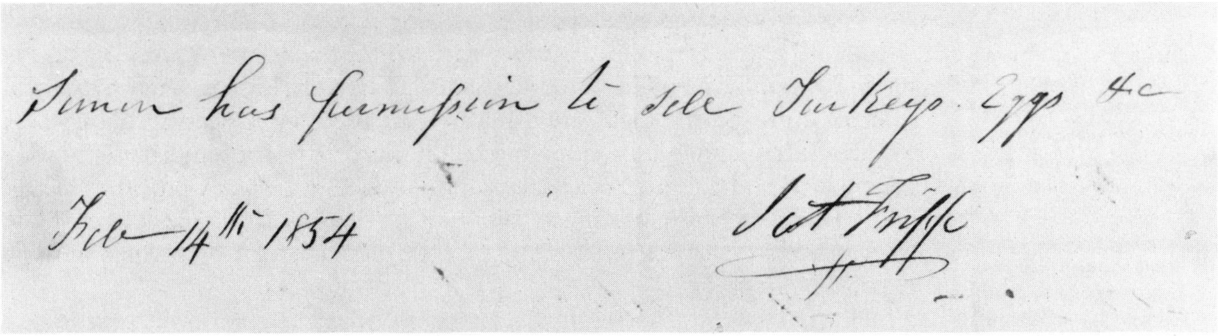

Simon has permission to sell Turkeys, Eggs etc. Feb 14th 1854

men); barbers (14); cooks and confectioners (18 men, 18 women); nurses and midwives (10); laundresses (45 women); fishermen; carpenters; and shoemakers.

The City Council regulated slave labor. In 1818 an ordinance was passed requiring owners to register slaves for hire with the city. The law obligated the slave to carry a ticket indicating his occupation. To give some idea of the extent of the practice, in 1849 the city collected $14,000 in this way. The purpose was to control the slave population, and a violation could cost the owner 20 dollars and the slave 20 "stripes on the bare back." Violations were common, and the system failed to stop a tendency toward more freedom for the slaves. Slaves began to hire themselves out, that is, they found their own employment, paid their owner a certain sum per month, and kept the rest. Such a system was profitable to the master. He did nothing and received "rent" for his slave. The slave, of course, was "free" to do what he could.

Black slaves and white owners lived together in a surprisingly integrated society. The master's family usually lived in the "big house" on the street, and the slaves occupied quarters behind the main house. The slaves' quarters had their own kitchen, storerooms, and stables. Rooms were small, frequently lacking windows and furniture was minimal. High thick walls gave the house and grounds a prisonlike atmosphere. Slaves could be watched more easily that way since the only exit was past the master's house. "They are divided out among us and mingled up with us, and we with them, in a thousand ways," wrote a minister.

By law the slave had to reside on his master's property unless he had a ticket giving him permission to reside elsewhere. But, despite the law, some slaves lived elsewhere, usually on the Neck outside the city limits. In 1848 one census taker found "that the slaves and free colored have removed to the Neck . . . where the class of houses suited to their condition are numerous and obtained at moderate rents."

The caption beside the image reads:

"Simon has permission to sell Turkeys, Eggs etc.": Slaves needed permission slips to travel or sell goods.

Selling sweet potatoes: "It is a common practice," said a contemporary account, "for masters to buy smart women and girls and send them into the streets to sell fruit and vegetables . . . These market-slaves are allowed a percentage of the profits, and manage sometimes to save enough to buy their freedom. Mostly, however, they seem satisfied with their condition, and laugh heartily and get fat."

A certain degree of freedom was inherent in Charleston's urban life. Slaves did have "free time." An errand to another part of the city might include a stopover at the home of friends, particularly free blacks. It might include a stop at one of the hundreds of grocery stores or grogshops where slaves could buy food and liquor and could socialize with each other (and with some whites). Local grocers and grogshop owners vigorously encouraged this illegal traffic because it was so profitable. In 1834 and 1835, when city officials tried to enforce tough new laws, the grocers and shop owners were up in arms.

Slaves could not marry legally, although free blacks could. Depending on the circumstances, varying from master to master, slaves did "marry," that is, they formed lasting relationships and raised children, but the marriage was always subject to being destroyed at the whim or death of the master. More than one black family in Charleston was torn apart when the master sold the

husband to one party and the wife and children to another. "Though he was living in the same town with them," one traveler noted of a slave husband, "he was never allowed to see them; he would have been beaten within an ace of his life if he ventured to go to the corner of the street."

The general standard of living of slaves in Charleston was far superior to that of slaves on the plantation. They had much better food and health care. Their dress was so different from that of the plantation slaves that it often shocked outsiders. One white visitor to Charleston in 1822 mistook what he called "a sable Dandy" for an "old acquaintance" and then he discovered "a couple of well dressed ladies . . . one in a black Canton crape, flounced with silk, black silk stockings . . . and a fashionable pair of high heeled shoes to correspond," only to discover later that the ladies were slaves. *"How much,"* he asked rhetorically in a letter to the newspaper, "could either *of you do* in a Cotton or Rice field?"

Dress became very important to the slaves of Charleston because it was one of the only ways to have a public identity or to own anything of value. A well-dressed slave was an affront to some whites who thought it "upitty." The Grand Jury even complained about it: "We recommend to the consideration of the legislature the regulation of the apparel of persons of colour — as we conceive the expensive dress worn by many of them highly destructive of their honesty and industry and subversive of that subordination which policy requires to be enforced."

Subordination of blacks — always official policy in Charleston — was not always effective. In fact, in a city of 40,000 people (Charleston's approximate population from the late 1840s to 1860), crowded onto a narrow peninsula, it was impossible for whites to fully supervise the black population. One Charleston jury complained that "the unrestrained intercourse and indulgence of familiarities between the black and white . . . are destructive of the respect and subserviency which our laws recognize as due from the one to the other. . . ." The grocery stores and bars, another jury charged, brought "the negro slave in such familiar contact with the white man, as to excite his contempt, or invite the assertion of equality. . . ." Miscegenation, common from the city's early days, continued.

It was illegal in Charleston to teach slaves to read or write. In 1800, the City Council authorized the police to "break doors, gates or windows" in preventing meetings "for the purpose of mental instruction" of blacks. But black Charlestonians wanted to learn and they did — in Bible classes, from free blacks, and from some masters and mistresses who disobeyed the law. "It

Funerals were major events for Charleston's black community because they were often held at night so slaves who worked during the day could attend. Whites complained that black funerals became carnivals or "a jubilee for every slave in the city" attended by "three or four hundred negroes and a tumultuous crowd of other slaves."

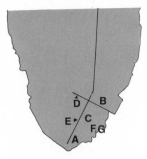

A. White Point Gardens (The Battery)
B. Centre Market
C. Old Slave Mart
D. Market St.
E. Meeting St.
F. Old Exchange Bldg.
G. Site of slave auctions

is probable," Thomas Pinckney concluded, "that, in spite of all endeavors to the contrary, the evil will increase. . . ."

Whites encouraged religious devotion among blacks. "The Gospel is our mightiest safeguard," one churchman stated, "for it governs in secret as well as in public." Blacks generally attended white churches throughout the colonial and antebellum period although seating was often (but not always) segregated. Reverend Paul Trapier estimated in the 1840s that 1,000 blacks were "connected with our six Episcopal Churches." Larger numbers attended services at the Methodist and Baptist churches. By the late 1850s there were at least 6,000 black Methodists in Charleston. In 1859 the Presbyterians built a separate church for the black membership because it had become so numerous. Whites debated whether separate black churches were a good thing. "Separate congregations . . . they *will* have," thought Reverend Thornwell, "if our laws and public sentiment of the community tolerate, they will be open, public, responsible. If our laws prohibit them, they will be secret, fanatical, dangerous."

In 1816 Northern black communities created the African Methodist Episcopal (AME) Church with congregations in Baltimore and other cities. Morris Brown, a black Charleston minister, was soon in communication with the first AME Bishop. Blacks had heretofore attended the Methodist Church with whites, but in 1818 a dispute over custody of a burial ground led to a break between white and black Methodists in Charleston.

The black leadership withdrew and founded the African Church. Three-fourths of the black Methodists followed. "The galleries, hitherto crowded, were almost completely deserted," wrote a white Charlestonian, "and it was a vacancy that could be *felt*. The absence of their responses and hearty songs were really felt to be a loss to those so long accustomed to hear them." The African Church did not survive long. Many of its members were to become involved in the Denmark Vesey slave insurrection of 1822, after which the city government demolished the church building. Morris Brown moved to Philadelphia, where he later became bishop of the AME Church. Most black Charlestonians returned to white congregations.

Ultimately separate black churches were established by the whites themselves. The black pew at St. Michael's and St. Philip's became so crowded that a separate congregation was organized with a few whites included as members (to keep watch, presumably). The Second Presbyterian Church did the same thing in 1850.

As difficult as it may be to understand today, the ownership of slaves was not limited to whites. There were black masters as well. William Ellison, whose extended family lived in Charleston, owned a cotton plantation and more than sixty slaves. He was one of the wealthiest men in the state. Ellison, of course, was extremely unusual, but there were numerous "free people of color," as they were then called, who owned slaves. Generally, the slave owners were mulattos, or light-skinned African Americans, but not always. And almost all of these members of the brown elite lived in the city and utilized slaves as mechanics and craftsmen, not as field hands.

Denmark Vesey: The black church was the only institution where blacks could genuinely govern themselves. They were, as one unfriendly white Charlestonian put it, "nurseries of self government." It was in the black churches and among the black community's elite that resistance to slavery was strongest. While no major slave revolt ever occurred in Charleston, the Denmark Vesey plot of 1822 belies the notion that black Charlestonians were somehow happy in slavery.

The full truth about the Denmark Vesey plot or rebellion will never be known because the white community and the newspapers controlled what was published about it. The policy of the times was not to print news of slave revolts in Charleston or elsewhere because the newspapers were read by free blacks and slaves. Thus, most of the information concerning Denmark Vesey comes from the official account published by the City Council in 1822.

On May 25, 1822, Devany Prioleau and William Paul, two slaves, met on the fish wharf. William, having told Devany that "something serious is about to take place," described a planned slave revolt. Devany then told his owner, Mrs. Prioleau, who alerted the city authorities. The police detained both William and Devany, and William was kept in solitary confinement and interrogated every day for a week. He finally broke down and named Mingo Harth and Peter Poyas as leading conspirators. When questioned, however, Harth and Poyas "behaved with so much composure and coolness, and treated the charges . . . with so much levity" that authorities believed them to be innocent. Nevertheless, the patrol was beefed up, and the city kept on alert.

On June 14 another slave confessed that a revolt was set for June 16. A military force surrounded the city. Two days later, ten slaves were arrested. On June 21 the authorities arrested Denmark Vesey. By July 2 at least six blacks had been hanged.

A special secret court established by the City Council set its own rules,

Denmark Vesey's favorite biblical verse was Joshua, chapter 4, verse 21: "And they utterly destroyed all that was in the city, both man and woman, young and old, and ox, and sheep, and ass, with the edge of the sword."

among them: that no black was to be tried except in the presence of his master or attorney, that everyone on trial should be heard in his own defense, and that no one could be executed on the testimony of one witness.

What emerged was evidence of a large slave conspiracy led by Denmark Vesey, a free black artisan who had been brought from Africa in his youth and had purchased his own freedom with part of a $1,500 lottery prize. He had probably planned the revolt for four years. He had studied the Bible, especially the biblical account of the deliverance of the children of Israel from slavery, and he had collected and read antislavery (abolitionist) writings from England and the north. He preached and encouraged other blacks, free and slave, to fight for their freedom. Other leaders included the cool Peter Poyas, a "first-rate ship carpenter"; Monday Gell, shopkeeper and harness maker; two slaves who belonged to the governor; and Gullah Jack, a witch doctor whose charmed crabs' claws were to protect those involved.

No one will ever know the details of the Vesey plot because the leaders never confessed, but apparently the plan included the organization of planta-tion slaves into a rebel army (Angolas, Ibos, and Carolina-born blacks were to be separately organized). Charleston was to be captured with arms secretly manufactured or seized from the two city arsenals. The terrified whites be-lieved the worst.

Vesey and the five other slaves who were the first to be executed main-tained their innocence to the last. Most of the 35 blacks ultimately executed died without confessing. One, Bacchus Hammett, "went to the gallows laugh-ing. . . ." Of the 131 suspects detained, 35 were executed, 31 were deported, 27 were acquitted, and 38 were questioned but not charged. Four white men (a German peddler, a Scotchman, a Spaniard, and a Charlestonian) were indicted and convicted of complicity in the plot. They served prison sentences ranging from 3 to 12 months.

The Denmark Vesey plot was the most dramatic indication of resistance, but there were others. Charlestonians of the colonial era, for example, had witnessed a major slave revolt — the Stono Rebellion — in 1739. On Septem-ber 9 of that year 20 slaves met near the Stono River, about 20 miles from Charlestown. The rebels went to a nearby store, took the guns and powder available there, killed the two storekeepers, and left their heads on the front steps. They traveled along the highway to Georgia and St. Augustine, killing, looting, and burning houses along the way. An innkeeper at Wallace's Tavern was not executed because "he was a good man and kind to his slaves." The uprising was stopped when Lieutenant Governor Bull just happened by, saw what was in progress, and escaped to sound the alarm. One account stated that the number of rebel slaves was "above sixty, some say a hundred." "They halted in a field and set to dancing, Singing and beating Drums to draw more Negroes to them." Late the same afternoon, a group of armed planters rode in to attack the rebels, and 14 blacks were killed in the ensuing battle. Most were eventually tracked down and hanged. According to one account, the planters "Cutt off their heads and set them up at every Mile Post they came to." More than 20 whites and probably 40 blacks died.

The odds against successful resistance to slavery were high. Blacks might outnumber whites in colonial South Carolina and in 19th-century Charleston, but unless an uprising involved almost the entire black population, it had little chance of success. Barriers to organization were great, and some slaves were loyal to their masters. Thomas Rose's slaves, for example, hid him from the rebels during the Stono Rebellion and were later rewarded. Vesey was betrayed by "loyal" Devany Prioleau. Most slaves could not read or write, which made communication difficult. Some were concerned about what would happen to their families. The whites had an organized military and the force of the government. And, in the unlikely event that a rebellion might succeed, where would the rebels go? The governments of other states would ultimately suppress any revolt.

But resistance to slavery was not limited to dramatic uprisings. It might take the form of insolence to the master, which was common. The Assembly actually debated a law giving the patrol the right "to kill any resisting or saucy slave." Or it might take the more serious form of arson or poisoning. Many slaves were executed for poisoning their masters or burning houses.

Whites came to dread uncontrolled blacks, and it is no wonder that white Southerners in general and Charlestonians in particular invented the myth of the happy-go-lucky, docile black. Such a racial stereotype was comforting to the white community, but, if it had been accurate it would have been unnecessary to control the black community so rigidly. The punishment of slaves, delegated to overseers on the plantation, was a governmental function in Charleston, where the municipal jailer replaced the overseer.

Slavery in Charleston declined somewhat during the 19th century. In 1820 there were 12,652 slaves and 10,663 whites. By 1860, there were 23,376 whites, 13,909 slaves, and 3,237 free blacks.

The biggest problem for whites was probably the free black who could own property, marry, read and write, organize churches, and engage in trade. The free blacks of Charleston were in no danger of losing their freedom and

Mistreatment of blacks was not a southern monopoly. In 1741, 13 blacks were burned to death, 8 hanged, and 71 banished in a "Negro conspiracy" — in New York City.

were generally protected by the law, although they were often treated unfairly. "The superior condition of the free person of color excites discontent among our slaves," Charlestonians fretted, acknowledging that "There is an identity of interest between the slave and the free person of color."

And indeed there was: free blacks were free, but they were still black. City ordinances relegated them to second-class citizenship. "No free person of color" was to be admitted "within the enclosure of the Garden at White Point" during certain hours, according to an 1838 ordinance. "All smoking of any pipe, or segar, within the enclosure of the said Garden" was prohibited. But "any white person who shall violate this clause" was fined five dollars. A "slave or free person of color, who shall smoke any pipe or segar within said enclosure" was "committed to the Guard House, and ordered to receive such corporal punishment as the Mayor may think proper to direct."

Slavery in Charleston was as varied as the slaves and masters themselves. Certainly there is overwhelming proof of widespread affection between the races. More importantly, the integrated nature of Charleston society, the close proximity of the races, the roughly equal numbers of blacks and whites made Charleston unique in the history of race relations. The very first line of Captain Martin's verse on Charles Town (at the end of Chapter 2) was, fittingly, "Black and white all mix'd together." The two races have lived side by side in Charleston for 300 years. Whatever else might be said about the subject, black folks and white folks have not been strangers to each other down through the centuries.

Many white South Carolinians worried about slavery. Mary Chestnut wrote in her famous diary, "I wonder if it be a sin to think slavery a curse to any land. Sumner said not one word of this hated institution which is not true. Men and women are punished when their masters and mistresses are brutes and not when they do wrong — & then we live surrounded by prostitutes. An abandoned woman is sent out of any decent house elsewhere. Who thinks any worse of a Negro or Mulatto woman for being a thing we can't name. God forgive *us,* but ours is a *monstrous* system & wrong & iniquity. Perhaps the rest of the world is as bad. This *only* I see: like the patriarchs of old our men live all in one house with their wives & their concubines, & the Mulattoes one sees in every family exactly resemble the white children — & every lady tells you who is the father of all the Mulatto children in everybody's household, but those in her own, she seems to think drop from the clouds or pretends so to think — Good women we have, *but* they talk of all *nastiness* — tho they never do wrong, they talk day & night . . .

My disgust sometimes is boiling over — but they are, I believe, in conduct the purest women God ever made. Thank God for my country women — alas for the men! No worse than men every where but the lower their mistresses, the more degraded they must be."

For better or ill, Charleston was the capital of Southern slavery. The city, which grew wealthy and powerful because of the institution, was its chief defender. But, at the same time, the city suffered inestimable pain because of it.

"If any negro or person of color, shall be guilty of whooping or halloing any where in the city, or of making a clamorous noise, or of singing aloud any indecent song, he or she shall, for each and every such offence receive at the Work House or Public Market, such a number of stripes, not exceeding twenty, as any Warden of the city shall adjudge."
— Ordinances of the City Council of Charleston, 1844.

The Antebellum City (1800–1860)

5

At the beginning of the 19th century, Charleston was among the five or six largest cities in the United States. Its population was about the same as that of New Orleans and twice that of Richmond, its only Southern rivals. Native sons included a presidential candidate, ambassadors to England and France, and a Justice of the United States Supreme Court. A future President, Andrew Jackson, spent part of his teenage years roaming the streets — learning to love gambling, horses, and cockfighting, and imitating Charleston aristocrats. The city was standing on what appeared to be the brink of a bright future.

And yet, by the 1820s and 1830s, trade had decreased, population growth had leveled off, and Charleston's position in the Union was less secure. Cold census statistics tell the story dramatically: By 1860 the city's population was about the same as that of Richmond and one-fourth that of New Orleans and St. Louis (a town half the size of Charleston in 1820). The simplistic picture of the "Queen City of the South" painted by Charleston's antebellum boosters — the gaiety, the cultural life, the handsome houses — was pretty, but inaccurate. Charleston's golden era was coming to a close. The antebellum period was a dynamic period for Charleston and not a Hollywood fable of the Old South.

Despite a population decline (relative to other cities) in the 19th century, Charleston grew in absolute numbers. In 1820 the population was 24,780 (10,653 whites, 1,475 free blacks, and 12,652 slaves). By 1860, the population was 40,552 (23,376 whites, 3,237 free blacks, and 13,909 slaves). By comparison, Savannah, with 22,292 people, was still a small town.

Physically, Charleston grew by leaps and bounds in the antebellum period. The Wragg Lands now became a booming residential suburb of the city.

Opposite page
A bird's eye view of Charleston in 1850.

The Charleston Style: The
Edmonston-Alston House
(1829), 21 East Battery, is
a museum operated by the
Historic Charleston
Foundation.

Wragg Borough was established in 1801 and boasted two parks, Wragg Square and Wragg Mall. The streets were named for the six Wragg children — Mary, Judith, Ann, Henrietta, Elizabeth, and John. These streets still exist today, as do Wragg Mall and Wragg Square (in front of the Second Presbyterian Church) at 342 Meeting Street. It was here that Joseph Manigault, a Wragg grandson, built his mansion. Designed by Gabriel Manigault, Joseph's

brother, the house (now a part of the Charleston Museum) still stands at 350 Meeting Street. Soon other antebellum mansions began to be built in Wragg Borough and adjacent Mazyckborough, formerly Alexander Mazyck's pasture, where the Liberty Tree once stood. Between Wragg Borough and the old colonial city lay Boundary Street (later Calhoun Street), Ansonborough, and a marshy area soon to become the City Market.

The eastern half of the city was also filling out. Large houses were built all along East Bay Street from Boundary Street to what is now High Battery. Christopher Gadsden's son, Philip, built a mansion on East Bay that still stands (329 East Bay across from Ansonborough Square). A row of grand mansions appeared on one extension of East Bay Street (now East Battery) called, variously, Front Street, "the New-street on East-Bay" or "New East-Bay." The great Battery mansions — The DeSaussure House (1 East Battery, built in 1850), the John Ravenel House (5 East Battery, built in 1849), the Roper House (9 East Battery, built in 1838), the William Ravenel House (13 East Battery, built in 1845), and the Edmonston-Alston House (21 East Battery, built in 1829 and now a museum open to the public) — are monuments to the grandeur that was antebellum Charleston.

The entrance to Manigault House.

The Battery itself — a marvelous place to stroll for the past 140 years — dates from the antebellum period when the stone wall and promenade were constructed. White Point Gardens was laid out in the 1830s, and the battery sea wall was constructed between 1848 and 1852. It was called High Battery after 1854 when the promenade was built at its present height.

In the 1830s Charleston's southernmost street was South Bay Street (now South Battery). William Gibbes's house (64 South Battery), built in 1722, stood overlooking docks, marsh, and the river. Grand houses were built all about the neighborhood: the Nathaniel Russell House (51 Meeting Street, built in 1809 by the "King of the Yankees" and now open to the public); the Thomas Heyward House (18 Meeting Street, built in 1803 by a signer of the Declaration of Independence); and 1 Meeting Street, built in 1846. Vanderhorst Creek was filled in and became (fittingly) Water Street.

A. Battery mansions
B. City Hall and Washington Park
C. 134 Meeting St. (Ordinance of Secession signed Dec. 20, 1860)
D. John Rutledge's home
E. Miles Brewton House
F. Planters' Hotel
G. Charleston Hotel
H. Broad St.
I. Meeting St.

The City Market was also built on filled-in land. The old colonial market at Broad and Meeting burned in 1796 and by 1804 the city had opened a new market (the present City Market) on Market Street. It was called the Centre Market and was designed to be the city's major marketplace for food. In an ordinance passed in 1807 the City Council set aside the land from Meeting Street to the Cooper River, established Commissioners of the Centre Market to operate it, and designated the area generally east of East Bay (then

Governor's Bridge) as a Fish Market. The market was kept clean by buzzards (or "Charleston eagles") who were "so tame that they crept about in the meat market among the feet of the buyers." This was the food market of Charleston until well into the 20th century.

The buying and selling of slaves was conducted in a small area bounded by Broad, East Bay, Queen, and Meeting. The busiest slave mart was just north of the Old Exchange Building. Here thousands of slaves were bought and sold from colonial days to the 1860s. In 1856, a slave mart opened on Chalmers Street. Now known as the Old Slave Mart, it is still standing and was once open to the public.

Charleston's chief retail area at East Bay, Broad, Tradd, and Elliott was noisy, dirty, commercial, and sometimes dangerous. It was distinctly unfashionable well into this century, but today is among the best addresses in town.

Broad, Elliott, and Tradd Streets comprised the retail district, and upper King Street (at least in the early 19th century) was host to a voluminous wagon trade from the surrounding countryside. Cotton was brought to town and traded along with goods of every description. Hundreds of small businessmen traded along upper King Street in its heyday, but the growth of Columbia as a trading center and the use of the Santee River for transportation to Charleston brought an end to upper King Street's business.

Charleston's first hotel was the Planters' Hotel on Church Street (now the Dock Street Theater). Prior to its erection, travelers stayed in taverns, inns, and boardinghouses, or in private homes where they were served dinner by the owners. Two of the best boardinghouses were kept by free blacks, one of whom was Jehu Jones. Jones's inn was described by the English traveler Thomas Hamilton as having "silver forks, clean tablecloths and all the luxuries of the table . . . [including] iced claret to convert Diogenes into a *gourmet.*" Other hotels included the American Hotel (1830), still standing at King and George, the Victoria (1840), and the Farmer's Hotel (1838), both on King Street.

The Planters' Hotel later became one of the centers of Charleston's social life. It played host to the great planters' families, visiting businessmen, and tourists of the antebellum period. Later still, in 1838, the grandest hotel ever to be built in Charleston, the Charleston Hotel was opened on Meeting Street (between Pinckney and Hayne). The distinguished architectural historian, Kenneth Severens, in *Southern Architecture,* tells us that the Charleston Hotel was the "architectural symbol of the new city. . . . The hotel introduced to the city the archaeological Greek Revival which Gallier had recently used in the St. Charles Hotel in New Orleans." The Charleston Hotel stood as a symbol of antebellum Charleston from 1839 until 1960, when it was demolished to make way for the Heart of Charleston Motel — a true calamity in the city's history.

Wharves and docks multiplied dramatically. A map of the city in 1855 shows more than 20 major wharves, including Adger's North and South Wharves, Atlantic Wharf, Accommodation Wharf, the Mt. Pleasant Ferry Wharf, Union Wharf, and docks for the Wilmington Steam Packet and railroad. A bathing house jutted out into the Ashley River at White Point Gardens. West of King Street (at White Point) were marsh, water, and ship-yards. Most of what is now Murray Boulevard west of King was either marsh or under water. On the west side of the city, on the Ashley River, were mill ponds and rice mills.

Great houses were built in Harleston Village north of Beaufain Street. The William Blacklock House (at 18 Bull) was built before 1800 by a wealthy merchant. At the time this house was built, its owner could look across the marshes of Coming's Creek (later filled in). North of Harleston Village was Radcliffe's Borough which had been planned in the late 1700s and had, by the 1820s, become the best address in Charleston.

The planters continued to build townhouses in the city, but in the 19th century their houses became larger and taller, the gardens and surrounding grounds grander still. Not unlike the suburbs of the 20th century, these Charleston suburbs were filled with the wealthy showing off their wealth with bigger houses and larger front lawns. The planter class clustered in these new areas, leaving older parts of the city (Broad, Tradd, Elliott, Church) to the merchants and common folk. Two great Episcopal churches were also built in these neighborhoods during the 19th century. St. Paul's Radcliffe Borough was built in 1815 at 126 Coming Street. It became known as the Planter's Church. Grace Episcopal Church at 100 Wentworth was built in 1847. Both are still in use.

The city grew steadily. Cannon Borough and Elliott Borough were opened north of Radcliffe's Borough. Hamstead and the Village of New Market were opened north of Wragg Borough. New street names appeared: Vanderhorst, Warren, Radcliffe, Coming in Radcliffe's Borough, Cannon, Spring, and Bridge Streets to the north. Line Street, named for the line of fortifications built during the War of 1812, eventually housed a passenger railroad depot. By the 1840s, the South Carolina Rail Road was an integral part of the city. Its tracks came down the Neck between King and Meeting Streets. Before the Civil War streets were laid out as far north as Grove Street (near the present Citadel). The "Neck" then became everything north of Boundary Street.

The economy of antebellum Charleston was based on rice, cotton, slave trading, shipping, and retailing. The Low Country planters continued to grow

The original Ashley River Bridge was built in 1819, and burned in 1865 to prevent General Sherman from entering the city. A wooden toll bridge was built in 1889 by a private company, and in 1926 a concrete span was built that is still in use.

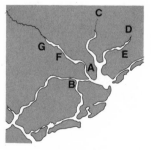

A. Lowndes Grove
B. Fenwick Hall
C. The Elms, Otranto, The Oaks
D. Medway
E. Boone Hall
F. Drayton Hall
G. Middleton Pl.

A. Wragg Lands
B. Wragg Borough
C. Joseph Manigault's
   Mansion
D. Mazyckborough
E. Harleston Village
F. Radcliffe's Borough
G. Cannon Borough
H. Elliott Borough
I. Ansonborough
J. Market St.

rice. Near the ocean they grew luxury cotton. Everywhere they used slaves.

Slave trading was big business. The slave trade with Africa was closed in 1808 by federal law, but the expanding southern states needed slave labor. On one day in 1860, for example, two Charleston newspapers, *The Courier* and the *Mercury*, advertised 2,048 slaves for sale in the near future. Those who sold slaves (politely called "brokers," not slave traders) were numerous and respectable. Some, like Thomas Norman Gadsden, were from the most prestigious of families. Gadsden's second cousin was a bishop and rector of St. Philip's Church.

Charleston, like the rest of early 19th century America, was eager to make use of steamboats and railroads to bring business to the city. The Santee Canal was constructed in 1801 to link the state's major river, the Santee, with the Cooper River. The goal was to provide cheap transportation so that upland cotton could be shipped to Charleston. Use of the steamboat increased shipments of cotton directly to the Bay, and the East Bay merchants and factors grew wealthy on this trade. But while the volume of trade increased, Charleston's percentage declined. Other ports (Savannah, Mobile, and especially New Orleans) drew on a wider area.

Charleston was ahead of its time in developing the railroad. In an effort to enlarge the city's markets and to cut into Savannah's trade, Charlestonians in 1833 built a railroad to Hamburg, South Carolina, a trading town on the Savannah River. This railroad was the second in the United States, and provided regular passenger service as well. When it was completed it was, according to G. R. Taylor, "the longest railroad in the world under single management." The city invested heavily in railroad schemes, the most ambitious of which would have connected Charleston with Cincinnati. The schemes all failed, and 20th-century Charlestonians were still paying the debts incurred in the previous century.

There was also significant manufacturing activity in Charleston during the 19th century. The city was ranked third in the South, manufacturing steam engines, railroad locomotives, and steamship machinery. Yet textile mills failed. Manufacturing as a major economic activity never reached its full potential because labor, expertise, and social acceptance were all lacking. In the early 1800s aristocratic Charleston firmly disapproved of trade as an occupation. Northerners and Europeans stepped in to fill the void, and many of the great merchants and financiers of antebellum Charleston were no longer native sons. This haughty attitude contributed further to Charleston's decline as a great port. Charleston was to remain a planter's city.

The Way of Life: Hedonism and love of pleasure, so prevalent in the colonial era, remained the accepted way of life, a social ideal for antebellum Charlestonians. "For some gentleman planters," William Freehling wrote in *Prelude to Civil War*, "contempt for work extended to agricultural endeavor. . . . An idle aristocracy which sometimes found its own profession distasteful, lowcountry planters had time to engage in politics, to study, to write." One planter noted that "dissipation — or to speak more correctly — idleness is the order of the day here. . . ." Young sons of the planter class often whiled away their time in Charleston bars, chased women, or wasted their time. Some went into the "honorable" but overcrowded professions of law, religion, or medicine. All disclaimed the work of merchants, mechanics, or overseers.

Visitors found antebellum Charleston in many ways the same as colonial Charlestown: "The men are of Idle disposition, fond of pleasures that lead them into a system of dissipation to which they are in a manner wedded. . . . Their principal amusements in the City in the morning is Billiards . . . and in the Evening cards and Segars. . . ."

Charlestonians created and joined still more clubs: the Ugly Club, the Three Pace Club (for duels), the Kolf Baan Club, the Golf Club, the Sons of Erin, and the Hibernian Society. The St. Cecilia Society held fewer concerts but more dances, balls, and suppers. The greatest club of them all, however, was the South Carolina Jockey Club, the first jockey club in the United States.

Race week in February was a special week in antebellum Charleston. The city's businesses closed, and everyone celebrated. The "courts of justice used daily to adjourn, and all the schools were regularly *let out.*" There was a Jockey Club dinner on Wednesday, a great ball on Friday, and numerous private parties. Horse races were held first at the New Market Course and later at the Washington Course (now Hampton Park). Spectators watched from one of the stands, such as the Jockey Club Stand, the Grand Stand, or the Ladies' Stand ("the ladies alighting from their carriages, protected by an arched way from the weather"). On either side of the saloon of the Ladies' Stand were "retiring and refreshment rooms." Finally, there was a "Citizens' Stand" for the ordinary citizen. According to the rules, "Respectable strangers from abroad, or from other States, are never allowed to pay for admission to any of the Stands on the Course. On their arrival they are immediately considered guests. . . ."

Race week was antebellum Charleston's version of Mardi Gras (or today's Spoleto Festival). "It is proverbial," John B. Irving wrote in his delightful 1857 account of the Jockey Club, "that all who come to Charleston during

One traveler found Charlestonians "devoted in debauchery and probably carry it to a greater length than other people." He observed that the Carolinian "may be compared with the Persians of old, for the more wine he can swallow the more accomplished he conceives himself."

It is fitting that the most famous Charlestonian of all time was a dashing, handsome, hard-drinking, womanizing rogue who traveled the world and knew the latest fashions — a man who took a Charleston girl out buggy riding then "refused to marry her the next day." Rhett Butler, fictional hero of *Gone With the Wind,* provides a better glimpse of antebellum Charleston than any account yet written by an historian.

In *Gone With the Wind*, Scarlett O'Hara visited Charleston — and hated it. "There was more social life . . . but Scarlett did not like the people who called, with their airs and their traditions and their emphasis on family. . . . She thought if she ever again heard voices that said 'paams' for 'palms' and 'hoose' for 'house' and 'woon't' for 'won't' and 'Maa and Paa' for 'Ma and Pa', she would scream. . . . Then she went back to Tara. Better to be tormented with memories of Ashley [Wilkes] than Charleston accents."

race week, do not find their way there merely to see the races. Many choose that time for a visit to the city. . . . Much money is foolishly spent (it is too true), but whatever is spent in this way circulates freely." Tourism thus has a long and illustrious history in Charleston.

Antebellum Charleston society was both a mellowed aristocracy, secure in its control of the city and state, and an open elite ready to absorb promising newcomers. The first Wade Hampton for example, was an unscrupulous upcountry planter who made a fortune in cotton near Columbia and in sugar in Louisiana. His grandson, Wade Hampton, the aristocratic Confederate leader, married a Charleston heiress, became a cultivated planter, and joined Charleston's elite. His brother-in-law, James Hammond, grew up impoverished in the upcountry, "the son of a Massachusetts adventurer." He, too, married a wealthy Charleston lady, built a great town house, bred racehorses, and became an insufferable snob. James L. Petigru, the greatest lawyer of antebellum South Carolina, originally from the Abbeville District, was welcomed into Charleston society. Thus did Charleston's elite absorb talented newcomers.

Not everyone found acceptance in antebellum Charleston, however. William Gilmore Simms, the South's greatest antebellum novelist, lived in Charleston and complained, "all that I have [done] has been poured to waste in Charleston, which has never smiled on any of my labours." Simms, the son of an Irish immigrant, worked as a druggist's clerk as a boy, married well, and became a planter, a lawyer, and a writer. At one time, he owned two plantations, a house in Charleston, ninety slaves, and was constantly in debt. After he began writing in the 1830s, he produced 25 "romances" or novels, a history of South Carolina, three plays, four biographies, a work of criticism, a collection of short fiction, volumes of speeches, and many magazine articles. He helped to edit nine magazines. His writings celebrated his native soil and described the history of the South in novel form in every age and place. He visited the emerging South (Alabama and Mississippi) and regaled his readers with stories of the "border country" as well as stories from Charleston's past.

"If Charleston had its St. Cecilia and its public library, there is no record that it ever added a single idea of any notable importance to the sum total of man's stock." So wrote W. J. Cash in *The Mind of the South*. For a city her size, however, Charleston had quite an active intellectual life in the antebellum period. How many ideas of "notable importance" are there anyway?

Simms's novels depict the worried Charleston of his time. Southerners, William R. Taylor has written, "had become obsessed by feelings of social decline. . . . They grasped for symbols of stability and order." Simms's novels reflect this uneasiness. In all of his romances — from *The Yemassee* (a historical novel about the Yemassee War of 1715) to *Border Beagles* (about an outlaw gang in Alabama and Mississippi) to *Katherine Walton* (a love story set in Charleston during the Revolution) — the theme is disorder and instability in

Southern society. Simms was more appreciated in Charleston than he thought. Certainly his great contemporary, Edgar Allan Poe, thought him one of the greatest of American writers, and the city erected a monument to him that still stands in White Point Gardens.

Poe also knew Charleston during the antebellum period. He served in the army at Fort Moultrie on Sullivan's Island, and was so taken with that mysterious island that he used it in three stories, "The Oblong Box," "The Balloon Hoax," and "The Gold Bug."

With or without Simms or Poe, and W. J. Cash notwithstanding, Charleston was the undisputed intellectual and literary capital of the South

"A number of gentlemen friends and Amateurs in musik": This 1827 painting by Thomas Middleton records two favorite Charleston activities: music and drinking.

The Fireproof Building, designed by Robert Mills, now houses the South Carolina Historical Society.

during the antebellum period. In addition to two newspapers, *The Courier* (edited by a Northerner from Massachusetts!) and the *Mercury,* Charlestonians published at least six successful magazines that had regional and national circulation: the *Southern Review* (an excellent literary journal founded in 1827), the *Southern Quarterly Review,* the *Magnolia, Russell's Magazine, Southern Rose, Southern Rosebud* (an offshoot of the *Rose?)* and *De Bow's Review,* probably the most influential Southern journal. De Bow subsequently removed himself and his journal to New Orleans, but his Charleston ideas did not change.

Writers, poets, and painters abounded. Charles Fraser painted miniatures that can still be seen today at the Gibbes Museum of Art (135 Meeting Street). Reverend Samuel Gilman, the Unitarian minister, wrote *Fair Harvard.* William Crafts celebrated race week in *The Raciad,* a poem after the fashion of Pope. So many of Charleston's antebellum writers were lawyers that one historian of the period concludes that "this literature was a literature of lawyers. . . . It was a Charleston pleasantry that John C. Calhoun had written a poem opening with the word 'Whereas.'"

The Literary and Philosophical Society was founded in 1815 by Stephen Elliott, one of Charleston's many Yale graduates. Elliott wrote widely on botany and became editor of the *Southern Review* along with Hugh Swinton Legaré, lawyer, classicist, and later Attorney General of the United States. Lecturers came in droves to speak before the Literary and Philosophical Society and other learned societies.

The Reverend Dr. John Bachman, minister of St. John's Lutheran Church of Charleston, participated widely in scientific circles and corresponded with the world's leading scientists and naturalists. Born in New York, Bachman came to Charleston in 1815 for health reasons. He was a lifelong friend of John James Audubon and, in one of the unscientific marvels of the history of science, two of Bachman's daughters married two of Audubon's sons. Bachman traveled widely with Audubon to study bird life, all the while urging Audubon to give up profanity, "grog and wine," and snuff. The two scientists coauthored a book, *The Quadrupeds of North America,* that became a classic.

Bachman studied the relationship between the environment and variations of species among animals. William Stanton in *The Leopard's Spots* indicates that "Bachman's observation on variation and its causes testify to his careful study and serve to place him in the front ranks of pre-Darwinian naturalists in the United States. . . . Bachman formulated a theory of his own that approached evolution."

A Short History of Charleston

Charleston's theater not only survived, it flourished. The Broad Street Theatre and the French Theatre presented plays throughout the period. And yet another new theater, the Charleston Theatre, was built in 1837 on Meeting Street.

A medical school founded in 1822 by the Medical Society became the Medical College by 1852. It was the forerunner of the present Medical University of South Carolina. But the College of Charleston, which graduated six students in 1794, gradually deteriorated. It could not sustain a college-level course of study and became, in essence, a grammar school. Though it became the first municipal college in the United States by act of the General Assembly on December 20, 1837, this was a dubious distinction. It appears that the City Council took it over in an effort to salvage it.

Despite the intellectual fervor of some Charlestonians, the state of the arts began to decline in the 1830s, when, according to George C. Rogers, Jr., Charlestonians "turned away from cosmopolitanism to a conservative sectional patriotism." The South Carolina Academy of Fine Arts, incorporated in 1821, held its first exhibition in 1823. In 1830 it closed. Perhaps it was only in architecture that Charleston made a truly lasting contribution to the arts.

Charleston Style: The Federal period (1793-1808) left a legacy of great homes. The Charleston single house adapted to the new century, indeed adapted to all centuries and styles. "Various styles, such as Georgian, Federal, Greek Revival and Victorian, can be distinguished in the treatment of the classical orders of the piazzas and the interior ornamentation," writes Kenneth Severens, but "the 'single house' as a vernacular type has transcended the vicissitudes of climate, taste, and prosperity."

Charleston's first real architect was a gifted amateur named Gabriel Manigault, who introduced the Adam style to Charleston. He designed the Orphan House Chapel (now demolished) on Boundary Street, the first United States Bank (built in 1800, now City Hall on the corner of Meeting and Broad), South Carolina Society Hall (built in 1804), and the remarkable Joseph Manigault House.

During the antebellum period, the nation's great architects, including a native son, designed buildings for the city. Robert Mills, the first native professional architect in the United States, was born and raised in Charleston and graduated from the College of Charleston. He studied under the great foreign-born architects of the time, including Benjamin Latrobe. He studied

In 1838 the actress Fanny Kemble wrote, "In walking about Charleston, I was forcibly reminded of some of the older country towns in England . . . and although the place is certainly pervaded with an air of decay, it is a genteel infirmity, as might be that of a distressed gentlewoman. It has none of the smug mercantile primness of the Northern cities but a look of state . . . a little gone down in the world, yet remembering still its former dignity."

with Thomas Jefferson, proposed and built the Washington Monument, and was the architect of the Treasury Building in Washington.

In Charleston, Mills inaugurated the Classical Revival with his design of the Congregational Church (1806, destroyed in the fire of 1861). He also designed the First Baptist Church (1822, 61 Church Street), the Fireproof Building (1822-1827, 100 Meeting Street), the Marine Hospital, and, rather unheroically, the city's drainage system.

William Strickland of Philadelphia and Edward Brickell White designed buildings for the College of Charleston. White also designed Market Hall (1840-1841, a part of the present City Market, on Market Street), the Second Baptist Church (1841-1842, the present Centenary Methodist Church), and the Rebuilt Huguenot Church (1844), at Church and Queen. The Gothic style had become so popular by mid-century that the Episcopalians followed suit with Grace Episcopal Church on Wentworth Street, also designed by White.

The Lutherans prospered, building St. Johannes on Hasell Street in 1842 and St. Andrew's Lutheran Church in 1840. The Jewish community rebuilt Beth Elohim Synagogue (90 Hasell Street) after a fire in 1838.

Charleston's Catholics did not, at first, share in the religious tolerance accorded other religions. For one reason, the early colonists were Protestant and English, and they brought with them a fear of "papists," the Roman Catholic Church, and England's historic enemies at that time, France and Spain. When two Irish Catholics arrived in Charleston in 1775, they were thought to be against the Revolution, tarred and feathered, and run out of town. Later, however, refugees from Santo Domingo arrived. They were French, like the Huguenots, but they were Catholic. It was these people whose tradition was compatible with that of Charleston, who established Catholicism in Charleston. Though the State Constitution of 1778 banned them from office, they formed their own community and prospered.

The first mass was celebrated in Charleston in 1786. Bishop John England, the first Catholic bishop in the South, came to Charleston from Belfast, Ireland, in 1820. He later wrote that "prejudice [against Catholics] at the time of the Revolution was so strong that any Catholics in Carolina kept their faith so secret that they were not even known to each other." Yet Charlestonians did not reject their tradition of religious freedom for long. By 1789, land was purchased on which to build a Catholic church. In 1800, St. Mary's was founded. The original church at 89 Hasell Street burned in the fire of 1838, but, like K. K. Beth Elohim across the street, it was rebuilt in 1839. St. Mary's was, thus, the mother church of Catholicism in the South.

As the century progressed, Irish Catholics poured into Charleston. By the 1820s and 1830s, fully one-eighth of Charleston's population was Irish, and St. Patrick's Day became a favorite holiday. One of the first Catholic newspapers in the country was published in Charleston. A convent was built in 1839. The Hibernian Society flourished and in 1840 erected a handsome hall at 105 Meeting Street (which still stands). By the 1850s, the Catholics of Charleston erected a great Cathedral at Broad and Legaré. It was called the Cathedral of St. John and St. Finbar and was named for the Bishop of Cork, Ireland, from whence Charleston's first and much-beloved bishop, John England had come. This cathedral burned in the great fire of 1861 and was replaced by the Cathedral of St. John the Baptist, which still stands.

Hibernian Hall.

Showing the Flag: Charlestonians have always been patriotic; and they enthusiastically prepared for the War of 1812. Numerous companies were formed, including the Washington Rangers, the Independent Greens (not football teams!), and the Federalist Artillery. (The state actually lent the federal government the funds for its defense.) The same enthusiasm prevailed for the War with Mexico in 1845. The City Council purchased equipment for a volunteer company of Charlestonians, part of the famous Palmetto Regiment that landed at Vera Cruz in 1847. The first flag to fly over Chapultepec when Mexico City was captured belonged to the Palmetto Regiment. Charlestonians, looking for military glory throughout the antebellum period, were soon to find it in abundance.

The city was always eager to celebrate its military history. When the Marquis de Lafayette returned to the United States in 1825, he visited Charleston, the city he had secretly entered 48 years earlier on his way to serve in the Continental Army. He stayed in Charleston four days and received the warmest public welcome since Washington's visit. At the corner of George and Meeting, the Marquis greeted both Charles Cotesworth Pinckney and Thomas Pinckney, former comrades-in-arms, with an embrace and kisses on the cheek after the French manner. It was the end of an era. Charles Cotesworth Pinckney died that same year. Thomas died three years later. They were buried "with all possible civil and military honour" — Charles in St. Michael's, and Thomas in St. Philip's churchyard. The last heroes of the Revolution were dead or dying.

Yet the democratic government won in the War of Independence was quite alive. The city government was busy. In 1819, a building was purchased at Broad and Meeting Streets to serve as a city hall, and it has remained City Hall ever since. The building had been a bank. However, the tellers' cages visitors see today were installed for the collection of city taxes after City Hall was rebuilt following a fire in 1882 which gutted the building. They do not date from the time when there was a bank on the premises. City government regulated everything from the theaters and auctions on East Bay Street to the weight of bread. Commissioners of Streets and Lamps were authorized to keep the streets and new street lamps in good repair.

Fires continued to be the greatest menace to public safety. Fire destroyed St. Philip's Church in 1835. (It was immediately rebuilt.) A great fire in April of 1838 burned a large segment of town, including much of Ansonborough and King Street. Fire engines were purchased early, and by 1857 Charleston had ten engines, ten volunteer white companies, and ten slave companies. But the largest fire yet struck in 1861. "The cause," Steve A. Channing wrote in *Crisis of Fear,* "was generally laid to pro-Union blacks in the City." Much of the city was destroyed. Meeting Street was badly damaged. Both the South Carolina Institute Hall and the Circular Congregational Church were lost. Much of Broad Street burned.

The fear that pervaded Charleston after the Denmark Vesey plot in 1822 had led to a multitude of civic and governmental efforts to keep the peace and prevent a slave rebellion. First and foremost was the establishment of the Citadel, an outgrowth of Charleston's earlier police department or guard. In the 1820s the city converted some tobacco inspection buildings on the green north of Boundary Street (Marion Square) into a guardhouse. In 1842 the General Assembly created the Citadel, and by 1843 twenty cadets were enrolled in the military college. There were, in addition, city constables, the City Guard (a city military organization), a city sheriff, city marshals, and, of course, wardens (later called Aldermen) and the mayor — all charged with the duty of keeping the peace.

Yet keeping the peace was a difficult task. South Carolinians in general, and Charlestonians in particular, were about to embark on the most tortured period of their political existence. Just as the city began to decline in stature, population, and economic and political importance, it began to feel the sting of criticism about the institution of slavery.

Charlestonians began to withdraw, to close their minds to the outside world. George C. Rogers, Jr., simply and eloquently describes the transition by entitling his chapter on Charleston prior to the 1820s "The Open City" and his chapter after the 1820s "The Closed City." The openness and cosmo-

Many Charlestonians foresaw the Civil War: "I see nothing before us but decay and downfall," Hugh S. Legaré wrote in 1833. And Senator Robert W. Barnwell wrote in 1845: "Our institutions are doomed and the Southern civilization must go out in blood."

politanism of the 18th century gave way to the fanaticism of the 19th century. The ardent nationalism of the early 1800s began to grow cold in the 1820s when periodic economic depressions deeply affected upcountry cotton planters, and the working people and retailers of Charleston. The planters were troubled by the emerging abolition movement, and most Charlestonians were unhappy about the federal tariff.

The original tariff of 1816 was designed to protect infant manufacturing. It had been supported by South Carolinians, but, while the tariff succeeded in protecting New England's textile mills, the South never developed industry and ended up paying higher prices for manufactured goods without receiving the benefits of the protective tariff. Resentment, nursed by both real and imagined economic problems, and, even more importantly, by the beginning of the crusade against slavery, led to a dramatic shift in South Carolina's political life. There now arose a radical states' rights party dedicated to fighting the tariff, the critics of slavery, "internal improvements" (that is, nationally financed turnpikes), and espousing a narrow construction of the Constitution to protect South Carolina's "rights." But the real underlying issue was slavery.

Eighteenth century Southerners had mixed feelings about slavery. Some saw it as a necessary evil. Some, like Henry and John Laurens, had deep reservations about it. (John Laurens had unsuccessfully urged the General Assembly to allow slaves to fight in the Revolution and earn their freedom.) And some, like John Wesley and Francis Asbury opposed it totally. In 1795 a group of 23 Methodist ministers met in Charleston and issued a statement: "deeply sensible of the impropriety, & evil of Slavery, in itself . . . And its baneful consequences, on Religious Society," the ministers agreed that "all such persons amongst us" — that is, slaveholders — should either emancipate their slaves or set them free at the slaveowner's death. Numerous Charlestonians criticized slavery, and many emancipated their slaves in their wills or during their lifetimes. Many joined the American Colonization Society, a movement dedicated to freeing the slaves and sending them back to Africa. The rector of St. Philip's and later bishop of South Carolina was the society's agent, and leading Southerners of the period applauded its aims. John Marshall, James Madison, and James Monroe had been members.

Thomas Jefferson had written eloquently about the evil effects of slavery. But the era of Southern history when slavery was a debatable issue was coming to a close. Mr. Jefferson died in 1826; Mr. Madison, 1836. The torch was passed from Virginians to South Carolinians, from the Jeffersons to the Calhouns. For the first time, the proslavery argument was heard.

"Charleston was the great cultural center of the Old South, a city with a flavor of its own and an air of cosmopolitan taste and breeding, and Charleston was the one part of South Carolina for which Calhoun had no use. . . . It may stand as a token of Calhoun's place in the South's history that when he did find culture there, at Charleston, he wished a plague on it." — Richard Hofstadter, *The American Political Tradition*.

Charlestonians of the 19th century rallied to the new ideology and wrote some of its chief works.

John C. Calhoun as a young man: Charlestonians rallied to Calhoun's passionate defense of slavery.

Enter John C. Calhoun: The greatest apologist for slavery, states' rights, and ironically, minority rights was not a Charlestonian at all, but a figure who towers over the city's history like a great cloud: John C. Calhoun. He is buried in St. Philip's churchyard, Calhoun Street is named in his honor, and a statue of him was erected on Marion Square. Although married to a Charleston heiress, he never cared much for the city. In 1807 he said that the fever in Charleston was "a curse for their intemperance and debaucheries."

The Calhouns were Scotch-Irish from the upcountry of South Carolina. John C. Calhoun was born at Abbeville in 1782. He was raised on a small plantation as part of a middle-class family, went to Yale College, and married a distant, but wealthy Charleston cousin, Floride Calhoun. He studied law in Charleston at the offices of Henry De Saussure, one of the leading lawyers of the state, and at the Litchfield Law School in Connecticut. He returned to South Carolina to practice law, became a planter, and entered politics.

Calhoun went to Congress in 1810 and became a "War Hawk," advocating, along with Henry Clay and others, a strong national defense. He was for the tariff, the national bank, national roads, and a strong army. He became Secretary of War under Monroe. It is ironic that Calhoun's entire early public life was built on nationalism, but the political winds in South Carolina were blowing the other way and Calhoun blew with them. In 1824 he pinned his hopes on Andrew Jackson, a fellow Southerner, in the hope of becoming President. He was elected Vice-President in both 1824 and 1828.

The tariff issue reached a peak in 1828 with the so-called Tariff of Abominations, and Calhoun secretly wrote the "Exposition and Protest" that expressed South Carolina's views. Because Calhoun hoped to succeed Jackson as President, he tried to play both sides by placating both Jackson and the militant nullifiers in South Carolina at the same time. It did not work. Calhoun fell out of favor with Jackson for a number of reasons, but the main reason was because he was outmaneuvered by Martin Van Buren, most dramatically in the Peggy Eaton affair.

Andrew Jackson's wife, Rachel, had been vilified in the election of 1828. She was accused of numerous indiscretions, including marriage to Jackson before her divorce was final. She died soon after the election, and Jackson

Old Hickory actually held a cabinet meeting about the Peggy Eaton Affair and officially pronounced her "as chaste as a virgin." Henry Clay rejoined: "Age cannot wither nor time stale her infinite virginity."

blamed her death on her critics. When Jackson came to Washington, he found what he considered to be another attempt to wrong a decent woman, Peggy Eaton. Peggy, while working at her father's Washington tavern, had met John Eaton, a friend of Jackson's and the new Secretary of War. She and Eaton were married after vicious gossip had spread about their relationship. Peggy, according to Samuel Eliot Morison, was "a luscious brunette with a perfect figure and a come-hither look in her blue eyes that drove the young men of Washington wild."

No proper Charleston lady, such as Floride Calhoun, would receive Peggy in her home, and other cabinet wives and wives of diplomats and congressmen followed her example. The affair became an open scandal. Jackson was furious at Calhoun, but Van Buren, who was a bachelor, went out of his way to show Mrs. Eaton a great deal of attention.

The Eaton affair, together with Jackson's discovery that Calhoun had misled him on a matter involving accusations against Jackson during Monroe's administration (when Calhoun was Secretary of War), led to a final break. Calhoun tried to defeat Jackson but failed. Having lost his opportunity to be President, he became, instead, the leader of the Southern cause in the United States Senate.

Calhoun became a very bitter man, obsessed with his mission. Mary Bates, a friend, said she "never heard him utter a jest." Clay described him as "tall, careworn, with furrowed brow, haggard and intensely gazing looking as if he were dissecting the last abstraction which sprung from metaphysician's brain, and muttering to himself, in half-uttered tones, 'This is indeed a real crisis.'" Harriet Martineau called him "the cast iron man who looks as if he had never been born, and could never be extinguished." Varina Howell Davis described him as "a mental and moral abstraction." Senator George E. Badger of North Carolina said of Calhoun: "On everything concerning niggers [he was] absolutely deranged."

This fanatical puritan nevertheless possessed a brilliant mind. Richard Hofstadter, in *The American Political Tradition,* wrote that Calhoun "was one of a few Americans of his age . . . who had a keen sense for social structure and class forces" and was "probably the last American statesman to do any primary political thinking." He was the first to affirm in the Senate of the United States that slavery "is, instead of an evil, a good — a positive good." Calhoun argued forcibly that black workers were better cared for than white laborers, that emancipation meant a race war in the South and the end of Southern civilization, and that Northern business interests ought to join the Southern

James L. Petigru: He stood by the Union but stayed in Charleston after secession. Mary Chesnut wrote of him in 1862, "He is as much respected as ever. Maybe his astounding pluck has raised him in the estimation of the people he flouts and contradicts in their tenderest points."

aristocracy in keeping working people (white or black) in their place. In his *Disquisition on Government,* he anticipated Karl Marx by identifying class conflict as inevitable. Indeed, Hofstadter has called him the "Marx of the Master Class." He wanted to protect the minority South, but he cared nothing for the rights of other minorities. He "created stereotypes in the minds of the Southern people that produced intolerance," concluded historian Clement Eaton.

Tension of the Times: Intolerance there was in abundance. When the Virginia legislature debated the merits of slavery in 1832, the Charleston *Mercury,* soon to become the leading secessionist newspaper in the South, argued against "the public discussion of such a topic." In 1822, in the wake of the Vesey plot, the state passed a law, the Negro Seaman's Act, requiring that all black seamen be jailed while their ships were in port in Charleston. The gentry began to organize extralegal vigilante groups like the South Carolina Association to enforce laws against blacks. Despite protests by the federal government that the Negro Seaman's Act was unconstitutional, it was continuously enforced.

The rise of the abolition movement pushed South Carolinians further than ever before. Even mild protests against slavery brought violent reactions. When the Ohio legislature recommended a moderate plan for emancipation in 1824 and when, in 1827, the American Colonization Society asked Congress for aid, South Carolina reacted with a vengeance. But strong forces were gathering against slavery. The Englishman William Wilberforce led a campaign to abolish it in the British West Indies, and as early as 1827 it was apparent that he would succeed. Barbados, the mother colony of Charleston, abolished the very institution it had exported to Carolina one hundred years earlier.

Calhoun fought the tide by promulgating the theory of nullification, which held that the States were sovereign before they entered the federal government and could, therefore, nullify or void any federal law — such as the tariff — that they found unconstitutional or dangerous to their existence. Charlestonians were bitterly divided on nullification. Merchant and mercantile interests favored Clay's policies and did not oppose the tariff. The great East Bay merchants had prospered under the Union, and they, together with many old Federalists such as the lawyer James L. Petigru, Joel Poinsett (minister to Mexico), Daniel Huger and others, opposed Calhoun and the radicals at every turn. One pro-nullification Columbia newspaper declared "the City of Charleston now, *is in fact* a colony of Yankee speculators, cherishing not a spark of Southern feeling."

The year 1831 was a watershed year in southern history. William Lloyd Garrison published the first issue of the *Liberator,* the radical abolitionist newspaper, and Nat Turner led his fellow slaves to kill their masters in Virginia. Garrison denounced the Constitution, which he felt protected slavery, as "a covenant with death and an agreement with hell." The greatest slave revolt, following the launching of the *Liberator,* was more than most white southerners could take.

In Charleston, the year 1831 also proved to be politically tense. There were unionist parades and nullification parades. Hugh Legaré, James Petigru, and Daniel Huger denounced nullification and read with delight a supportive letter sent by President Jackson. The nullifiers began creating local political and military organizations. In July a statewide nullification convention was held in Charleston. The organizers were good politicians. They tapped all classes of white South Carolinians and made the lowliest Charlestonian feel at home with the greatest aristocrat. The younger sons of the aristocracy, so disdainful of work, had now found a cause. Fear of slave revolts, a growing feeling of isolation from world opinion, economic hardship, the political acumen of the Calhoun party — these factors nursed the Nullification Crisis. The Unionists were dismayed. "Can we get a gang to oppose robbers, as easily as robbers unite in gangs?" Petigru wondered. "I think not."

By 1832 fights between unionists and nullifiers had spilled over into the city streets. In October the nullifiers won a large majority of the seats in the General Assembly and tension mounted. The state government then proceeded to organize a nullification convention to forbid the enforcement of the tariff in South Carolina. Robert Hayne resigned his seat in the United States Senate to become Governor of South Carolina. Calhoun resigned as Vice-President of the United States, the first person to do so. (Spiro Agnew later joined him in that select company.)

While the nullification convention resolved to ignore federal law, President Jackson resolved to enforce it. He sent spies to Charleston and troops to Fort Moultrie and Castle Pinckney. Yet Jackson was cool under fire. When the General Assembly sought the removal of federal troops from the Citadel, Jackson removed them. He was going to make the South Carolinians fire the first shot. Abraham Lincoln was to learn a great deal from Andrew Jackson.

Jackson next issued a Nullification Proclamation in which he denied the legality of nullification. "Disunion by armed force," he said, "is treason." The other southern states were loath to follow South Carolina's lead. The nullifiers

Angelina Grimké left her prominent family in Charleston to live up north. She was a leading spokeswoman for the abolitionist movement and an early feminist. She wrote many pamphlets condemning slavery including one entitled "An Appeal to the Christian Women of the South." She told the Massachusetts legislature, "I stand before you as a southerner, exiled from the land of my birth by the sound of the lash and the piteous cry of the slave. I stand before you as a repentant slave holder."

had problems at home, too. In their determination to win they had passed a law that required all voters to swear paramount allegiance to the State. This greatly offended the many unionists who viewed the oath as treason to the United States. Nonetheless, Charlestonians prepared for war. James Hamilton, Jr., a former governor, prepared military defenses. Governor Hayne ordered volunteer troops to drill in preparation. Joel Poinsett organized a unionist force to come to the aid of the federal authorities.

In the end, of course, there was no war. Henry Clay orchestrated a compromise on the tariff issue. The people of South Carolina realized that they could not fight alone, and the crisis passed — for the time being.

Yet the issue of slavery would not fade away. The American Anti-Slavery Society was formed in 1833, and Congress began to receive thousands of petitions against the institution. In the same year, Parliament abolished slavery in the British West Indies. As southerners began to feel even more isolated, they perfected the pro-slavery argument. Calhoun, in his effort to reconcile slavery with democracy, repudiated Jefferson's doctrine of the equality of man.

Charlestonians led the fight against abolition. When anti-slavery tracts arrived in Charleston, the local postmaster would not deliver them. A mob appeared on one occasion to enforce this censorship of the mails. The classic pro-slavery work was published in Charleston in 1852. *The Pro-Slavery Argument* contained essays by regional and state figures quoting the Scriptures and Aristotle, and citing pseudoscientific works to prove that blacks were inherently inferior. One of the leading pro-slavery philosophers was William J. Grayson, once collector of the port of Charleston. Grayson wrote a long poem in 1856 entitled *The Hireling and the Slave*. His argument, like that of many other pro-slavery writers, was that slaves were better off than industrial workers. The arrogance of these writings was not lost on the average citizen of the North.

Ironically, two of the most famous abolitionists of the antebellum period were Charleston aristocrats, Sarah and Angelina Grimké. Their father was a prominent planter, lawyer, and slaveholder, but his two daughters grew up in Charleston detesting slavery. After her father's death, Sarah became a Quaker, and worse (in the opinion of all proper Charlestonians), she decided to leave Charleston and move to the North. Angelina, Sarah's younger sister, also came to hate slavery and also became a Quaker. She later married Theodore Weld, one of the most famous of the abolitionists. Together, the Grimké sisters became founders of the early feminist movement. On February 21, 1838, Angelina Grimké spoke against slavery before a committee of the Legislature of the Commonwealth of Massachusetts and became the first woman in

American history to speak to a legislative body. She spoke constantly against slavery and published a pamphlet, an *Appeal to the Christian Women of the South*, in which she wrote, "The women of the South can overthrow this horrible system of oppression and cruelty, licentiousness and wrong."

The Storm Gathers: During the 1840s and 1850s agitation over states' rights and the expansion of slavery in the West increased. A few South Carolinians had begun to urge secession as far back as the Nullification Crisis, though Calhoun was opposed to secession except as a last resort. In 1842 there were rumors of a conspiracy to burn down the city. By 1855 arson (presumably caused by dissatisfied slaves) had become so common that the City Council offered a $2,000 reward for information about suspected arsonists. In 1856 Mayor Miles established a mounted police force and strengthened the City Guard.

The long history of conflict over slavery — the Missouri Debates, the Wilmot Proviso, the Compromise of 1850; domestic and foreign anti-slavery opinion; the advent of the Republican party (dedicated, so the South thought, to the abolition of slavery); growing local tensions in Charleston — all strengthened the movement for secession. By the late 1850s, most white southerners viewed themselves as prisoners in their own country, condemned by what they saw as a hysterical abolition movement.

In March 1850 the great nullifier, John C. Calhoun, died. His body was transported by ship to Charleston, accompanied by a congressional delegation. His funeral was unsurpassed in ceremony. A huge parade followed the funeral car (modeled on Napoleon's!) down King Street to Hasell, from Hasell to Meeting, down Meeting to South Bay (now South Battery) then to East Bay, up East Bay to Broad and down Broad to City Hall. Ten divisions of troops, organizations of every description, a 200-man honor guard (including James L. Petigru, Calhoun's old foe), and ordinary citizens participated in the funeral march. Calhoun's body lay in state at City Hall for 24 hours before the "cast iron man" was buried in St. Philip's graveyard. In 1880 the present memorial was placed on his grave by the General Assembly.

By 1858 a consensus was building in the northern states that the expansion of slavery must stop and the institution itself put on the road to eventual extinction. "Shall I tell you what this collision means?" William H. Seward thundered in Rochester, New York in 1858. "They who think that it is accidental, unnecessary, the work of interested or fanatical agitators, and

"The desolated, ruined South; . . . the Slaves unloos'd and become the masters, and the name of Southerner blackn'd with every shame — all that is Calhoun's real monument," Walt Whitman wrote in 1865. But Calhoun's Monument in Charleston is a tall pedestal and statue at Marion Square on Calhoun Street.

James Petigru, one of Charleston's last unionists, said of secession: "South Carolina is too small for a republic and too large for an insane asylum." In 1861 Stephen A. Hurlbut, President Lincoln's secret emissary, wrote the President that Mr. Petigru "is now the only man in the City of Charleston who avowedly adheres to the Union . . . [he is] the only citizen loyal to the Nation." Later on, when a friend told him Louisiana had seceded, Petigru replied, "Good God Williams, I thought we had *bought* Louisiana."

therefore ephemeral, mistake the case altogether. It is an irrepressible conflict between opposing and enduring forces, and it means that the United States must and will, sooner or later, become either entirely a slaveholding nation, or entirely a free-labor nation. Either the cotton and rice-fields of South Carolina and the sugar plantations of Louisiana will ultimately be tilled by free labor, and Charleston and New Orleans become marts for legitimate merchandise alone, or else the rye-fields and wheat-fields of Massachusetts and New York must again be surrendered by their farmers to slave culture and to the production of slaves, and Boston and New York become once more markets for trade in the bodies and souls of men." Seward was a Senator from New York and the leading Republican candidate for president.

In October 1859, John Brown raided Harper's Ferry in Virginia in an effort to incite a slave rebellion. This was the beginning of the end. Charlestonians, ever the staunchest foes of abolition, began to lead the fight for secession. Perhaps it was the depressed economy, perhaps it was the high percentage of slaves, or perhaps it was the vigorous commitment to slavery as an institution that placed South Carolina and Charleston at the forefront of secession. Maybe Charlestonians really believed, as George C. Rogers, Jr. argues, that "they had the perfect society," that Charleston was "the center of an idea, a southern way of life." Scarlett's mother, in *Gone With the Wind*, said, and it was true: "If the nice people of Charleston feel that way, I'm sure we will all feel the same way soon."

Yet there was something else. That ancient Charleston hedonism, the love of posturing, the unrestrained Low Country aristocracy whose power knew no bounds, the lack of any real challenge to the elite's views — all of these factors contributed, too. When an individual planter had the power of life and death over his slaves, when the state government did as the planters willed, when no other class or faction could fight back, it is easy to understand why the radical secessionists of Charleston could believe that no one would dare oppose them. They believed there would be no war, that gentlemen of noble birth could stare down the nation. "Why, all we have," said Rhett Butler at Twelve Oaks, "is cotton and slaves and arrogance. They'd lick us in a month." But, then, Rhett had been run out of Charleston.

Whatever the reason, events moved rapidly after 1859, though not rapidly enough for the radical secessionists. The Charleston Vigilance Association was formed to protect the peace and suppress slaves. Secession activists redoubled their efforts. Moderates like Christopher Memminger reluctantly concluded that slavery would only be safe outside the Union. Soon, only a

·&? THE QUESTION

IF LINCOLN
will be elected or not, is one which interests all parties, North and South. Whether he

IS ELECTED
or not, the people of

SOUTH CAROLINA
(whose rights have been for a number of years trampled upon) have the advantage of supplying themselves with CLOTHING, at the well-known CAROLINA CLOTHING DEPOT, 261 King-street, at such prices as

WILL LEAD
them to be satisfied that the reputation of this Establishment has been

BOLDLY
and fearlessly maintained

FOR A
number of years, supplying us

SOUTHERN
Customers with all the Latest Styles, and at as low prices as any Clothing House in *the present*

CONFEDERACY
of all the States.
Thankful for the liberal patronage extended, the Proprietors desire merely to inform their customers and the public generally, that their present STOCK OF CLOTHING is COMPLETE in all its departments, and are now prepared to offer Goods on the most reasonable and satisfactory terms. A call is therefore solicited by
OTTOLENGUIS, WILLIS & BARRETT,
November 6 261 King-street.

Between the lines one sees that the Carolina Clothing Depot has prices that WILL LEAD customers to know that its reputation has been BOLDLY maintained . . . and so on.

handful of unionists remained.

What John Brown's raid started in 1859 was finished by the nomination of Abraham Lincoln as the Republican Party's candidate in 1860. Lincoln was viewed as a radical opponent of slavery, though he had consistently said he would never interfere with slavery where it existed. Lincoln did, however, argue against the spread of slavery, and this appealed to the workingpeople of America who wanted the West to remain free so white labor could prosper. The Democrats, who convened in Charleston in 1860, were badly divided. The secessionists and moderates both disliked the leading Democratic contender (and eventual nominee), Stephen A. Douglas. He was seen as untrustworthy since he had once championed popular sovereignty in the western territories (allowing the settlers themselves to decide about slavery). In short, no "true" southerner could be elected, and, in the view of the secessionists, Douglas' election would only postpone the fight. Charlestonians were not necessarily of one mind, however, on tactics. Some still thought that a compromise candidate could be nominated in Charleston and that war could be averted. When the convention convened in April, no one knew what to expect.

What Charleston witnessed was the most divisive national party convention in American history. "There are radical and inextinguishable feuds in the Democratic Party," Murat Halstead, a reporter, wrote from Charleston, "and they must come out here and now." The political fabric of the nation began to tear in Charleston that April, one year before Fort Sumter. "No American political convention has ever held so much meaning for party and nation," wrote Robert W. Johannsen in *Politics and the Crisis of 1860,* "as that conclave of determined Democrats which gathered in Charleston, South Carolina, in April, 1860, to nominate a candidate for the presidential office. Upon the decision at Charleston rested not only the future of the Democratic Party but also the continued existence of the Union. . . . All the forces of sectional animosity that had been building up between the North and the South for over a decade were focused on those ten fateful days."

Indeed, politically speaking, the first shot of the Civil War was fired in Charleston long before Sumter.

South Carolina's delegation was unionist, as the secessionists had boycotted the state party proceedings. Yet the other southern states had come to believe in secession, and most of the southern delegates walked out, urged on by Charleston's radicals. The city's newspapers, the *Mercury* and the *Evening News,* bombarded the delegates, urging no compromise. Meetings were held, and intemperate speeches were the order of the day. The streets of Charleston

James Petigru refused to acknowledge the legality of secession. Mary Chesnut noted in her diary: "Mr. Petigru alone in South Carolina has not seceded." Born in 1789, James Louis Petigru came to be the greatest lawyer in the history of South Carolina. When he died in 1863 the city closed down to mourn him — despite his refusal to recognize the Confederacy. He is buried in St. Michael's churchyard. His epitaph so moved Woodrow Wilson that he had it cabled to him at Versailles: "In the great Civil War/He withstood his People for his Country/ But his People did homage to the Man/ Who held his conscience higher than their praise."

and the galleries of the convention at Institute Hall (now demolished) were filled with secessionists, most of whom wanted Lincoln to be elected, thereby hastening the confrontation to come. The tension in the city itself prolonged the convention and helped to deadlock it. Douglas could not get enough votes in Charleston. The nation, Emerson Fite wrote, was "awestruck." The convention adjourned and reconvened in Baltimore, where Douglas was duly nominated. "The last party, pretending to be a national party, is broken up," said the *Mercury*, full of glee, "and the antagonism of the two sections of the Union has nothing to arrest its fierce collisions."

Charleston and Charlestonians had helped disrupt the Democratic Party which was, until that May of 1860, the governing party of American politics. It was the party of Jefferson and Jackson. It was the party of the incumbent President, James Buchanan. There had never been a Republican President. The night after the walkout by Southern delegates, Halstead described the city as follows:

> There was a Fourth of July feeling in Charleston last night — a jubilee. There was no mistaking the public sentiment of the city. It was overwhelmingly and enthusiastically in favor of the seceders. In all her history Charleston had never enjoyed herself so hugely.

Robert Barnwell Rhett, the Father of Secession, thought he ought to be the President of the Confederacy. No one else did. "Rhett," T. R. R. Cobb wrote his wife, "is a generous hearted and honest man with a vast quantity of cranks and a small proportion of common sense."

Lincoln defeated Douglas and John C. Breckinridge, a third party nominee. No one in South Carolina was surprised. Lincoln's victory was what the majority wanted — a reason to secede. To Charlestonians, wrote Steven A. Channing in *Crisis of Fear*, "Lincoln's election *meant* convulsive slave insurrection — *meant* emancipation of the Negro hordes. . . ." The Civil War was fought to preserve slavery and the southern civilization slavery made possible.

As late as September 1860, however, secession and Civil War did not appear inevitable. James Petigru thought "no possible issue could be more untenable than to make [Lincoln's] bare election a *casus belli*, without any overt act against the Constitution. . . . If our planter were in debt, or cotton was at 5 cents. . . . [secession] might be likely; but our magnanimous countrymen are too comfortable for such exercise." He worried, though. "The Constitution," he wrote his daughter Susan, "is only two months older than I. My life will probably be prolonged till I am older than it is."

But on November 7, 1860, when it was clear Lincoln had been elected, high federal officials in Charleston resigned. On November 9, a large public meeting was held at the Institute Hall. "It was plain, from a brief glance," wrote J. W. Claxton, "that the respectable citizens of Charleston were there.

A Short History of Charleston

The speakers were persons of note. They, one after another, in burning phrase, counselled immediate secession. . . . As they uttered their fierce words, the multitudes rose from their seats, waved their hats in the air, and thundered forth resounding cheers." The president of the South Carolina Senate, William O. Porter of Charleston, wrote, "The city which is most exposed and must bear the brunt in great part, is clamorous for secession." Even the mercantile community was caught up in the frenzy. They, too, after all, believed Lincoln's election meant the end of slavery, and even the most conservative businessman could not abide abolition. "So unanimous is public sentiment," wrote William Grimball, "that in the city of Charleston[,] formerly from its commercial interests the most union loving and conservative portion of the State, no other candidates will present themselves to the people."

As Frederick Jackson Turner pointed out, "Charleston was peculiarly suited to lead in a movement of revolt. It was the one important centre of real city life." It was a focal point, a gathering place for the planters. "Thus South Carolina, affording a combination of plantation life with the social intercourse of the city, gave peculiar opportunities for exchanging ideas and consolidating the sentiment of her leaders." Charleston was the political center of the state and its only real city. She was located in the center of the Low Country black belt, surrounded by a huge black population. She was, as James M. Banner, Jr., points out, "at one with the surrounding land." The planter influx made her both cosmopolitan and provincial, urban and rural.

Fear of slave revolts and fear of arson and poison, so much a part of Charleston's history, now took over the white community. "The negroes are all of the opinion that Lincoln is to come here to free them," Petigru's niece wrote to her husband, yet "they are perfectly quiet and *nothing* is apprehended from them." But the quiet was ominous, and the city was tense with rumors of slave revolt.

On December 17, 1860, the Secession Convention met in Charleston. On December 20, in St. Andrews Hall in Charleston, the State of South Carolina voted to secede from the United States. The "Ordinance of Secession" was signed at Institute Hall that evening. Six days later, Major Robert Anderson removed his federal troops from Fort Moultrie, where the new nation's first important military battle had been won, to a new fort built on a sandbar in Charleston harbor. It was called Fort Sumter.

Circular Church and Institute Hall. It was at Institute Hall that the Democratic National Party Convention was held and the Ordinance of Secession was later signed.

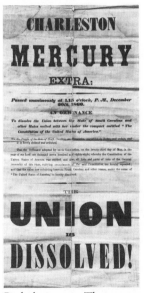

Prelude to war: The most famous front-page story in Charleston's history.

Confederate Charleston (1861–1865)

6

President James Buchanan, whom most Americans justifiably do not remember, was followed in office by President Abraham Lincoln, whom most Americans venerate. Buchanan, however, was still President in December 1860, and he gave the distinct impression that the federal government had accepted nonviolent secession. There was even a preliminary agreement to negotiate the ownership of federal property in South Carolina. "I informed them [a delegation of South Carolina Congressmen]," Buchanan wrote in December of 1860, "that if they [the federal forts] were assailed this would put them completely in the wrong & [make] them the authors of the civil war."

That, in a nutshell, was the situation when Lincoln took office in March 1861. The Confederate States of America had been established on February 8, 1861, before his inauguration on March 4. He promised in his Inaugural Address not to interfere with slavery, but made it clear he would not brook secession: "In your hands, my dissatisfied fellow-countrymen, and not in mine, is the momentous issue of civil war. The government will not assail you. You can have no conflict without yourselves being the aggressors."

Major Anderson, the Union commander at Fort Sumter, whose father had been stationed at Fort Sullivan, who himself had been a slave owner, and who was married to a Georgian, provided the Confederates with no excuse for aggression. One could argue, as Milby Burton does in *The Siege of Charleston, 1861-1865,* that "the first overt act of war" was not the firing on Sumter, but the seizing of Castle Pinckney, another federal fort in Charleston harbor. But federal forts had been taken by the Confederacy elsewhere. Or one could argue that the war started on January 9, 1861, when Citadel cadets fired on the *Star of the West* as that vessel attempted to supply Sumter.

"Why did that green goose Anderson go to Fort Sumter," Mary Chesnut complained to her diary. "Then everything began to go wrong."

Opposite page
Charleston watches the bombardment of Fort Sumter.

Pierre Gustave Toutant Beauregard: A Louisiana Creole won the hearts of Charleston's ladies and was the Confederacy's man of the hour at Fort Sumter.

One officer of the *Star of the West* said, "The people of Charleston pride themselves upon their hospitality, but it exceeded my expectations. They gave us several balls before we landed."

But Anderson sat peacefully at Fort Sumter through January, February, March, and the first part of April. Charleston was the stage, but the play was being directed from Montgomery, the capital of the Confederacy, and from Washington. When asked by representatives of the Confederacy to surrender, Anderson politely refused. When Brigadier General P. G. T. Beauregard, of Louisiana, arrived to take charge of the Confederate military command at Charleston, the drama began.

The critical events of March and April are both obvious and mysterious. Did Lincoln manipulate the Confederacy into firing the first shot? Who was really in control of the situation? What really happened?

In March, after Lincoln became President, Anderson remained at Sumter. The Confederates occupied Fort Moultrie and Castle Pinckney. The *Star of the West* had been repulsed in January. Only seven states had seceded. Three federally controlled forts lay in seceded territory: Fort Taylor in Key West, Fort Pickens in Pensacola, and Fort Sumter. By general consensus in both the North and the South (and contrary to Scarlett O'Hara's feelings about the matter), Fort Sumter was to be the testing ground because it was a direct threat to Charleston, the Cradle of Secession.

or Each, A Dilemma: President Lincoln's dilemma was that if he withdrew Union troops from Sumter, he would be acknowledging the end of the Union. By doing so he would abandon his oath to "preserve, protect, and defend the Constitution of the United States." If he sent troops to defend Sumter, however, he would be the aggressor in a contest no one — North or South — wanted.

President Jefferson Davis's dilemma was that if he allowed the Union to hold Sumter, he would be acknowledging that he headed a government so weak it allowed a foreign government to hold a fort in the harbor of one of its largest cities. He would be losing the respect and perhaps the recognition of foreign governments. On the other hand, if he attacked a small band of soldiers who had given no provocation, he would seem a warmonger. If he fired on the flag, he would be causing millions of Northerners who did not want war to rally to Lincoln for a noble cause — the preservation of the Union. The people of Charleston looked to their new country and their new President for the right decision.

Each side was circling the other. The Confederates wanted to take Sumter peaceably. Lincoln wanted to avoid a confrontation but maintain his

A Short History of Charleston

position until something could be worked out. Supplies at Sumter were running low. It would take 20,000 federal troops to hold the Fort. Radical Republicans pushed Lincoln to start the war, and radical Confederates pushed Davis.

Did Lincoln conceive of a plan during those months to force the issue at Charleston — to bring on the first shot by the Confederates — so that he could unify and rally Northern opinion? The evidence is very strong that he did.

On March 13, Captain Gustavus V. Fox, a former naval officer and a trusted Lincoln lieutenant, presented the President with a plan for a naval expedition to reinforce Sumter. Fox came to Charleston on March 21, visited with Major Anderson, and learned (and presumably told Lincoln) that Anderson could only hold out until April 15.

On the same day Fox was at Sumter, Lincoln sent Ward H. Lamon, another trusted friend, to Charleston. Lamon, in his *Recollections,* states that he was sent "on a confidential mission." On March 23 he met with James Petigru, the last Unionist in Charleston, who told him that "peacable secession or war was inevitable." Lamon also met with Governor Pickens, who told Lamon that reinforcement of Sumter meant war. Lamon apparently told Pickens that the fort would probably be abandoned, though he had no authority to give such assurances. Lincoln also sent another friend to assess the situation in Charleston, an Illinois lawyer and Charleston native, Stephen A. Hurlbut. He, too, found "there is no attachment to the Union" in the city. Thus, by March 27, when Lamon and Hurlbut returned, Lincoln knew for a fact that any attempt to relieve Fort Sumter would result in war.

On March 29 Lincoln met with his cabinet, which was divided on the issue of Sumter, and then issued a secret order to prepare a naval expedition. The destination was not given, but the force was to sail on April 6. Lincoln made other secret preparations, preparations so secret they were kept from the Secretary of War and the Secretary of the Navy. Seward was opposed. "I do not think it is wise," he wrote, "to provoke a civil war beginning at Charleston."

On April 4 Lincoln held a meeting with a number of Republican governors known to favor a strong stand at Sumter. No one knows what transpired at that meeting, though some historians conjecture that Lincoln told them of his plan and warned them to get ready for war. On the same day Lincoln also met with John B. Baldwin, a Virginia Unionist, who told Lincoln that the only solution was to evacuate Fort Sumter. According to Baldwin, Lincoln became excited and said, "Why was I not told this a week ago? You have come too late!"

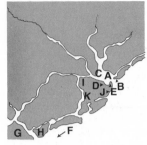

A. Ft. Sumter
B. Ft. Moultrie
C. Castle Pinckney
D. Ft. Johnson
E. Cumming's Pt. Battery
F. Port Royal
G. Edisto Is.
H. Seabrook Is.
I. James Is.
J. Battery Wagner

Gov. Frances W. Pickens, the feisty governor of South Carolina during the firing on Fort Sumter.

Gustavus V. Fox presented President Lincoln with a plan for a relief expedition to Fort Sumter. He later became Assistant Secretary of the Navy during the Civil War.

Actually, it was not too late. Lincoln met that day with Captain Fox, the commander of the naval expedition destined for Charleston Harbor. Fox received his orders from President Lincoln personally. Anderson would be relieved, Lincoln told Fox, but Governor Pickens of South Carolina would be notified first, before Fox arrived at Sumter. Members of the cabinet objected to this notification, but it was a key element in Lincoln's plan. A letter was then sent to Major Anderson.

On April 6 Lincoln drafted the following notice to Governor Pickens in his own handwriting:

I am directed by the President of the United States to notify you to expect an attempt will be made to supply Fort Sumter with provisions only; and that, if such an attempt be not resisted, no effort to throw in men, arms, or ammunition will be made without further notice, or in case of an attack upon the fort.

As numerous historians have pointed out, the message (read it carefully!) was a masterpiece of ambiguity. Lincoln, master of the English language, most eloquent of speakers, author of the Gettysburg Address, drafted a message he knew all parties would read differently. Let the great Southern historian, Charles W. Ramsdell, explain:

To the suspicious and apprehensive Confederates it did not merely give information that provisions would be sent to Anderson's garrison — which should be enough to bring about an attempt to take the fort — but it carried a threat that force would be used if the provisions were not allowed to be brought in. It was a direct challenge! How were the Southerners expected to react to this challenge? To Northern readers the same words meant only that the government was taking food to hungry men to whom it was under special obligation. Northern men would see no threat; they would understand only that their government did not propose to use force if it could be avoided.

Late on the night of April 6 and into the morning hours of April 7, an intriguing episode took place. The *Powhatan,* the flagship of Fox's naval expedition, left New York under a new commander, Lieutenant David D. Porter. Lincoln had given command to Porter, but Seward, the Secretary of War, after conferring with Lincoln, wired "DELIVER THE POWHATAN AT ONCE TO CAPTAIN MERCER. (signed) SEWARD." But Porter apparently had other orders. He replied, "HAVE RECEIVED CONFIDEN-

Typically, Charlestonians enjoyed life to the brink of war. Mrs. Mary Boykin Chesnut attended "the merriest, maddest dinner we have had yet. Men were audaciously wise and witty.
We had an unspoken foreboding that it was to be our last pleasant meeting."

A Short History of Charleston

TIAL ORDERS FROM THE PRESIDENT AND SHALL OBEY THEM. (signed) D. D. Porter." Was Porter under secret orders from Lincoln *not* to go to Sumter and thereby ensure that no attack would take place? (Fox could not attack without the powerful *Powhatan*.) Or was Porter really ordered to go to Fort Pickens, not Sumter, because there was a mix-up between Seward and Lincoln? We shall never know.

On April 8 Lincoln's ambiguous message was given to Governor Pickens and General Beauregard. But the Confederates already knew from intelligence and even newspaper reports that a large naval expedition was on its way. Theoretically, no one knew the destination of Captain Fox's ships, but Lincoln's message had implied that force would be available. It was assumed that Fox's expedition must be that force. Some of the ships were actually heading to Pensacola, but that fact *was* kept secret, so secret that the Confederates assumed incorrectly that the entire expedition was headed for Charleston.

The ball was now in Jefferson Davis's court. His alternatives were both dangerous. Either Sumter must be captured before the federal naval expedition arrived, or Sumter would be forcibly relieved by the federal fleet. It was a Hobson's choice: If Sumter were attacked, the South would be the aggressor and appear to be wrong. If Sumter were relieved, Davis's government would lose face. The Secretary of State of the Confederacy, Robert Toombs, was against attacking Sumter: "It is unnecessary; it puts us in the wrong; it is fatal!"

What could Davis do? If he allowed Lincoln to peaceably reprovision Sumter, Lincoln might then give him "further notice" that he was throwing in "men, arms, or ammunition." Had not the message clearly said so?

On April 9 Beauregard discovered, by seizing the mail from Sumter, that Anderson had been informed of the federal fleet's imminent arrival. On April 10, the Confederate government learned definitely that the naval expedition had left New York and decided to act before the fleet could arrive. Time was now of the essence. Beauregard was ordered to proceed.

The general brought in 5,000 more soldiers because he believed the Yankees were on the way to attack Morris Island. The 2,000 men at Morris Island scurried in anticipation. More than 6,000 Confederate troops now surrounded the small band at Sumter. The *Courier* editorialized: "We are sick of the subject of evacuation. . . . Let the strife begin." The city was crowded with soldiers, wagons, horses, and people waiting for the war to start. The harbor was full of boats transporting troops.

On April 11 Beauregard learned that one of Fox's ships was only a few miles away. That afternoon three Confederate officers went to Sumter to hand

Ironically, the tune of "John Brown's Body" was taken, according to the historian Henry Steel Commager, from an African-American melody "popular in the Carolina low country, where it was sung to the refrain,

Say, brothers, will you meet us?

On Canaan's happy shore?"

Other historians believe that a free black Charlestonian, William Steffe, wrote the song and that a Vermonter, Tom Bishop, picked up the tune while traveling in South Carolina. Bishop used it in writing "John Brown's Body." Bishop later joined a Massachusetts infantry battalion. Julia Ward Howe heard the melody as Bishop's battalion marched through Washington, and used it to write "Battle Hymn of the Republic." Thus, as John Mitchum, a filmmaker, explained to a reporter for the *News and Courier* in 1991, "the song is black music, with white words, and welded the whole union back together."

Fort Sumter from the battlements of Fort Moultrie: Note the palmetto flag upper left; see note, page 53.

Anderson a message from Beauregard. "I am ordered by the Government of the Confederate States," it read, "to demand the evacuation of Fort Sumter." Anderson replied that the demand to evacuate was one "which I regret that my sense of honor, and of my obligations to my Government, prevent my compliance." When Anderson asked if he would be notified prior to the commencement of firing, he was told that he would be warned. "I shall await the first shot," Anderson replied, "and if you do not batter us to pieces, we shall be starved out in a few days."

Anderson's remarks were reported to Beauregard. Still anxious to avoid bloodshed, Beauregard again sent his aides to Anderson to inquire as to when he would be "starved out" — and could then honorably surrender. Anderson played for time, knowing the fleet was on its way. Finally, he replied that he would evacuate on April 15 at noon (his men would have been without food for three days by then) "should I not receive prior to that time controlling instructions from my Government or additional supplies."

James Chesnut, Jr., Beauregard's aide, knowing that the fleet was on the way, would not agree to Anderson's stalling. He had waited too long already at Sumter for Anderson's reply. As he stood at Fort Sumter he wrote to Anderson:

> SIR: By authority of Brigadier-General Beauregard, commanding the provisional forces of the Confederate States, we have the honor to notify you that he will open the fire of his batteries on Fort Sumter in one hour from this time.

For a while, a little-known general named Robert E. Lee was in charge of Charleston's defense. His main concern and that of his successors was to keep the railroad line open between Savannah and Charleston. He was sent to Virginia to command the Confederate army, being replaced by General John C. Pemberton.

First Shots: It was 3:30 a.m., April 12, 1861. The war that no one wanted, that no one really believed would ever happen, was about to begin. The bombardment of Fort Sumter, a truly glorious spectacle (if it were not so pregnant with tragedy), began at 4:30 that morning. Three Union vessels — Fox's fleet — remained outside the bar, unable, and to all appearances unwilling, to enter the harbor.

Colonel Chesnut and his men had left Fort Sumter and gone to Fort Johnson on James Island. Either Chesnut or Lieutenant Stephen D. Lee gave the order to fire to Captain George S. James. The first mortar shot, aimed high into the air so as to form an arc, was the signal to start the Civil War. Tradition has it, probably incorrectly, that the first shot was fired by one Edmund Ruffin of Virginia, the 67-year-old radical secessionist, writer, philosopher, and fanatic. He supposedly jerked the lanyard of a columbiad gun at the Iron Battery on Cummings Point, Morris Island. Whoever fired it, the war's first shot was a direct hit against the parapet of Fort Sumter.

All the guns in the harbor — except those on the Battery — then commenced firing. By 5:00 a.m., more than 40 cannons were firing on Sumter from two batteries on James Island (including Fort Johnson), Cummings Point Battery on Morris Island, a battery in Mt. Pleasant, and four batteries on Sullivan's Island (including Fort Moultrie).

The bombardment was furious and constant for the first two and one-half hours. Fort Sumter's defenders fought back and fought bravely, but they were no match for Beauregard's artillery. Charlestonians climbed atop roof-

Scarlett O'Hara was unimpressed by the firing on Fort Sumter. Those Charlestonians "took so much upon themselves about Fort Sumter! Good Heavens, didn't they realize that if they hadn't been silly enough to fire the shot that started the war some other fools would have done it?"

In May 1862 a slave and harbor pilot named Robert Smalls sparked national attention with a dramatic daytime bid for freedom. He stole a Confederate steamer, the *Planter*, and sailed out to the Union blockade. When passing a rebel sentinel, "I gave the [correct] signal — two long blows and a short one. I put on the captain's straw hat and stood so the sentinel could not see my color." He was received with cheers at the blockade. After the war Smalls became a Congressman and customs collector.

Robert Smalls, the first African American hero of the Civil War.

tops to watch the attack and cheer on the Confederacy. The Battery and all the wharves were crowded with spectators. The sounds of the cannon were loud and terrifying. The city's houses and buildings shook and rattled.

The attack continued into Saturday, April 13. Firebombs or "hot shot" were hurled into Sumter. The fort still fired back, and its defenders were cheered by the Confederates who admired the bravery of their enemies. But the firebombs had their effect; Sumter exploded and caught fire. Anderson could not hold out, and the fleet did not come to his rescue. On April 14 he surrendered. The Stars and Stripes was lowered — the fort was taken. Charleston and the Confederacy celebrated. The harbor was soon filled with boats as Charlestonians came to see the site of the first battle of the Civil War.

Yet, in truth, the victory belonged to a man far away from Charleston — Abraham Lincoln. His strategy had worked. He had forced the Confederacy to fire at Fort Sumter, thereby electrifying the North. Public opinion in the North, once divided, now united behind the President. He had only tried to send food to loyal, starving soldiers. The Rebels had opened fire on a federal fort for no reason. On May 1, Lincoln wrote to Fox: "You and I both anticipated that the cause of the country would be advanced by making the attempt to provision Fort Sumter, even if it should fail; and it is no small consolation now to feel that our anticipation is justified by the result."

Lincoln's two secretaries, John G. Nicolay and John Hay, wrote later: "President Lincoln in deciding the Sumter question had adopted a simple but effective policy. To use his own words, he determined to 'send bread to Anderson'; if the rebels fired on that, they would not be able to convince the world that he had begun the civil war."

In the days following the fall of Sumter, Stephen A. Douglas went to see Abraham Lincoln. The former opponents met so that Douglas's support — and therefore the support of the Democratic party — could be enlisted in the war effort. Douglas told Lincoln he had best call out 200,000 men, not the 75,000 he originally called for in his proclamation. "Why?" the President asked the Senator from Illinois. Remembering the battering he had taken at the Charleston Democratic National Convention just one year before, Douglas replied, "You do not know the dishonest purpose of those men as well as I do."

City at War: Charlestonians now settled in for war. Troops came and went. Fortifications were built all over the area. The Union Navy blockaded Charleston harbor, but, at least in the early years of the war, the blockade was ineffective. "Old Abe has at last fulfilled his threats of blockading us by sending the *Niagara* here," Emma Holmes confided to her diary. Blockade running became a way of life, a lifeline for the South.

Port Royal (50 miles from Charleston, near Beaufort) was soon occupied by the Union. What E. Milby Burton described as "the most formidable armada ever assembled under the American flag" sailed into Port Royal Sound in November 1861 and captured the area. Thirty-six transport ships carrying nearly 13,000 troops arrived, together with 14 men-of-war. It was the first significant Union victory of the Civil War. They then advanced from Port Royal to the Stono Inlet, to Edisto Island, to Seabrook Island and then to John's Island. Finally, they landed on James Island just outside Charleston. A vigorous battle was fought on James Island at Secessionville in June 1862, a battle the Confederates won. In hand-to-hand combat, the Union lost 700 men; the Confederates, 200. The Union troops ultimately withdrew to Port Royal.

On December 11, 1861 the city experienced the most tragic fire in its history. At 8:30 in the evening alarm bells sounded. The fire spread from Hasell Street at East Bay to the market, to Meeting Street, and eventually to the Ashley River along Tradd Street. It destroyed the Circular Congregational Church, the Art Association, and whole sections of Meeting Street and Queen Street. Ironically, it destroyed both St. Andrew's Hall on Broad Street, where secession had been debated and enacted, and Institute Hall on Meeting Street, where the Ordinance of Secession had been signed. Some said the fire had been deliberately set by African-Americans; others, that slave refugees from the Sea Islands had just not been careful about a camp fire. In later years pictures of burned-out portions of Meeting Street would illustrate the destruction of the war, but in reality the damage was done by The Great Fire of 1861. 540 acres had burned and 575 homes had been destroyed.

Charleston remained a high-priority target for the Union because it was the South's second largest port and because it was the "Cradle of Secession," the symbolic mother city of the Confederacy. From their base at Port Royal, the Union Army and Navy built a war machine to attack Charleston.

Between the Battle of Secessionville in June 1862 and the beginning of the real siege of Charleston in April 1863, the city enjoyed a relative calm interspersed with some Confederate victories. One such victory was the capture of the Union gunboat, the *Isaac P. Smith,* in January 1863. General Beauregard, a daring and inventive commander, ordered a sneak attack on the gunboat in the Stono River off James Island by land forces and artillery.

The siege of Charleston began on April 7, 1863. The most powerful

History's first su... submarine attack o... Charleston harbor on February 17, 1864, when ... Confederate submarine *Hunley* sank the *Housatonic.* The *Hunley* and its crew were lost in the waves caused by their exploding torpedo. The vessel has never been found. A memorial to the crew was erected at the Battery in 1899.

Judah Benjamin grew to young adulthood in Charleston where his father ran a dry goods store on King Street. Young Judah was educated at the private academy of Rufus Southworth on St. Michael's Alley. He later became a United States Senator from Louisiana and served successively as Attorney General, Secretary of War, and Secretary of State of the Confederacy.

armada of the war was assembled at Port Royal, and soon the deadliest ships of the Union Navy — seven ironclad monitors, the experimental *Keokuk,* and the *New Ironsides,* an armored frigate — arrived in Charleston.

Beauregard had established excellent defenses for the city: obstructions in the harbor, mines, and well-placed fortifications. He had even approved building the first submarines to be used successfully in warfare. The Confederacy did not have much of a navy, and submarine warfare was its only chance. The first submarine, named *David* in honor of the engineer who built it, was semi-submersible, with a torpedo attached to a pole 30 feet long. It was used successfully against the *New Ironsides* in October 1863. Other boats, called "Little Davids" (designed to fight the Union Goliaths), were soon in production.

The Union fleet's attack on Fort Sumter began on April 7, 1863, and continued on and off throughout the remainder of the war. There were eleven major and minor bombardments of the fort, attacks by small boats, and shelling from land and sea. Fort Sumter never surrendered. It was held tenaciously until February 1865 when the end of the war was certain.

But during the spring and summer of 1863, Charlestonians still thought they might win the war. They and the Confederacy had determined that Charleston would never surrender. And the siege of Charleston, which had begun in April with the attack on Fort Sumter continued. In July 1863, after weeks of secret preparations on Folly Island and Coles Island, the Union Army attacked strategically important Morris Island, which protected both Fort Sumter and Charleston Harbor. The island was really a sandbar, but, in terms of lives, it was an expensive piece of real estate in 1863. The goal of the attack on Morris Island was Battery Wagner, a fort near the tip of Morris Island that commanded part of the harbor and a main ship channel. With Wagner intact, no base would be available to the Union Army from which to launch an attack against Charleston.

The assault on Battery Wagner lasted from July 10 to July 18, 1863. Losses were heavy on both sides, but Union losses were especially heavy. Some of those killed belonged to the 54th Massachusetts, a regiment of black troops led by white officers and commanded by the aristocratic Bostonian Robert Gould Shaw.

The 54th Massachusetts had been organized in the wake of the Emancipation Proclamation in 1863 by Governor John A. Andrews of Massachusetts, a zealous abolitionist who promoted the then unpopular idea of using black troops. It was to be "a model for all future Colored Regiments." Shaw, the 25-year-old Boston Brahmin and battle-seasoned veteran of Cedar Mountain and

early
l "be
f life
. Lee,
eston
dered.
He told remberton...o fight "street by street and house by house as long as we have a foot of ground to stand upon."

Christopher G. Memminger served as Secretary of the Treasury of the Confederacy. Memminger was perceived as cool-headed, "a tactician instead of an ideologue," according to Emory Thomas. "Memminger," T.R.R. Cobb wrote his wife "is as shrewd as a Yankee, a perfect —— metamorphosed into a legislating lawyer." Memminger School is named in his honor.

A Short History of Charleston

Antietam, accepted command. The regiment departed from Boston's flag-draped streets in May, arrived in Hilton Head in June, and arrived on James Island in July.

The soldiers of the 54th Massachusetts were chosen to lead the final assault on Battery Wagner on the night of July 18. Six thousand Union troops stormed the battery, some invading the fort itself before being repulsed. There were 1,500 Union casualties, including Shaw. Nearly half of the 54th Regiment was killed. The attack failed. Historians disagree about the effectiveness of the 54th, but the loss at Battery Wagner had a large impact in the North. "Hardly another operation of the war," Dudley T. Cornish has written in *The Sable Arm*, "received so much publicity or stirred so much comment. Out of it a legend was born. As a result of it Robert Gould Shaw came as close to canonization as a New England Puritan can."

The significance of the actions of the 54th Massachusetts was just this: African-American troops could and would fight and die for their country. It was a simple proposition, but one which most whites — North and South — did not believe before that battle. "It is not too much to say that if this Massachusetts 54th had faltered when its trial came," said the New York *Tribune*, "two hundred thousand troops for whom it was a pioneer would never have put into the field . . . But it did not falter. It made Fort Wagner such a name for the colored race as Bunker Hill has been for ninety years to the white Yankees."

Robert Gould Shaw was buried by the Confederates on Morris Island, with the dead of his regiment, or, as the Southern press described it, in a ditch "with his niggers." Northern reaction was vehement, and many insisted Shaw's body be buried with dignity elsewhere. Shaw's father, however, wrote General Quincy Adams Gillmore, the Union commander, that "a soldier's most appropriate burial-place is on the field where he has fallen."

Despite the heroism of men like Colonel Shaw, the Union Army was not ready to march into Charleston. The siege of Charleston was to become bloodier still. On August 21, 1863, General Gillmore sent a message to General Beauregard demanding "the immediate evacuation of Morris Island and Fort Sumter" within four hours, or else "I shall open fire on the city of Charleston." Beauregard wrote a blistering reply:

> Among nations not barbarous the usage of war prescribes that when a city is about to be attacked, timely notice shall be given by the attacking commander, in order that noncombatants may have an opportunity for withdrawing beyond its limits. . . . It would appear, sir, that despairing of

Col. Robert G. Shaw, the hero of the Union assault on Battery Wagner. There are monuments to Robert Gould Shaw in both Charleston and Boston. On the Boston Common Colonel Shaw's statue bears the inscription: "Together they gave . . . undying proof that Americans of African descent possess the pride, courage and devotion of the patriot soldier." In present-day Charleston, at 22 Mary Street, there is a community center for black youths named the Robert Gould Shaw Boys Center.

The Union's bombardment of Charleston, directed from a marsh near Morris Island (the Yankees called their eight-inch gun the Swamp Angel), reached its nadir when Union artillery officers began using St. Michael's spire as a marker.

Margaret Mitchell, the author of *Gone With the Wind,* was a pretty good historian. She researched her facts and created the character Rhett Butler very carefully. In 1936 she wrote a letter explaining his origins: "I made him a Charlestonian because I had to make him a blockade runner, and there was little or no blockading done from Savannah." She came up with the name Rhett because she was looking for a "one-syllable South Carolina Coast first name." Butler was a "Georgia Coast last name."

"Should you capture Charleston, I hope that by some accident the place may be destroyed, and if a little salt should be sown upon its site it may prevent the growth of future crops of nullification and secession." — General Henry W. Halleck to General Sherman, 1865.

Mrs. Ravenel wrote Charleston's epitaph: "With the fall of the city and of the Confederacy went out the old life of Charleston."

reducing these works, you now resort to the novel measure of turning your guns against the old men, the women and children, and the hospitals of a sleeping city, an act of inexcusable barbarity. . . .

On August 29, Gillmore began the bombardment of the city. President Lincoln himself gave the order to fire. In fact, President Lincoln was quite interested in and knowledgeable of weapons technology. One historian has described him "in his own person as the Union's closest approach to a weapons research and development agency." The President, formerly a surveyor, an amateur inventor, as well as a lawyer, had long been interested in incendiary shells and Greek fire. "Such shells, he thought, would be especially valuable in siege operations, as at Vicksburg and Charleston," Richard N. Current wrote in *The Lincoln Nobody Knows.* "Vicksburg surrendered before a thorough test could be made, but behind Fort Sumter the City of Charleston remained exasperatingly out of reach. After a long range, 200-pound Parrott Gun (the 'Swamp Angel') had been set up on Morris Island, Lincoln himself gave the order to shoot into the city with incendiary shells." The lower part of Charleston was bombed and shelled on and off until the surrender a year and a half later. Those who could left Charleston for Columbia or the upcountry. Others removed themselves north of Calhoun Street, where the shells generally did not reach. Downtown Charleston became a ghost town. President Jefferson Davis visited Charleston in November of 1863. He spoke to the assembled citizens from the portico of City Hall and said it was better to leave the city "a heap of ruins" than "prey for Yankee spoils." The crowd agreed and chanted "Ruins! Ruins!"

There were few civilian casualties, but the city was almost destroyed. "By 1864, the town presented the most extraordinary appearance," wrote Mrs. Ravenel. "The whole life and business of the place were crowded into the few squares above Calhoun Street, and along the Ashley, where the hospitals and the prisoners were and the shells did not reach. . . . To pass from this bustling crowded scene to the lower part of the town was . . . like going from life to death."

By the fall of 1864 the end was in sight. Battery Wagner had been evacuated by the Confederacy in the face of an overwhelming Union force. Fort Sumter lay in ruins, though it was still occupied by Confederates living underground. The city was desolate. Lawlessness prevailed as Confederate troops ransacked empty houses looking for loot. Young Gus Smythe wrote, "Our own soldiers are doing us more damage than the shells."

Charleston was abandoned by the Confederate Army in February 1865, following General William Tecumseh Sherman's capture of Atlanta and then Savannah in December 1864. The "March to the Sea" was naturally expected, as late as February 11, to lead to the Cradle of Secession, but the natural geography of the Low Country protected Charleston from Sherman just as it has protected it against 20th-century highways that would destroy the coast. Sherman would have bogged down in any attempt to march and transport through the Low Country marshes. Instead, he headed inland toward Columbia, which he burned, destroying valuables sent from Charleston for safekeeping.

On the morning of February 17, 1865, the Confederates at Fort Sumter raised the Confederate flag. That evening it was lowered for the last time. Later, the soldiers left under cover of darkness. The next day no flag appeared over Sumter and the fort, which had received the first shots of the war, was again in federal hands. "And thus after a siege which will rank among the most famous in history," a Union officer wrote, "Charleston becomes ours."

The city was occupied by Union troops on February 18. In keeping with Charleston's history, a small child lit a fire near a large stockpile of powder left at a railroad station by the Confederate Army. Soon a great fire began near the Cooper River. On the other side of town, the Ashley River Bridge was intentionally burned, and it, too, started a major fire. The fires soon met in the center of the peninsula. As Milby Burton succinctly puts it in *The Siege of Charleston:* "The night of February 17-18 was one of horror and chaos, undoubtedly the worst ever experienced in the history of the city . . . with the evacuation a certainty [the cotton piled in public squares] was set on fire . . . casting an eerie glow over the entire city." The city was at the mercy of roving mobs and looters. Explosions rocked the city — from a magazine on Sullivan's Island and from the destruction of the gunboats *Palmetto State* and the *Chicora.*

Gradually federal troops entered the city. Some looted. Some restored order. The 54th Massachusetts Colored Regiment, among others, paraded down the streets of Charleston. "Any one who is not satisfied with war," General William Tecumseh Sherman wrote, "should go and see Charleston, and he will pray louder and deeper than ever that the country may in the long future be spared any more war."

George A. Trenholm succeeded Christopher Memminger as Secretary of the Treasury of the Confederacy. A dashing millionaire, probably the wealthiest man in the South, Trenholm made millions as a blockade-runner during the war and his overseas companies acted as virtual banks for the Confederate government.

"The truth is the whole army is burning with insatiable desire to wreak vengeance upon South Carolina. I almost tremble at her fate." — General Sherman to General Halleck, 1865.

Reconstruction Charleston (1865–1877)

7

A northern reporter for the *Boston Advertiser* and the *Chicago Tribune* named Sidney Andrews, came to Charleston in September 1865 and saw: "A city of ruins, of desolation, of vacant houses, of widowed women, of rotting wharves, of deserted warehouses, of weed-wild gardens, of miles of grass-grown streets, of acres of pitiful and voiceful barrenness — that is Charleston, wherein Rebellion loftily reared its head five years ago, on whose beautiful promenade the fairest of cultured women gathered with passionate hearts to applaud the assault of ten thousand upon the little garrison of Fort Sumter!"

Physically, the city was in ruins. The great damage done by the fire of 1861 had never been repaired, and the bombardment of the city below Calhoun Street had left a virtual ghost town. Charleston had survived, but its way of life was forever altered. For the white aristocratic elite, civilization seemed almost at an end: "No one in the country in which you live," Williams Middleton wrote his sister in Philadelphia, "has the slightest conception of the real condition of affairs here — of the utter topsy-turveying of all of our institutions. . . ." Slavery had been abolished, and many former slaves had run away or refused to work. Beautiful Middleton Place, like many other plantations, had been burned by Union troops, and capital for rebuilding was nonexistent. Family fortunes, invested in Confederate bonds or currency, had disappeared. Town houses were looted by Union troops and criminals of both races. People took what work they could find. Lieutenant General Richard H. Anderson worked in the railroad yards. The James Heyward family took in sewing. Other Charleston aristocrats rented rooms in once fashionable homes or ran boarding schools. Some drove streetcars; others became tellers in banks. There were also attempts to get plantations back in working order. Slowly life began to return to some new kind of order,

Opposite page
The victorious 55th Massachusetts: The black regiment entered Charleston February 21, 1865, singing "John Brown's Body."

The flag raising ceremony at Fort Sumter, April 14, 1865.

but the poverty and even outright hunger during the first year was grinding.

The gloom that pervaded white aristocratic Charleston, however, was unknown in black Charleston. For black Charlestonians, life was different. Civilization was not at an end; it was just beginning. They would have agreed with Williams Middleton's remark about the "utter topsy-turveying of all our institutions." The difference was that they were happy about it. Slavery was at an end. The "Day of Jubilee" had arrived. Charleston was now the promised land. For the city's blacks it was a time of celebration.

And celebrations were frequent. On March 3, 1865, a huge crowd of black Charlestonians assembled at Marion Square and watched as 13 black women, elegantly dressed to symbolize the 13 original states, presented the Union commander with a flag, a bouquet of flowers, and a fan for Mrs. Lincoln. On March 4, Major Martin R. Delany, editor, explorer and the highest ranking black military officer in the army arrived in Charleston. On March 29, one of the largest parades ever held in Charleston began at noon. Four thousand blacks participated. There were companies of soldiers, tailors, coopers, 50 butchers, 1,800 school children and their teachers, eight companies of firemen, sailors, and many other tradesmen. They were followed, most dramatically, by two carts, one carrying an auction block with an "auctioneer" auctioning two black women and their children. The other carried a coffin with the signs "Slavery is dead" and "Sumter dug his grave on the 13th of April, 1861."

The greatest celebration was held on April 14, 1865, when Robert Anderson returned to Charleston to raise the garrison flag he had taken with him on that fateful day in April 1861. The city closed down for the festivities. Three thousand blacks went to Fort Sumter to watch the ceremonies. Robert Smalls was there with the *Planter*. Denmark Vesey's son was there. Leading abolitionists Henry Ward Beecher and William Lloyd Garrison were there. The Reverend Mr. Beecher made a speech to the assembled crowd urging national unity and education for black South Carolinians. He blamed the war on the "the polished, cultured, exceedingly capable and wholly unprincipled ruling aristocracy who wanted to keep power." A ball, a supper, and a fireworks display were also part of the festivities. It was later that same night, in Washington, D.C., that Abraham Lincoln was assassinated.

White Charlestonians, seething with anger, had little grief to spare for the murdered President. The Rector of St. John's Episcopal Church refused to say the traditional Episcopal prayer for the President. And what was said was said behind closed doors.

The die of Reconstruction had been cast before the surrender at Appomattox. Class antagonism between blacks and whites, the racial animosity

A Short History of Charleston

of centuries, was now out in the open. Sidney Andrews summed it up this way in 1865: "The whites charge generally that the negro is idle and at the bottom of all local disturbance, and credit him with most of the vices and very few of the virtues of humanity. The negroes charge that the whites are revengeful, and intend to cheat the laboring class at every opportunity, and credit them with neither good purposes nor kindly hearts."

The history of Reconstruction Charleston reflects this fundamental disagreement. On one hand is the traditional school boys' story of wicked "carpetbaggers" (northern adventurers come South), "scalawags" (native whites who cooperated with blacks), and blacks bent on taking over the government, stealing, and plundering, a story full of bribery, violence, ignorance, and thievery ending in corruption so complete that by 1877 the old aristocracy could take over the reins of government once more. On the other hand is the story of newly emancipated blacks led mainly by free, native black Charlestonians, former Union soldiers, and some idealistic whites from the North (government officials and New England schoolteachers) trying to reform a narrow and racist society steeped in hostility to the American ideals of equality and democracy and struggling to achieve a more democratic constitution, better schools, and a chance for people who had been poor, oppressed, and ignorant for centuries to better themselves. White Charlestonians and, later, white northerners saw only the first version. Black Charlestonians and, still later, white northerners saw the second.

Blacks from the countryside came to Charleston in great numbers in the early years and throughout Reconstruction. Contrary to historical myth, most slaves deserted their plantations and their masters. And the defection of the house servants was, according to Joel Williamson in *After Slavery,* "almost complete." Many, just liberated, never having been allowed to leave their immediate area, had an understandable desire to see the world. For whites, the inpouring of blacks was horrifying. "No negro is improved by a visit to Columbia," J. K. Robertson wrote Mrs. Smythe in 1865, "& a visit to Charleston is his certain destruction." Charleston was a mecca for the freedman (as the newly freed slave was called) because of its large free black population, the social and religious opportunities for blacks, and the cosmopolitan character of the big city. Charleston was where the action was. The city's black population increased by 3,000 between 1860 and 1870. In 1870 there were 4,000 more blacks than whites in Charleston. As one black said, "freedom was free-er in Charleston."

The behavior of blacks toward whites changed. Old courtesies were still shown by many blacks to their old masters, but many others were determined to exercise their new independence. One white Charlestonian found

After emancipation, blacks had to adopt surnames because in slavery they had none. Many blacks from the Charleston area took the names of large slaveholders. Thousands of Charleston's blacks today have names like Middleton, Pinckney, Hayne, and Manigault. Blacks also took the names of great leaders like Washington, Lincoln, and Grant. There were not many black Calhouns, however.

"Negroes shoving white person[s] . . . [off] the walk. Negro women dressed in the most outré style, all with veils and parasols for which they have an especial fancy. Riding on horseback with negro soldiers and in carriages." Black Charlestonians now could talk in public in groups, keep dogs and guns, and smoke cigars. They could even go to the Battery, a place legally off limits to them prior to the war. One white aristocrat noted, in 1866, that "On Sunday afternoon the ethiops spread themselves on the Battery." Yet A. T. Smythe wrote his wife in 1865 that the blacks he met were "as civil and humble as ever. All I met greeted me enthusiastically as 'Mass Gus.'" An elderly Middleton wrote in 1866 that, "The negroes about town behave as far as I see extremely well. I have met with nothing but respect and good-will from them."

A New Order: The violence of the Reconstruction period resulted from the extreme changes of the time. Four hundred thousand blacks were freed in South Carolina. Black troops occupied a city that was once the proud capital of black slavery. Centuries of social habits came dramatically to an end. The wonder, really, is why there was not more violence. Whites still believed slavery was right, and that blacks were innately inferior. Blacks, however, were now free — and about to take over the government. It was a strained situation. Something had to give.

What gave was the peace. There were two major race riots in Charleston during 1865 and 1866. In July 1865 white Union soldiers from a New York Zouave regiment clashed with black soldiers of the 21st U.S. Colored Troops. The riot stopped when the Zouaves were sent to Morris Island. On June 24, 1866, a mob of blacks started a fight on the corner of Tradd and King Streets by assaulting a white. The instigator of the riot was one Scipio Fraser, who led an assault in which a white man died. Later, Fraser bragged about the killing: "I, and no one else, killed the rebel son of a bitch, and he is not the first, nor he will not be the last I will kill." Rioting went on for at least a week.

As blacks rose to political power and many whites were disenfranchised because they had fought for the Confederacy, tension increased. There were rumors of violence on John's Island in 1868. There were murders of both whites and blacks on various plantations.

The conflicts inherent in Reconstruction Charleston were worsened by the political realities of the situation. Nothing would satisfy the whites except a return to slavery, or failing that, a form of pseudoslavery in which blacks would be controlled by whites. Many whites of good will sincerely believed that blacks would perish in freedom, that they would die of disease and hunger, and some actually did. The overall health of the black community declined in the postwar years. While native whites urged blacks to trust them, pointing out their common background, blacks were doubtful. "We have played together, you say," one black campaign banner read in 1870, "but were we ever whipped together?"

On the national level, Lincoln's assassination ended hopes for a moderate treatment of white southerners. President Andrew Johnson, Lincoln's successor, established a provisional government in South Carolina in June 1865 and appointed an old Unionist, Benjamin F. Perry, as governor. In September a new Constitution was drawn up, but white conservatives still dominated the government. They immediately passed a code "for the regulation of labor, and the protection and government of the Colored Population of the State." These laws became known as the Black Code, and, while it was passed in some measure to protect blacks from unscrupulous whites, it also harked back to slave days. The Black Code, the rejection of the Fourteenth Amendment by southern legislatures, the election of former Confederates to high public office, and the realization that, with the abolition of slavery, the South's percentage of congressional seats would *increase* (slaves had only been counted as three-fifths of a person in the original Constitution) — all led to a movement in Congress to take Reconstruction out of the hands of President Johnson and place it in the hands of the Radical Republican Congress. The state was again put under military rule, and the government was reorganized on the basis of equality of the races. In November 1867 the first elections in which blacks could vote were held.

A new constitutional convention met in Charleston on January 14, 1868, and continued through March 18. The convention was attended by 124 delegates, mostly Republicans. There were 76 blacks and 48 whites. "The character of the professional Republican politicians in South Carolina during Reconstruction has often been debated," writes Joel Williamson. "The Redeemers, who wrote most of the history of the period, damned them all. . . . Negro politicians were either Northern-sprung zealots in various stages of mental derangement or ignorant and deluded freed-men who moved directly from the cotton fields into office without so much as a change of clothes. Even a cursory survey of these groups reveals the inaccuracy of such a description."

The scalawags actually came from every social strata of South Carolina. The notorious Reconstruction governor, Franklin J. Moses, was the secessionist governor's secretary! Carpetbaggers varied widely. The last Republican governor, D. H. Chamberlain, for example, was a graduate of Yale Law School and a distinguished lawyer.

And the blacks? "The one thing that most native Negro leaders were not was fresh from the cotton fields," concludes Williamson. Fifty-nine black members of the Constitutional Convention of 1868 were either born in South Carolina or had settled there before the war. Twelve had been free prior to the war. They had been tradesmen, not field hands. Many were teachers working for the Freedman's Bureau, an agency of the federal government. Francis Louis Cardozo, a mulatto whose mother was half Indian and half black and whose father was Jewish, was educated at the University of Glasgow, studied at Edinburgh and London, and was an ordained Presbyterian minister. Of the 38 delegates who were former slaves, none had worked in the fields. Some were ministers, carpenters, blacksmiths, shoemakers, or coachmen. There were barbers, tanners, teachers, and carriage makers, but no field hands. It was, in truth, reminiscent of the rise to power of the artisans after the Revolutionary War — except that the participants were black and the aristocracy was not represented at all.

The convention wrote a new constitution based on those of the northern states. "In letter it was as good as any other constitution the state has ever had, or as most American states had at that time . . . the Conservative whites were content to live under it for eighteen years after they recovered control," concluded F. B. Simkins and R. H. Woody in their study of Reconstruction. Actually, much of the Constitution of 1868 survives today in the present South Carolina Constitution.

The Constitution was more democratic than any before or since (until very recent times). It provided for universal male suffrage and for a free public school system, the first in the history of South Carolina. It protected the rights of property owners. At no time did the Reconstruction government confiscate land. True, its policy was to raise taxes, but, for the first time in its history, South Carolina was going to support public education and minister somewhat to the needs of the poor.

Scalawags and Scandals: During the next eight years, South Carolina was governed by a Republican Reconstruction government. The oft-told story was made famous by James S. Pike in his classic *The Prostrate State: South Carolina Under Negro Government* (1874). Scandals abounded, the greatest of which involved the illegal issuance of state bonds. Millions of dollars were siphoned off by the corrupt Republican governors, Scott and Moses, and their cronies. Millions were stolen by United States Senator John J. ("Honest John") Patterson and his pals in a railroad scam in which the state "invested" in the Blue Ridge Railroad.

Corruption affected life in Charleston as it did life throughout the state.

When the military government was removed in 1868, a Republican was elected mayor. Mayor Pillsbury won the election by 23 votes, out of 10,000 cast! The city's debt grew to $5 million by 1873. The position of the collector of the port of Charleston, always a powerful position, went to a Patterson henchman, H. C. Worthington, a former congressman and Union general. Whites complained that blacks held all of the government posts. Yet no black Mayor was elected and, in fact, the Conservatives actually won the municipal elections of 1871 when they ran John A. Wagener for mayor on a "fusion" or "cooperationist" ticket composed of both whites and blacks.

Black Charlestonians served in a variety of positions in local government. A black was postmaster of Charleston throughout the period. The police force was half black and half white. The state judges were white and apparently honest, as were the solicitors. The entire legislative delegation was black throughout most of the period. Blacks filled lower judgeships. Some performed fairly and honestly; others did not.

Some, though not all, elections were corrupt. Republicans, set on winning the mayor's race in 1873, imported as many black voters as they could. Four hundred blacks came to the city from Edisto Island to vote! One travel account indicates that: "Governor Moses told an editor in Charleston that every citizen of South Carolina could vote in that city, if he chose, without hindrance."

It was an age of corruption. While this does not excuse Reconstruction South Carolina, the entire country suffered corruption after the Civil War. As the idealism of the war faded, cynicism replaced it. The administration of President Grant and the age of the Robber Barons coincided with Reconstruction in the South.

In 1865, the Union Army seized Charleston's school system and installed a leading abolitionist, James Redpath, as superintendent. Redpath soon opened the Morris Street School to blacks and whites, though few whites attended. Teachers in the new school system were black and white. Northern white churches contributed people and money to the effort. Episcopalians taught blacks at the Franklin Street School after 1866. "The teachers all but one are Charleston ladies," reported one visitor in 1874. The New England Freedman's Aid Society supported the Shaw Memorial School, named for Robert Gould Shaw.

Segregation was outlawed by the Constitution of 1868, but it is doubtful that much integration took place as a result. Many leaders of the black community agreed with the black leader, F. L. Cardozo, when he said, "colored people would prefer separate schools, particularly until some of the present prejudice against their race is removed."

Advanced training for blacks became available, too. In 1865 the American

We have planned for the dedication of the bleak spot where so many hundred of our soldiers were covered in long trenches; in heaps-four short rows containing 249 of our men, the dead of less than a week. These were white soldiers—prisoners of war. The colored men have built a fence about the spot a free offering, and a fine monument is to be erected as soon as we have sufficient means. The cloudless sky and hot sun of an August morning was over us as the school children formed in procession and marched from the Morris St. School to the Club House on the racecourse where the opening ceremonies are to be held. We rode slowly up King St. to the race course. There it was thronged with vehicles of every description and pedestrians of all ages, from the baby in arms to the white hairs of bent old age. All faces wore the sweetest smiles and nearly every hand bore bunches of baskets laden with beautiful flowers.

— *The diary of Dr. Esther Hill Hawks, May 1, 1865.*

Zion Presbyterian Church, one of the city's first African American churches, was built in 1859 on Calhoun Street between Anson and Meeting Streets.

Missionary Society established a school for black teachers in Charleston, the Avery Normal Institute, which continued in existence until 1946. (From 1947 until 1954, Avery was part of the public school system.) The Citadel was closed. Its buildings were used by federal troops for a time. The College of Charleston continued to function on a reduced scale.

One of the most dramatic social changes of all occurred in the religious field. Black Charlestonians withdrew from white churches *en masse*. Not only were they not expelled, but certain sects, such as the Presbyterians, tried to keep black worshippers in the fold out of a profound belief that their souls were in danger if not properly instructed. A few months after the war ended, blacks were largely to be found in their own segregated churches. "In fact," J. K. Robertson wrote Mrs. Smythe in June 1865, "the colours are separated now as to churches. The Blacks now have Calhoun & Zion, Old Bethel, also I believe another Methodist church, Morris Street Baptist and perhaps some other old churches to themselves." What was at work was the age-old dream of black people to minister to their own needs, as well as the missionary zeal of northern and black churches.

Typical of the situation that arose in many white Charleston congregations was the history of Charleston's Trinity Methodist Church. Timothy Lewis, a Northern Methodist missionary, arrived to organize new Methodist congregations and to minister to the needs of Charlestonians, black and white. The whites did not want the blacks to leave Trinity. In fact, they pleaded with them "to stay with us in your old places in the galleries." Lewis countered with the nondiscriminatory Northern Methodist doctrine that "there will be no galleries in heaven . . . go with a church which makes no distinctions." The black Methodists left to form Centenary Church, still one of the strongest Northern Methodist churches in the South.

Black ministers came to Charleston, and former Charlestonians returned to their hometown. Charleston attracted black intellectuals, ministers, and politicians. After all, there was unlimited opportunity for black people to make a contribution. Take Daniel Alexander Payne. He had been born free in Charleston in 1811, and had been a shoemaker, a tailor, and a teacher. In the 1830s he left for Pennsylvania, where he became a leader in the AME Church. After he was ordained a bishop, Payne returned to Charleston in 1865.

It was from this crucible that most of Charleston's leading black churches — the Zion Church (Presbyterian), the Emmanuel AME Church, the Morris Street Baptist Church, St. Mark's (Episcopal) — emerged. They were religious, social, political, and educational centers. They were welfare agencies. They were community meeting halls and focal points of organized community efforts. These churches remain to this day the central institution of black community life in Charleston.

The best example of the political power of the black churches can be seen in the life of Richard Harvey Cain. A mulatto born free in Virginia, Cain grew up in Ohio, studied at Wilberforce University, and became a minister. He left his Brooklyn pulpit in 1865 to come to Charleston and immediately organized the Emmanuel Church at a cost of $10,000, a considerable sum at that time. He attended the Constitutional Convention of 1868, was elected a state senator, and served as a lobbyist. Cain is probably best remembered as the founder of Lincolnville, a small black community near Charleston, which he organized in 1871. In 1872 he was elected to Congress. He was editor of the *Missionary Record* and became a bishop in 1880.

The offices of the *News & Courier* on Broad Street in the 1880s. The *News & Courier* was created when the *News* merged with *Courier*. In 1991 the name of the newspaper was changed to *The Post & Courier* when the *Evening Post* and the *News & Courier* merged.

Postbellum Recovery: Charleston's economy recovered gradually from the trauma of war. The Freedman's Bureau, contrary to popular myth, did not promise "40 acres and a mule" to every freedman and, in fact, refused to give food or any relief to those who refused to work. Federal policy was to send "vagrants" back to the plantations to work. But the bureau insisted that the rights of freedmen be protected and that fair wages be paid. Cotton production started immediately after the war and the number of bales shipped from Charleston doubled between 1866 and 1869. The same was true for rice, but rice became less important to the Carolina economy since it was too costly and too difficult to grow without free labor. By 1873 Charleston was beginning to show some signs of prosperity.

In addition to the cotton trade and other port business, Charleston began to expand its railroad lines. Lumber exports grew. Phosphate mining along the rivers became a major industry. Phosphate was mined, then baked, then ground to a powder and mixed with ammonia and sulfuric acid to make fertilizer that was shipped and sold to grow cotton. The manufacture of doors, blinds, sashes, and machinery became another major industry. Retail and wholesale establishments flourished once again. King Street became a crowded, bustling retail district, while East Bay regained its reputation as a regional wholesale and shipping district.

The intellectual life of Charleston, though, was sadly afflicted by Reconstruction. On the bright side was the temporary increase in newspapers: the Charleston *Courier*, the *Daily Republican*, the *Mercury*, the *Charleston Daily News*, and the *Weekly Republican*. Out of all this emerged the *News and Courier*, which became the only daily morning newspaper in Charleston. In 1873 the owners of the *News* merged with the venerable *Courier*, which had been founded in 1803. The newspaper's offices were originally on Broad Street, and its powerful editor, Francis

Editor Dawson was probably involved in Reconstruction scandals himself. He may have helped the bond ring (see p. 126) transfer business to London, according to historian Joel Williamson. He clearly used bribery to defeat Republican Governor D. H. Chamberlain, who complained, "They beat me out by using more money than I had." Even conservative historian David Duncan Wallace asserts that Dawson paid graft to the state treasurer for some of the state's printing business.

Warrington Dawson, an Englishman, was no stranger to Reconstruction politics. Dawson, in fact, championed the idea of fusion, that is, native whites voting for "decent" Republicans rather than boycotting elections. He greatly influenced the course of city politics, as the idea of fusion worked well in city elections.

In 1873 Edward King described Charleston as "very lovely . . . lying confidingly on the waters . . . fronting on the spacious harbor, over whose entrance the scarred and ever memorable Sumter keeps watch and ward." Numerous ships lay at anchor off the new marble customs house on East Bay.

King Street sported a new Academy of Music where Charleston's theater tradition continued. Elliott Street did not fare too well during Reconstruction. In 1870, three black women were arrested "in a house of bad repute on Elliott Street, while engaged in a free fight, during which they made use of violent and horrible language," the *Daily Republican* reported.

A new form of transportation, the streetcar, made its debut during Reconstruction. Inaugurated in 1866, Charleston's streetcars looked like the later trolleys, but were horsedrawn along tracks. They were operated by the Charleston Street Car Company along the Blue Line (Broad Street), the Red Line (Rutledge), and the Yellow Line (Meeting Street). They were used until 1897. The whole enterprise almost failed in 1867 when a number of blacks insisted on riding in the car instead of on the platform as required by the company's rules. Police and soldiers were called to restore order. But once blacks won the right to ride on the streetcars, whites stopped using them.

An Inglorious End: By 1876 both North and South had run out of steam when it came to Reconstruction. Eleven years of Radical Republican rule and the idealistic fervor of the past fifteen years had taken their toll. The great emigration of blacks to the North had done nothing but strengthen racism in the North and lessen concern for blacks in the South. The North finally concluded it could not reconstruct the South.

The election of 1876 in South Carolina actually produced two rival governments. Republican D. M. Chamberlain claimed the governorship backed by federal troops. Democrat Wade Hampton claimed the governorship backed by his Red Shirts, Rifle Clubs, and Sabre Clubs. Hampton, an aristocratic former Confederate general, had the universal love and respect of the whites, particularly in the upcountry of South Carolina, where violence was the chief means of preventing blacks and Republicans from voting. In Charleston, bribery was probably more common. A number of Charleston blacks, unlike

The Ku Klux Klan, powerful in South Carolina's upcountry, was never very active in Reconstruction Charleston.

blacks elsewhere in the state, supported Hampton.

Hampton eventually won out, but his election caused still more violence: the Hamburg Riot, the last major race confrontation of the Reconstruction era. Hamburg, a black village on the Savannah River near Augusta, Georgia, was known to Charleston history as the terminus of the state's first railroad. By 1876 it was almost a ghost town. In the summer of 1876 whites in the upcountry had organized Rifle Clubs and Sabre Clubs to resist the Reconstruction government. In Hamburg whites started a fight with blacks and murdered a number of them. The reaction in Charleston was instantaneous. On July 10 a mass meeting was held to condemn the atrocities. A week later another meeting was held, and the city grew tense.

On September 6 a riot broke out. "The rioters held King Street, the main thoroughfare, from midnight until sunrise, breaking windows, robbing stores, and attacking and beating indiscriminately every white man who showed his face," reported the *New York Times.* The rioting continued for some time, both in Charleston and in the surrounding areas. At Cainhoy, ten miles from Charleston, one black and four whites were killed. At least eight people died in the riots: six whites and two blacks.

Wade Hampton: This hero of what his contemporaries called "The Confederate War" became a hero of Post-Reconstruction South Carolina.

When the Southern Democrats assented to the election of Rutherford B. Hayes in the disputed presidential election of 1876, Hayes removed federal troops from South Carolina and agreed not to enforce the former slaves' newly won rights. Reconstruction was at an end.

Despite the tumult that surrounded his election, Wade Hampton was the undisputed hero of post-Reconstruction South Carolina. Hampton's policy was paternalistic, it is true, but it was not antiblack; he had sincerely appealed to black voters, promising, and keeping his promise, to respect their rights and to appoint blacks to responsible positions. The Great Redeemer of South Carolina was to stamp the next 14 years of South Carolina history with his philosophy. Throughout the 1870s and the 1880s blacks participated in the political process under Hampton's protection. Once Hampton left office, black South Carolinians were at the mercy of lesser men.

Born in Charleston at the Rhett House on Hasell Street, the oldest home now standing in Charleston, Wade Hampton was the quintessence of the southern gentleman. After all, his father's thoroughbreds had won all of the races held by the Jockey Club in 1800. He owned a huge plantation in Mississippi and had fought valiantly for the Confederacy. He was a fair and compassionate leader. There are monuments to him all over the state, and at least two in Charleston: at Hampton Park and on Marion Square. His greatest memorial, however, was a peaceful society in impossible times and a legacy of goodwill in the most difficult of situations.

Porgy's City
(1877–1941)

8

Fallen from its rare grace as it was, how bad could life have been in Charleston during the 1880s? Well, in the movie version of *Gone With the Wind,* Rhett left Scarlett to go back to Charleston, "where there's a little bit of grace and charm left in the world," or, as Rhett says in the novel, "to try to make peace with my people." Scarlett (in the novel) cries, "But you hate them!" Scarlett wasn't going to Charleston, and, as we know Rhett didn't give a damn.

What kind of city was Rhett Butler coming home to in the 1870s and 1880s? Charleston had yet to recover from the Civil War. Parts of the city were unrepaired well into the 1880s. The great wealth of the antebellum period had not returned. Great suburbs like Harleston or Radcliffborough and Wraggsborough would never be built again.

But Charleston survived. Like other cities in the South, it tried to look to the future. From 1877 to 1890, the city retained its role as the political — if not the official — center of the state.

The spirit of the "New South" movement gripped the city in the 1880s. That movement, epitomized by Henry Grady's Atlanta, preached national reconciliation, economic regeneration and diversity, industrialization, and an "amicable" adjustment of the "Negro question." The young men of the 1880s looked to Americanization and industrialism as solutions to the South's problems, and Francis W. Dawson, the young editor of the *News and Courier,* was one of the movement's prime spokesmen.

Dawson, an Englishman by birth, had been sympathetic to the Confederacy and came to Charleston after the war at the age of twenty-five. He paid tribute to the past, but urged Charleston to look to the future. He coined the slogan "Bring the Cotton Mills to the Cotton" (recalled by Lillian Hellman in

Opposite page
Inspiration for "Catfish Row": Cabbage Row, 89–91 Church Street, as it looked in the 1920s. Gershwin's *Porgy and Bess* (1935), set here, wasn't performed in Charleston until 1970.

The Cotton Palace: Nothing remains of the South Carolina Interstate and West Indian Exposition of 1901 but the bandstand in Hampton Park.

her play *The Little Foxes*) and argued for the location of the textile industry in Charleston. Charleston did get on the New South bandwagon, and cotton mills did come. The Charleston Cotton Mill, for example, continued in business until the early 1900s. Other factories opened, including the Charleston Shoe Factory. Charlestonians were trying to forget the past and learn the American way of life.

One of the staples of the New South movement was the exposition, industrial fair, or what we now call a "world's fair." Numerous expositions such as the Atlanta International Cotton Exposition, and the Piedmont Exposition were held in the South in this period, and Charleston, though a little late, played host to the South Carolina Interstate and West Indian Exposition, a truly fantastic world's fair that attracted international attention, brought President Teddy Roosevelt to Charleston, opened up a whole new section of the city, and left a lasting legacy, Hampton Park. The exposition was organized by a private corporation on land donated by Captain F. W. Wagener, president of the company. It generally encompassed what is now known as Hampton Park and Wagener Terrace in the Northwest Section of the city.

The exposition opened on Sunday, December 1, 1901. There were 14 main buildings, palaces (like the Cotton Palace which was lit by electricity at night), manmade lagoons, gardens, and a variety of exhibitions. The Midway featured Akoun's Beautiful Orient and Streets of Cairo, Fair Japan, and the Cuban Theatre. Captain Wagener entertained President Roosevelt in the Women's Building at "The Grove" (a plantation house still standing at the end of St. Margaret Street). There was a Negro Building, as well as a Negro Department, organized by Booker T. Washington and prominent black Charlestonians. There were Eskimos and tigers. As a result of the exposition, the American Cigar Company located in the city, the oyster-canning business got started, and the United Fruit Company began shipping bananas through Charleston.

After the exposition, more people began to move to the area south of the grounds (south of present-day Hampton Park). Legend has it that wood and other materials from the exposition went into the building of houses in the neighborhood. The old bandstand, once located at the center of the exposition, was moved and still stands in Hampton Park today. The Citadel moved to the Hampton Park area in 1922.

But for all of Charleston's boosterism, the city was in a deep decline. Port business fell dramatically from the 1870s to World War I. The mills failed. Railroads either bypassed Charleston, or their discriminatory rates hindered the city's economic recovery; it was cheaper to ship cotton from Spartanburg to New York by rail than it was to ship it to Charleston by rail and then by boat to New York. The poverty was a crushing problem, and remained so until World War II.

In 1883 the city celebrated its Centennial of Incorporation, and on August 13 Charlestonians assembled to hear speeches honoring Robert Y. Hayne and James L. Petigru. (Their busts, dating from this celebration, now reside in City Council Chambers at City Hall.) At 8 p.m., 15,000 Charlestonians gathered at the Rutledge Street Pond (now Colonial Lake) to witness a great display of fireworks, striped balloons, and colored fires. The fireworks included inscriptions such as "Fort Moultrie, June 28, 1776," and "Charlestown 1670."

Catastrophes and Demagoguery: As if the city had not suffered enough, two catastrophes struck in the 1880s: a cyclone in 1885 and an earthquake in 1886. The cyclone badly damaged the Battery seawall and flooded parts of the city, but it was only a taste of what was to come.

At 9:45 p.m., on August 31, 1886, the Great Earthquake struck. Buildings collapsed and people ran into the streets to escape falling walls. Twenty-seven people were killed immediately, sixty people ultimately died. Damage was estimated at six million dollars. Roads out of the city were impassable for days, and the railroad lines were destroyed. Many buildings were badly damaged or destroyed. The old Guard House and Police Station at Broad and Meeting Streets was so damaged it had to be torn down. It was ten years before the present-day Post Office Building was erected on the site.

Hundreds of Charlestonians were left homeless by the earthquake. A tent city was set up in Washington Park, where people lived while their homes were being reconstructed. Other Charlestonians erected tents in their yards. But Charlestonians were encouraged by expressions of sympathy from all over the world. Queen Victoria sent a telegram; a benefit concert was given in Paris.

As if Charleston had not had enough, the Great Hurricane of 1893 struck the city seven years later. The lower peninsula was covered with five feet of water and the western section of town under six to ten feet. Hundreds of people were killed on Ladies Island near Beaufort. The founder of the American Red Cross, Clara Barton herself, took charge of the sea island relief efforts and had a headquarters on East Bay Street. Miss Barton had last been to Charleston in 1863 to nurse Union soldiers on Morris Island. A hurricane or two later, and the rice fields were in such bad condition that rice planting

Many Charleston buildings had "earthquake rods" driven through them after the earthquake of 1886. Round discs, some ornamented, on the sides of local buildings are reminders that the worst earthquake in the history of the eastern United States occurred in Charleston.

Earthquake, 1886: Charleston (and Boston) are as prone to earthquakes as San Francisco. Here is the corner of Cumberland and East Bay Streets.

ended forever.

Charleston accepted genteel poverty gracefully. In 1905 Henry James came to the city and described a remnant of the Old South. He could see it "in one case by the mere tragic of the manner in which a small, scared, starved person of color, . . . an elderly mulattress . . . just barely held open for me a door through which I felt I might have looked straight and far back into the past. The past, that of the vanished order, was hanging on there behind her. . . . So, it seemed to me, had I been confronted, in Italy, under quite such a morning air and light, quite the same touch of a tepid, odorous medium, with the ancient sallow crones who guard the locked portals and the fallen pride of provincial *palazzini.*"

The disasters of the 1880s — cyclone, earthquake, economic stagnation

A Short History of Charleston

— were compounded further by the next shock waves to hit Charleston: Pitchfork Ben Tillman, Populism, and the rise of the southern demagogue.

From colonial times to 1890, Charleston had maintained disproportionate political clout in South Carolina despite the state's growing upcountry population. The city had more representation than it was entitled to, and its political and business leaders dominated South Carolina. The war and its aftermath had linked all white South Carolinians against common foes: black South Carolinians, carpetbaggers, and the federal government. Confederate officers became the natural leaders of the white community during Reconstruction. After Reconstruction, the same conservative class of planters, aristocrats, and Confederate officers (now called "Bourbons" or "Redeemers" by historians) aligned themselves with the new business elite (from the railroads, cotton mills, factories and banks), many of whom were Northerners come South.

The Redeemers stayed in power through the 1880s by a combination of the personal charisma of Wade Hampton and other popular Confederate officers, fear of blacks and Republicans, inertia, and poverty. But the economic and social frustration of the mass of rural whites came to the forefront during the 1890s.

From this popular movement arose the greatest demagogues and race-baiters in the history of South Carolina: Benjamin Ryan ("Pitchfork Ben") Tillman and Coleman Blease. These men and others were elected by irate, downtrodden white farmers on a platform of agrarian and educational reform, intimidation and lynching of blacks (Both "Cotton Ed" Smith and Ben Tillman defended lynching on the floor of the United States Senate), and a general hostility toward the only cosmopolitan city in South Carolina — Charleston.

Charleston had come to epitomize everything the Populist demagogues were angry about. They hated aristocrats and were tired of old Confederate generals (by 1890 the war had been over for 25 years). Charleston was a city full of aristocrats, and it symbolized the war. They hated aristocratic and intellectual institutions. Tillman attacked the University of South Carolina and the Citadel ("that military dude factory"). They detested blacks. Charleston was half black. They were for prohibition. Charleston was a drinking city. Tillman called Charlestonians "the most self-idolatrous people in the world." William Watts Ball recalled in his memoirs that the Tillmanites "preached their jehad against Charleston and for no good reason save that Charleston would not bow the knee to Captain Tillman. . . . It seems unbelievable now [1932], but it is the simple truth that the political leaders of that day inflamed the people to look upon Charleston as the hatchery of their woes, imagined or

The Upcountry saw Charleston, in the words of one up-country writer, as a "worldly place, a sea city trading with remote London and Canton in heathen China. It had silks and a theatre and . . . was worldly and sumptuous with the wicked walking on every side."

real . . . and politically they crushed Charleston."

The ascendancy of the demagogues forced Charleston to turn in on herself. She was now feeling the pent-up resentment of hundreds of years. No Charlestonian was elected governor from 1865 until 1938. "Charleston's reply was feeble and futile," Ball wrote. "After 1890 it accepted the verdict. Its leaders scattered and retired to their tents." Because they could not succeed in statewide politics, Charlestonians turned all of their attention to local races. Ball noted in 1932 that Charleston's "local contests are of a heat seldom observed elsewhere . . . outsiders gaze upon a Charlestonian election with wonderment, sometimes with merriment."

Tillman's chief attack on Charleston's way of life was his program of prohibition, and his government instituted what was called the State Dispensary, a state monopoly on selling alcohol. The Dispensary Act, which went into effect in 1893, was never really enforced in Charleston. Private businesses continued to sell liquor in defiance of state law. Tillmanite governors sent raiding parties of state constables to Charleston to enforce the statute which the local police refused to do. In 1896 the governor suspended the City Council's control of the police force and placed Charleston under the metropolitan police law, appointing a Tillmanite (one J. Elmer Martin) as chief of police — all to enforce the unenforceable liquor laws. Charlestonians continued to drink at illegal saloons called "blind tigers."

Centuries of Charleston hedonism would not give way to anything so transient as Ben Tillman. Eventually the mayor promised to try to enforce the liquor laws, and the city regained control of its police force. Soon the Dispensary Act was repealed. Charlestonians continued to drink — and to thumb their noses at the rest of the state.

Tillman was elected to the United States Senate, and, by 1900, both he and Charleston realized that a truce was in order. One result of the truce was the location of a United States Naval Station in Charleston in 1901.

The location of the old Naval Station at Port Royal was a legacy of the Civil War. In 1899 the battleship *Indiana* was badly damaged while entering the dry dock at Port Royal, and the navy, dissatisfied with the facility anyway, began looking for a new location. Mayor J. Adger Smyth saw the possibility of locating the navy yard in Charleston and began to campaign for it. Tillman, a member of the naval committee, joined in the campaign, and by 1901 the most important economic decision in the modern history of Charleston was made. The Navy Yard came to Charleston. Later administrations enlarged the facilities dramatically, and it became the largest employer in the Charleston

---

In 1906 Charleston received 213 of the 297 liquor licenses issued to South Carolina. From the earliest years of the 20th century to the 1960s when it was cleaned up by reform mayor J. Palmer Gaillard, Market Street was the center of Charleston's underworld.

It is ironic that the federal government and the United States Navy have both destroyed and rebuilt Charleston. The building of the Navy Yard in the early 20th century was Charleston's economic salvation just as the Civil War had been its undoing.

area and a force that permanently changed its character.

Charleston was changing in other ways. In 1904 there were 55,807 inhabitants, 24,238 of them white. A substantial number were newcomers. Immigrants had begun flooding America in the late 19th and early 20th centuries. By 1904 perhaps one-third of the city's white population was of German ancestry, for example. Until well into the 20th century, some Lutheran churches in Charleston conducted services in German. The business community was heavily populated by people of German background, and they dominated the wholesale and retail grocery trade. The Irish constituted 10 to 15 percent of the white population, and there were also Italians, Swedes, Syrians, Jews, Russians, and Poles.

The Irish community had grown in importance. An editor of the *News and Courier* repeated to President Taft a saying about Charleston in that era: "The Germans own it, the Irish control it, and the Negroes enjoy it."

John P. Grace

John P. Grace and Changing Times: Ethnic Charleston spoke out politically in 1911 with the advent of a dapper Irish politician named John P. Grace. Grace was one of those people who defies easy description. He was raucous, loud, aggressive, and contentious. He fought for the common man, for more and better municipal services, for aid to the underprivileged. He was not proud of Charleston's role in slavery or the Confederacy. ("And notoriously it was here," he once wrote in his annual message, "that the Ordinance of Secession was signed, and the first shot of the Civil War was fired.") He believed in the Declaration of Independence and loudly denounced the aristocrats, whom he accused of exploiting working people and harboring contempt for democracy.

Grace was born in Charleston in 1874, of second-generation Irish parents. He was educated in the city and was one of Captain Wagener's office boys. He worked in the cotton business in Greenville, in the steamship business in New York, and sold encyclopedias in the Midwest. In 1899 he went to Washington as secretary to the local congressman. There he attended Georgetown University Law School and became a lawyer. He then became the partner of W. Turner Logan, a prominent aristocratic Charleston lawyer.

Grace's position on race was progressive for his times. He hated slavery. According to John J. Duffy, Grace "accepted the results of the Civil War. Unlike many of his contemporaries, he considered the results just retribution for the crime of slavery, 'the worst form of avarice because it put gold above even human lives and liberty.'" He personally argued the case that led to the abolition of legal peonage of blacks in South Carolina.

Yet Grace was a man of his times and a bit of a demagogue himself. He

Grace's predecessor was Robert G. Rhett, whose greatest achievement was Murray Boulevard around the Battery. Beginning in 1909, the city filled in 47 acres of mud flats from the western boundary of White Point Gardens to Chisolm's Mill. The city sold 191 lots, a seawall was built, and the Boulevard was constructed.

used race-baiting as a tactic when it suited his purpose, and he aligned himself with one of the worse race-baiters in South Carolina history, Governor Coleman Blease.

It was Grace's support that helped Blease win the governorship, and that victory led Grace to run for mayor of Charleston in 1911. He was opposed by a candidate of the "aristocrats" or "boni," Tristram T. Hyde, a banker. It was a wild campaign. Grace campaigned against "special privilege," against monopoly, and against the "bluebloods." The *News and Courier,* "the Old Lady of Broad Street," wailed against Grace daily. Grace won, but by a very narrow margin, 2,999 to 2,805.

Grace's first administration (1911-1915), saw improvements in a variety of city services. The streets were paved, with the abutting property owners paying part of the bill. Health laws were passed and enforced. Playgrounds began to be built in earnest for the first time in the history of the city. Grace tried to buy the electric company (the Consolidated Company) so that the city could deliver cheaper electricity, but failed. His greatest achievement, however, was in bringing new railroads to Charleston and securing better rates.

Charleston's traditional love of pleasure (or what Grace's opponents called "vice") thrived under the Grace administration. Charlestonians continued to drink at "blind tigers" contrary to state law. Grace's political ally, Governor Blease, did not interfere. Bribery of state constables was apparently commonplace. A local group called the Law and Order League protested that the vice laws were not enforced. Grace's attitude was that he could not control sin, that no one had ever stopped Charlestonians from drinking and gambling, and why should he waste time trying? Grace's enemies accused him of political payoffs to owners of blind tigers, bribery, and just about everything else, but Grace's honesty was never successfully questioned. As for gambling in Charleston, Governor Blease asked, "Do they expect me to dress up like a preacher and beg them [the Charlestonians] not to race?"

In the mayoral race of 1915 Grace was again confronted by his old opponent, Tristram Hyde. A new reform governor, Richard Manning, sent in the militia to guard against a stolen election, an *Evening Post* reporter was killed, and a number of people were wounded as the votes were counted. It was as bitter an election as Charleston had ever seen. "We shall be voting or rioting," Tom Waring wrote a friend. Grace even blasted the St. Cecilia Society. The word was out, Grace said, that no one would be admitted to the St. Cecilia ball if he voted for Grace. In the end Grace lost.

Although Grace was out of office between 1915 and 1919, he was hardly quiet. He opposed World War I, and his newspaper, the *American*, blasted Wilson, Great Britain, and the League of Nations. Most Charlestonians supported the war, which brought an increase in jobs for the Navy Yard and spurred the growth of North Charleston.

In 1919 Grace again ran for mayor against Hyde. This time Grace campaigned on one theme: city control of the docks. The docks were a disaster. The waterfront had been neglected for years. The once proud wharves, pride of 18th century Charleston, had rotted. Many were abandoned. The railroads, which controlled the docks through the Terminal Company, did nothing either to remedy the situation or to help the city. Grace attacked them savagely, and his opponents retaliated. Once again the *News and Courier* railed against Grace as an unpatriotic radical socialist. The paper warned that Grace's election would be seen as a victory for pro-Germans and that it would hurt the Navy Yard. Despite vicious personal attacks against him, Grace barely won.

In his second term (1919-1923), Grace fulfilled his promise and bought the waterfront from the Terminal Company for $1.5 million, a great deal less than the railroads wanted. After long and difficult negotiations, a public referendum, and state legislation, the Ports Utility Commission was created to operate the port. That step led eventually to the establishment of the State Ports Authority, which has modernized and greatly enlarged the port of Charleston.

In his second administration Grace remained an activist, liberal, and probusiness mayor. He made both the High School of Charleston and the College of Charleston tuition free. The city donated the land for the Fort Sumter Hotel and encouraged the building of the Francis Marion Hotel on King Street. And, once again, he did little to control vice.

In 1921 Turner Logan, Grace's law partner, replaced Richard S. Whaley in Congress. It was a great victory for Grace and his organization, but it contained the seed of his political demise.

In 1923 Grace faced an entirely new kind of opponent, a man with solid ties to the "downtown aristocrats," who lived "uptown" in Hampton Terrace in the new northwest section, was himself an aristocrat, but was as feisty and tough a street fighter as Grace himself. Thomas P. Stoney was what John Duffy called "a 34-year-old dynamo, and a master of the same tactics of mass manipulation which had brought Grace to the fore."

John Grace had a ready wit. He once told an audience in Mt. Pleasant: "Mt. Pleasant is neither a mount, nor is it pleasant. When I ran two years ago, one man in the town voted for me. He has since died. I came [to the rally] only for the ride."

Thomas P. Stoney

The Stoney Challenge: Stoney was a lawyer, a great orator, and a great politician. He came from an old aristocratic family, and had the support of former Mayors Rhett and Hyde, the *News and Courier*, and the old ruling elite, but he was not one of them at heart. He realized very early that the old patrician way of politics was dead. In other words, he combined the best of the aristocratic tradition and a respect for the city's past with the best of the democratic tradition and a genuine respect for and affinity with the workingman. He did not live "South of Broad," but, unlike Hyde, he was not afraid to face Grace in debate at mass meetings. Nor was he afraid to deliver a little demagogic speech himself when necessary.

Stoney accused Grace of "bossism." He called Grace a power-hungry tyrant who used the police for political purposes and was a puppet of the Consolidated Electric and Gas Company. Grace charged that Stoney was a tool of the old elite, that he was a member of the Ku Klux Klan and was anti-Catholic. It was a typical Charleston mayoral race.

Stoney won in an upset, 7,595 to 6,330. The Grace era had ended, although Grace lived on as determined as ever. Perhaps his greatest legacy to Charleston was yet to come: the Cooper River Bridge.

The Cooper River Bridge was opened to traffic on August 8, 1929. Until the erection of the second Cooper River Bridge (the Silas Pearman Bridge) in 1966, it was the only route between Charleston and Mt. Pleasant, Sullivan's Island, the Isle of Palms and beyond. The purpose of Grace's Cooper River Bridge was to make the Isle of Palms a great tourist attraction.

By the early 20th century the Isle of Palms boasted a Pavilion for dancing, a large hotel (the Seashore Hotel, which burned prior to the opening of the bridge), and an amusement park (with a ferris wheel as early as 1911). Florida was rapidly becoming a popular winter resort, and Charlestonians were then, as now, trying to attract some of that tourist traffic. "In the twenties, the Tourist Era really began," wrote Robert Molloy in *Charleston: A Gracious Heritage*. "It was then that Northern millionaires, in the cutting phrase of Jonathan Daniels, became 'the real cash crop of Charleston.' The great Grace Memorial Bridge was set over the Cooper River. . . ." The Bridge was built at a cost of $6,000,000 by a private company, the Cooper River Bridge, Incorporated, of which Grace was president. The bridge was to be financed by a 50-cent per vehicle toll. As Grace said, "At the time the Bridge deal was made, assurances were given at Chicago (and we all believed it) that the Isle of Palms was backed up by a representative group of the strongest interests in this section; that all it needed to make it the premier beach resort of the south was someone to build a bridge. . . . Beautiful maps were shown of the projected Isle of Palms, its lakes, its golf links and hotels that were only waiting for the word 'bridge.' "

Perhaps no public facility in Charleston is more a memorial to one man. Grace planned the bridge; he nurtured it; he went to Columbia to lobby for appropriate legislation; he pressed his friend the governor to delay signing the bill so as to give the Bridge Company more lead time before the 90-day expiration date of the enabling legislation; he went to Chicago to negotiate a contract; he went to New York to receive the bids ("When the bids were opened I was present in Byllesby and Company's office in New York. We sat around the table in fear and trembling"); and he even argued the test case personally before the South Carolina Supreme Court. Yet, for all John Grace's exertions the great beach resort the bridge was to make possible never developed.

The old bridge failed to live up to another promise, too. A souvenir pamphlet entitled "The Story of the Bridge" issued at the huge three-day ceremonies accompanying the grand opening in August 1929 stated: "Indication of the strength of the bridge is the stated fact, that if a 10,000-ton steamer should collide with the piers of the bridge, it would be the steamer alone which would suffer damage." But on February 24, 1946, the *Nicaragua Victory* slipped anchor, and the tide pushed the 10,000-ton ship into the bridge, ripping it in two. A crushed auto was found below. Five people were killed.

The bridge failed financially as well. Nineteen twenty-nine just was not the year to invest $6 million in a bridge to the Isle of Palms. The stock market crashed, and the Bridge Company was in trouble from the beginning. Funds to pay off the bonds and to protect the stockholders' investments were to come from tolls, but the traffic never materialized. The company reorganized under the bankruptcy laws, and Charleston County bought the Cooper River Bridge for $4.4 million in 1941. Soon after, L. Mendel Rivers, then in the legislature, and others finally got the state to buy the bridge for $4.15 million. State Senator O. T. Wallace, who took office in 1943, announced his intention to remove the tolls. They were lifted on June 29, 1946, with a public celebration. Wallace paid the last 50 cents and introduced a bill naming the span for Mayor Grace.

Following World War I, Charleston continued to expand. The northwest section and Hampton Park grew in terms of both population and political power. In 1926 Mayor Stoney's administration saw the opening of the new Ashley River Bridge (it is still in use). In 1929 the city opened a new municipal airport on the site of the colonial French Botanical Gardens. The Union

There is a memorial to John Grace in City Hall. Carved in 1923, it was a victim of political animosities until rescued in 1981 by the city's second Irish mayor, Joseph P. Riley, Jr. Charleston Corporation Counsel William Regan tells the story that upon his election Riley was handed an aged envelope addressed to "The Next Irish Mayor" by the Bishop of Charleston. Inside was the message: "Get the Stoneys."

People seem fascinated by suicides and attempted suicides from the bridge. Twenty-two have jumped. Five have survived, one from the highest point.

The Academy of Music was a renovated building. In 1869 John Devereux remodeled the Adger Building at the corner of King and Market and created a new theater which accommodated 1,200 people. Sarah Bernhardt, among others, performed there. The building was demolished in the 1930s to make way for a modern movie theater, the Riviera. The new "moving picture theatre" was owned by a young Sicilian immigrant to Charleston, Albert Sottile.

Pier at the end of Market Street opened. Electric streetlights went up. King Street boomed from the 1880s through the 1940s and became by far the largest retail district in South Carolina.

In 1931 Burnet Rhett Maybank became mayor. In many ways he followed the trail blazed by Tom Stoney. He, too, was an aristocrat who could relate to the average person. He served as mayor until 1938 when he successfully ran for governor supported by 90.9 percent of the vote in Charleston County. A solid New Dealer, he enthusiastically backed Franklin D. Roosevelt for President. Maybank went on to become a United States Senator, and he and his fellow Charlestonian, James F. Byrnes, brought Charleston back into the national political limelight. Maybank's political machine was certainly more powerful and longer-lived than anything envisioned by John P. Grace. V. O. Key wrote in the 1940s that one "erstwhile gubernatorial candidate reported that the Charleston leaders had asked him at the time of his campaign what size vote he wanted from Charleston." The old saying went that Charleston withheld its votes until the rest of the state reported in — so that the local Democratic machine could see "how many votes are needed."

Maybank was a remarkable mayor. He brought in a new paper mill in the midst of the Depression. He built five public housing projects and a yacht basin. One of Mayor Maybank's greatest achievements was the charming Dock Street Theater, a product of the New Deal and the Works Progress Administration. Maybank conceived the idea of a replica theater for Charleston, and convinced the WPA to give the city $350,000 in the mid-1930s to build a community theater inside the now defunct Planters' Hotel. The present Dock Street Theater is a replica of London theaters of the 1730s. It was built inside the shell of the Planters' Hotel and the facade, entrance, and balcony were all retained from the antebellum hotel. Much of the interior came from old Charleston homes.

In November 1937 the Dock Street Theater opened (or reopened) with the same play that had opened the original Dock Street Theater, *The Recruiting Officer*. Harry Hopkins, Works Progress Administrator, formally presented the key to the theater to Mayor Maybank "on behalf of the United States Government. . . ."

In the early 20th century Charlestonians had turned in on themselves in every facet of life, not just politics. After enduring the agony of war, the humility of Reconstruction, poverty, defeat, political isolation, and moral rejection by the rest of the state, Charlestonians began to brood and to write. By the early 1920s, writes George B. Tindall in *The Emergence of the New*

South, "The Poetry Society of South Carolina (mainly Charleston) stood in the vanguard of the Southern Renaissance." The group grew around three local writers, DuBose Heyward, Hervey Allen, and John Bennett, the author of *Master Skylark.*

The Poetry Society, organized in 1920, published a *Year Book* and began to awaken the South to its literary possibilities. It was the first statewide poetry society in the country and brought famous poets to Charleston, including Carl Sandburg and Robert Frost. It awarded prizes that gave recognition to such unknowns as Robert Penn Warren. DuBose Heyward traveled extensively to preach the gospel of the new literary South-to-be.

Charlestonians contributed significantly to the Southern Renaissance. Out of it came the poetry of Heyward and Allen in *Carolina Chansons* in 1922; Heyward's *Porgy, Angel, Mamba's Daughter, The Half Pint Flask,* and *Peter Ashley;* Allen's *Anthony Adverse;* John Bennet's *Madame Margot;* Samuel G. Stoney's *Po' Buckra';* Ambrose Gonzales's *The Black Border,* and much more. The city began to be a home to writers and artists again. Josephine Pinckney, Archibald Rutledge, Janie Screven Heyward, Herbert R. Sass, and many others came out of this period.

The same was true in art. The Gibbes Art Gallery opened in 1905. Alfred Hutty, Alice R. Huger Smith, and Elizabeth O'Neil Verner began painting, drawing, and etching scenes of Charleston and the Low Country.

In 1922 a group of white Charlestonians who lived on plantations organized the Society for the Preservation of Spirituals, an organization dedicated to preserving black spiritual songs and music. In 1931, a number of prominent Charlestonians produced *The Carolina Low-Country,* a collection of black songs and essays about Charleston and the Low Country.

Porgy and Bess: Charleston began to glorify its past, its present, its people, and its places. "Local color" became Charleston's stock-in-trade in the arts, in literature, and in song. That local color was very deep and very colorful indeed, for it produced nothing less than the most famous American opera ever written, *Porgy and Bess.*

The story of the opera begins with DuBose Heyward, a descendant of rice planters and an insurance salesman living on Church Street in Charleston during the 1920s. Heyward was taken with a way of life he could only glimpse: that of the poor blacks of Charleston. He said of himself later: "I think without realizing it, I started to write 'Porgy' when as an employee of a

The Dock Street Theater, the jewel of Charleston's cultural scene as well as a monument to Roosevelt and the New Deal, had an ironic early problem: who could use the theater! The director of the first resident company in 1938 scorned "outside people." Later, when the Footlight Players took over production, "outside people" came regularly as guest directors, players, musicians, writers. Many visiting companies during the Spoleto Festival are booked into the theater.

Alicia Rhett, great-granddaughter of Robert Barnwell Rhett, the father of secession, played India Wilkes in *Gone With the Wind,* which opened to raves in Charleston in January 1937. Miss Rhett, a Charlestonian, continued her family's traditional loyalty to the Confederacy — with a little help from Hollywood. The distinguished old name, Rhett, lives on.

Scene from the opera, *Porgy & Bess.*

cotton warehouse on the Charleston waterfront, I first came into close contact with the negro life of the city. I was young and impressionable, and the drama that was enacted before me moved me profoundly. . . ."

Heyward was well acquainted with a local crippled black beggar named Goat Sammy who for many years sat begging in his goat cart at the corner of King and Broad. Goat Sammy's real name was Samuel Smalls. One day in March 1924, Heyward picked up the *News and Courier* and read a story under the headline "Busy Time for Police." It read as follows: "Samuel Smalls was arrested, charged with shooting at Maggie Barnes on premises at 4 Romney Street. His markmanship, however, being poor, the Barnes woman escaping [sic] unhurt."

Smalls was arrested on March 24, 1924. The assault occurred at 4 Johnson Court, Romney Street, near Smalls's real residence in Green Tenement near Mt. Pleasant Street. The "real" Porgy languished in jail until the charges were dismissed on June 3.

But Smalls's passion electrified Heyward. Here was a pitiful beggar who had real man-sized feelings. "To Smalls I make acknowledgement of my obligation," Heyward wrote in the introduction of his play. "From contemplation of his real, and deeply moving, tragedy sprang Porgy, a creature of my imagination . . . and upon whom . . . I could impose my own white man's conception of a summer of aspiration, devotion, and heartbreak across the colour wall."

The rest is a part of American cultural history. Heyward gave up his work to write. He went to the MacDowell colony in New Hampshire where he wrote *Porgy.* The novel was published in 1925 and set in Charleston "in the 1920's in the Golden Age. Not the Golden Age of a remote and legendary past . . . but an age when men, not yet old, were boys in an ancient, beautiful city that time had forgotten before it destroyed." It was the story of a black beggar named Porgy; Bess, his woman; Crown his rival; and Sportin' Life and others who inhabit Catfish Row, the poor black Charlestonians of the 1920s.

The novel was a great success. Dorothy Heyward, Heyward's wife, wrote a script for a play, and, despite Heyward's doubts that a play could be successfully produced with such a large black cast, even in New York, *Porgy* was produced by the Theatre Guild on Broadway.

Before the play was ever written, George Gershwin expressed an interest in writing an opera based on the novel. Gershwin had already made his mark, having written *Rhapsody in Blue* and a number of Broadway musicals. He came to Charleston in the summer of 1934 and stayed on Folly Island. For

Dubose Heyward, author of *Porgy,* lived at 76 Church Street. Down the street was Cabbage Row, a black tenement that became the model for Catfish Row. Both Heyward's house and Cabbage Row still stand.

A Short History of Charleston

months he and Heyward roamed the sea islands around Charleston, going to black churches, listening to gospel music, and to "shouts." Heyward recalled later: "I shall never forget the night when, at a Negro meeting on a remote sea-island, George started 'shouting' with them, and eventually to their huge delight stole the show from their champion 'shouter.' I think that he is probably the only white man in America who could have done it."

And what happened to Goat Sammy? We shall never know for sure. He disappeared from Charleston, never knowing that the character Porgy was based on him. A few years after *Porgy* had become successful, people in Charleston began to refer to the missing Smalls as "Porgy." Some insisted that Porgy was his real name. A number of prominent Charlestonians started looking for Smalls (including Mayor Stoney, who sent the City Police out!). Two patient investigators, Police Chief Healy and Henry Church finally found a grave — which no one has been able to find since the 1920s — on James Island. Apparently Smalls had a wife on the island. Her name was not Bess. It was Normie.

According to Dorothy Heyward's account in the *News and Courier*, Normie said that "De ole goat follow' Sammy . . . very close. He ain't eat nuttin aftuh Sammy gone. Dere nuttin' we can do. He jus' grieve an' die. He want to be wid' Sammy." And according to Normie (through Dorothy Heyward), Sammy shot Maggie Barnes because she stole his watch, not out of jealousy. But, then, that's what Sammy told his wife.

In 1911, another terrible hurricane hit the Low Country and finished off the rice growing industry which had flourished since colonial times. It had winds of 105 m.p.h. and left seven dead. Ironically, it was this 1911 hurricane which DuBose Heyward had described in the novel *Porgy*. An entire chapter (Part V) is devoted to a hurricane in Charleston. It began, as they all do, in September. The church bells clanged twenty times, the signal for a hurricane. "At its first stroke, life in Catfish Row was paralyzed," Heyward wrote. A blue flag was raised over the Customs House. "And now from the opaque surface of the screen came a persistent roar that was neither wind or water, but the articulate cry of the storm itself," *Porgy* continued. "The buildings huddled closer and waited. Then it crossed the strip and smote the city."

The hurricane of 1911 was immortalized in the words and music of George Gershwin. After the great storm scene the sheet music for *Porgy and Bess* reads as follows: "(Clara is at window looking through crack in the shutter. She holds baby as she sings); Clara (with great feeling): 'One of these mornings you goin' to rise up singin', Den you'll spread yo' wings an'

Heyward and Gershwin describe the hurricane which terrified Porgy and Bess:

Dem Septembuh storm due soon, an' fish ain't likes eas' win an muddy watuh.

DuBose Heyward, *Porgy* (1925)

Lawd Shake de Heavens an' de Lawd rock de groun'

Lawd Shake de Heavens an' de Lawd rock de groun'

Brudder an' my sister, when de sky come a-tumblin' down

George Gershwin, *Porgy and Bess* (1935)

The house Gershwin stayed at while writing Porgy and Bess is still on Folly Beach at 706 West Ashley Avenue.

The Battery after the Hurricane of 1911.

you'll take to de sky. . . .'" Thus, the most famous song of America's most famous opera is about the feelings of Charleston's survivors of a great hurricane.

Neither *Porgy* nor *Porgy and Bess* played in Charleston in the 1920s or 1930s. Nor did they play in the 40s, 50s, or 60s. The reason was segregation. The black community would not participate in producing a play about black Charlestonians and watch it in a segregated theatre.

In 1954, an attempt was made to produce *Porgy* locally. Parts were cast, and a theater was secured, but the seating arrangements could not be agreed upon. The leaders of the black community, Arthur Clement and Mrs. R. L. Fields, indicated that local black actors would not play to a segregated hall. *Porgy* was cancelled.

Segregation: The black community had come a long way from slavery and Reconstruction. Charleston may not have been paradise for blacks in the late 19th and early 20th centuries, but it was not hell, either.

A Short History of Charleston

There were no lynchings in Charleston throughout the dark days of the Tillman-Blease hysteria. The Ku Klux Klan, "the legitimate offspring of the patrol," as George Tindall calls it, operated all over South Carolina, but its activities in Charleston were not great. There were at least 73 lynchings in South Carolina between 1882 and 1900 alone, yet Charlestonians would not countenance such violence. The *News and Courier* was in the vanguard of opposition to both dueling and lynching. Charlestonians of both races settled into a period of relatively peaceful coexistence.

In politics, most blacks were disenfranchised by the Tillman Constitution of 1895. During the 1880s, though, many still held office: George Washington Murray, for example, was Inspector of Customs in 1889 and Benjamin Baseman was postmaster. Blacks were staunch Republicans and remained with the party of Lincoln until 1932 when Franklin Roosevelt brought them into the Democratic Party.

Black voters were cheated and intimidated out of the vote throughout the state and in Charleston during the 1880s and 1890s. The Democratic primary — for whites only — became the real election. And blacks were Republicans when they could vote at all.

Segregation slowly became a way of life. It will be recalled that the newly freed blacks of the Reconstruction era had themselves sought segregation in religion: They wanted to control their own churches. Others sought segregation in housing. Freedom meant freedom from the watchful eye of whites. But in public accommodations — restaurants, hotels, public transportation, and education — black Charlestonians strongly resisted segregation.

Actual figures are difficult to find, but in terms of housing patterns Charleston was certainly not a segregated city from 1880 to the 1940s. Blacks continued to live where they had lived for centuries — in the slave quarters behind the great houses, in houses of their own throughout the city, in villages on the edge of town. The most obvious statement about residential segregation in Charleston is found in *Porgy* itself. *Porgy* is set in Charleston in 1925, and Porgy lived in fictional Catfish Row on East Bay Street. Catfish Row was based on Cabbage Row, a real black tenement, located on Church Street. It was a simple fact of life in Charleston that black Charlestonians lived all over what is now referred to as "South of Broad" through the 1920s and the 1930s.

Gradually, though, blacks began to move. Many left the city altogether and moved North — the greatest emigration in American history was the movement of blacks from the South after the Civil War. Following their emancipation most moved from their former slave quarters and lived elsewhere, but elsewhere was not necessarily in a segregated neighborhood. But in time black and white neighborhoods did begin to form.

Segregation was not established overnight. The state civil rights law, passed during Reconstruction, was only repealed in 1889. As late as 1897 the *News and Courier* was opposed to the new segregation or "Jim Crow" laws: ". . . we have no . . . need for a Jim Crow car system," the paper editorialized in 1897, arguing *against* segregation on the railroads. In 1898, though, the state began legislating segregation. Thus, the theaters in Charleston were integrated between 1865 and 1900. Thereafter segregation became a hallmark of every southern city, including Charleston. The trolley cars, and later buses, required blacks to sit in the rear. Signs were posted everywhere: "White" and "Colored." Rest rooms, drinking fountains, doctors' waiting rooms, schools, hotels, and restaurants (white or black only), parks and playgrounds — all were segregated.

Excluded from the mainstream of white culture, blacks founded their own newspapers. During the 1880s and the 1890s, there were at least seven black newspapers published in Charleston, including the *New Era,* the *Enquirer,* the *Observer,* the *Messenger,* and others. They formed their own schools, including the Charleston Training School for Nurses (later McClellan-Banks Hospital) and the Charleston Industrial Institute. Blacks joined trade unions and became stevedores; they worked in knitting mills, cotton mills, shoe factories, and phosphate mines; they farmed and produced truck crops for the northern market. The number of black lawyers and black doctors multiplied.

The most famous of Charleston's black institutions by far was the Jenkins Orphanage, made internationally famous by the Jenkins Orphanage Band. The orphanage was organized in 1891 by Reverend D. J. Jenkins, a black Baptist minister who, the story goes, made it his life's work when he found six young black orphans shivering on a cold winter day. The orphanage opened in 1892 and was funded by local and northern contributions, and eventually by the City Council and by funds raised by the Jenkins Orphanage Band. For much of its existence, the Jenkins Orphanage was housed in the Old Marine Hospital on Franklin Street (which still stands and now is the office of the Housing Authority).

The band was organized in the early 1890s and went to London on a fund-raising trip. According to John Chilton, in *A Jazz Nursery*, the band began playing in the streets of London, where it attracted the attention of Major Augustine Smythe of Charleston and his family, who happened to be in

Black Charlestonians listened enthusiastically to speeches about the "Back to Africa" movement in 1878, but not many left. In March of that year 5,000 people attended a religious service at the battery to consecrate the *Axor,* which would take 206 emigrants to Liberia. Martin R. Delany, the father of the movement, had a long and illustrious career in Charleston.

London at the same time. When the English courts enjoined the band from playing on the streets and they could not raise the funds to return home, Major Smythe paid their way. The Smythe law firm thereafter represented the orphanage, and the band played outside the major's home each Christmas morning until his death in 1914.

The band played regularly in New York and traveled extensively. It was known as the "Piccanninny Band," and Reverend Jenkins was known as the "Orphanage Man." It appeared at the St. Louis Fair and Exposition and the Buffalo Exposition, at President Taft's inauguration, at the London Hippodrome, and at the Anglo-American Exposition in London in 1914. And, of course, it played in the streets of Charleston throughout the early 20th century.

The band wore old Citadel uniforms and played the popular music of the day, ragtime and some jazz. It starred in the opening of the play *Porgy* in New York in 1927. The program indicated that the band was "the original band of the Jenkins Orphanage in Charleston, and is part of the actual aggregation described in the lodge parade of Mr. Heyward's novel."

Black Charlestonians gave something else to the Jazz Age. They gave it "the Charleston," the dance that was and remains the very symbol of the Roaring Twenties. The origin of the Charleston is obscure. Some authorities claim the dance was originated on King Street by the Jenkins Orphanage Band. Others claim a black Charlestonian named Russell Brown did a "Geechie Step" in the black dance halls of Harlem, and, as black jazz pianist Willie "The Lion" Smith recalled, people "would holler at him, 'Hey, Charleston, do your Geechie dance.' Some folks say that is how the dance known as the Charleston got its name." Smith wrote that the dance "had been around New York for many years before Brown showed. The kids from the Jenkins Orphanage Band of Charleston used to do Geechie steps when they were in New York on their yearly tour."

What is not obscure is how the Charleston became famous. Black dances had become the rage in New York, and *Runnin' Wild,* a 1923 Broadway musical comedy featured the new dance. James P. Johnson wrote the music, which had come out of a Harlem nightclub called "The Jungles." Johnson recalled that "The people who came to *The Jungle Casino* were mostly from around Charleston, S.C., and other places in the South. Most of them worked for the Ward Line as longshoremen, or on ships that called on southern ports. . . . It was while playing for these Southern dancers that I composed a number of Charlestons, eight in all, all with the same rhythm. One of these later became my famous Charleston when it hit Broadway."

The Rev. Daniel J. Jenkins, whose portrait hangs in City Hall, was the founder of the Jenkins Orphanage and the famous Jenkins Orphanage Band.

The Jenkins Orphanage Band made regular appearances at the Abyssinian Baptist Church in Harlem, where a former Charlestonian named Adam Clayton Powell was the minister. The band produced some of America's greatest jazz musicians. Gus Aitken played trumpet with Louis Armstrong, "Cat" Anderson played with Lionel Hampton and Duke Ellington; Freddie Green has been with Count Basie since 1937; Speedy Jones played drums with Hampton, Ellington, and Basie.

Gates, 61 Tradd Street.

In 1929 the St. Louis Museum of Art paid $5,000 for the early Georgian panelling from one room of the Jacob Motte house at 61 Tradd. It is now an exhibit at the museum — "The Charleston Room."

Charleston survived from the 1880s to the 1940s by preserving her heritage, by celebrating her local color and her history, and by celebrating herself. Preservation became a way of life. So it was no coincidence that a movement for the preservation of the old buildings also began in Charleston in this period. DuBose Heyward was preserving the past in poetry and literature. The Society for the Preservation of Spirituals was preserving the past in music. The Society for the Preservation of Old Dwelling Houses would preserve the city's houses and, indeed, the city itself.

Charleston's introspection in the 1920s brought the city face to face with its architectural treasures. While the rest of the nation was booming, while New York, Philadelphia, and Boston were becoming great cities fueled by the Industrial Revolution, Charleston rotted in genteel poverty. There were few great brownstones or Victorian mansions built in Charleston and certainly no skyscrapers. Life in late 19th and early 20th century America passed Charleston by.

Yet, in the 1920s, there were people still alive who remembered the Civil War. There were two generations of children, now grown, who had lived through Reconstruction and after and who had heard a glorified version of the city's history. They looked back, as Heyward did, to Charleston's "Golden Age" and wanted to preserve it. Luckily, Charleston had not been destroyed by development. The historic district was isolated even from the north-south highways.

Ironically the threat to Charleston in 1920 came from museum directors and other collectors who had bought up houses and parts of houses for museums. The houses were not valuable, but their mantels and paneling were. A group of dynamic citizens banded together to do something.

Susan Frost and Mr. and Mrs. Ernest Pringle founded the Society for the Preservation of Old Dwelling Houses in 1920. One of the Society's earliest triumphs was saving the Joseph Manigault House from destruction. It was a start. Samuel G. Stoney, storyteller and writer, and Albert Simons, architect, wrote books, attended meetings and urged civic action to save Charleston's architectural heritage. Mayor Stoney, unhappy over Standard Oil Company's plan to put gas stations all over the city, pushed through the city's first zoning laws in 1929 to protect the historic district. Later, in October 1931, professional planners came, and Charleston adopted the first historic zoning ordinance in America.

Charleston became the leader of the preservation movement in the United States. Under the city's Old and Historic District Ordinance, still in effect, no exterior architectural changes could be made to buildings in the Old and Historic District unless they were approved by the city's Board of Architectural Review. Other cities copied the "Charleston Ordinance."

But the first ordinance was not Charleston's only contribution to the preservation movement. The city also pioneered other techniques. Soon the Preservation Society bought famous houses and opened them to the public. The idea of a revolving fund to encourage the preservation of historic houses was originated by Sidney Rittenberg, a member of City Council. Still later, in 1944, the city produced the first citywide architectural survey, *This is Charleston,* ever done in the United States. It is still in print.

The Historic Charleston Foundation was organized in the 1940s to do what the Preservation Society had failed to do: raise substantial money to buy historic properties for resale. The Foundation, which has led the preservation movement in Charleston, began its famous house tours in 1947. Two years later a dynamic young businesswoman, named Frances Edmunds, was chosen to head the tours, and they made a profit for the first time. (The idea of house tours had come from Natchez via Dorothy Legge, who, incidentally, pioneered the rehabilitation of Rainbow Row on East Bay Street in the 1930s.)

Why did the preservation movement succeed in Charleston? There were many people dedicated to the proposition that as Charles B. Hosmer has written in *Preservation Comes of Age,* "something was sacred about the city." Charleston had no industrial or economic machine eager to develop it. It produced leaders capable of leading. And it was a conservative city that respected its traditions even before the Civil War. As Robert P. Stockton has written, "Charlestonians, in rebuilding the ruined city after the Civil War, often chose traditional (ante bellum) forms rather than styles nationally current in the 1870's and '80s, and the single house form, in fact, survived into the early part of the 20th century." The city seal reads: "She guards her buildings, customs and laws."

Charlestonians, like Rhett Butler, enjoyed living in a city where a little bit of grace and charm was left in the world.

The Americanized City (1941–)

9

On December 14, 1940, President Franklin D. Roosevelt visited Charleston. He was asked by a reporter what role the South would play in the new defense buildup, and he answered with a question of his own: "Of these million four hundred thousand people who are going to be trained, how many are going to be trained in the South?" The answer to that simple question explains much of Charleston's recent history.

On December 7, 1941, one year after Roosevelt's visit, the Japanese attacked Pearl Harbor and Charleston would never be the same. War has always been a prime force in Charleston's history, and World War II had a more profound effect on Charleston than any other war except, perhaps, the Civil War. Between 1930 and 1950, Charleston County grew from 101,050 to 164,856, while the city grew very little. Charleston itself, which had been two-thirds of the county in 1910, now became a small part of an Americanized "metropolitan area." By 1960 the city would account for about only one-fourth of the population of the county. As the county grew by leaps and bounds, the city either lost population or gained only by the annexation of suburban areas. Why?

In the aftermath of World War I, North Charleston was still a small suburb of Charleston. The city had no other suburbs. North Charleston was originally developed by a group of investors that included former Mayor Robert G. Rhett, B. L. Montague, a lawyer, and E. W. Durant, a real estate investor. A trolley line ran to North Charleston from Charleston, but the various companies that owned the land did not fare well. In 1932, the North Charleston development company went into bankruptcy.

During World War II the Navy Yard and the Charleston Shipyard and

Opposite page
Charleston today: Historic peace and quiet prevail in the old city. These "single houses" on Church Street date to 1759-1807.

Drydock became by far the major industry in the area, attracting workers to the old northern suburbs. In some ways life north of Charleston was like a western boom town as thousands of new people — war workers, their families, and those who came to service the new industries — came to the "North Area" from rural and small-town South Carolina, from Georgia, and from all over the South. In 1938 there 1,632 workers at the Navy Yard. By the mid-1940s there were in excess of 25,000!

North Charleston and Charleston Heights were the center of this new migration, which was mostly white and mostly southern. People slept in their cars and in makeshift apartments, and they were packed into every type of accommodation. Workers often lived as cheaply as they could in order to send money home. The Great Depression had meant poverty and want; World War II meant jobs and money.

World War II permanently changed Charleston's way of life, for the boom at the Navy Yard proved not to be temporary. When the war ended, there was a decline in the number of people employed, but the number never returned to prewar levels. Both the Navy Yard and the North Area became a permanent part of the Charleston landscape.

The Americanization of Charleston continued with the creation of other suburbs west of the Ashley River, beginning with the building of the concrete Ashley River Bridge in 1926. The bridge allowed those with automobiles to move into St. Andrew's Parish and beyond, to old Windermere, the Crescent, and Wappoo Heights in the 1930s and to Byrnes Downs (named for Jimmy Byrnes) in the 1940s.

The old peninsula city began losing population in the 1940s and 1950s. In 1940 Charleston's population was 71,275, the largest in its history. The affluence of the era, the invention of the automobile, the building of better roads and bridges — all led to the movement to the suburbs. Then, in the 1950s, shopping centers sprang up. Like all American cities, Charleston witnessed a movement out of the crowded center city to the greener pastures of suburbia. The northwest section of the peninsula (Hampton Park), itself a suburb, grew as well. Ward 12, the ward in which the northwest section lay, became the most populous ward in the city and the center of political activity.

Huger Street ran through the center of Ward 12. And it was on that street that two giants of postwar Charleston politics lived: former Mayor Tom Stoney at 573 Huger and Gedney M. Howe, Jr., at 554 Huger. A lawyer, Howe served on a PT Boat during World War II, saw action in Africa and returned home a hero. In 1946 he ran for Solicitor with Stoney's blessings.

The Class of 1946 at North Charleston High School had more Georgians than South Carolinians. In 1972 the City of North Charleston, a product of the Navy Yard, was incorporated.

Postwar growth of the Navy Yard and military-related industries was due in part to the efforts of L. Mendel Rivers, congressman from the First District for 30 years and later chairman of the House Armed Services Committee. It was said in the 1960s that Charleston was surrounded by three rivers — the Ashley, the Cooper, and the Mendel Rivers.

"Howe, Long, must our Road be Stoney?" read a civil rights placard in the 1960s. Long was J. C. Long, a former state senator.

A Short History of Charleston

(Howe's father, Gedney M. Howe, Sr., had been city engineer under Stoney, and he supervised the construction of Murray Boulevard.)

Gedney Howe served as Solicitor from 1946 to 1956. During that time, he built a reputation as a brilliant politician and a formidable lawyer. Recognizing the potential impact of the growing union vote and being philosophically committed to the labor movement, he early championed labor causes and wielded great influence in labor councils. He was also committed to racial equality at a time when Charleston was almost totally segregated and soon gained the trust of the black community. He never sought another elective office after serving as Solicitor, but he became the key figure in Charleston's political history from the 1950s to the 1980s.

The city government had greatly expanded its functions between the time of Grace and Stoney and the New Deal Era. By the 1950s it was operating a municipal airport, a waterworks department, a marina, a golf course, incinerators, swimming pools, and a housing authority. Under William McG. Morrison, the position of mayor became a full-time job.

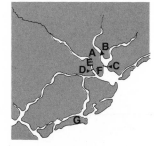

A. North Charleston
B. U.S. Naval Base and Shipyard
C. Cooper River Br.
D. Ashley River Br.
E. The Citadel and Hampton Park
F. Author's House
G. Kiawah Is.

In 1959 a young reform candidate, J. Palmer Gaillard, Jr., ran for mayor with the support of Stoney and Howe. His slogan was "We Need a Change." Gaillard was elected, and change the city did. For the first time since before the Civil War, Charleston's boundaries were expanded to take in a portion of St. Andrew's Parish, urban renewal was begun, the marina was expanded, and a municipal auditorium was built. There was also a shake-up in the police department.

Charlestonians once again celebrated their past in the Civil War Centennial of 1961. A postage stamp commemorating the firing on Fort Sumter was issued at Charleston. Citadel cadets "fired" again on the *Star of the West*. And in 1970 the city joined with the state to celebrate the tricentennial of the founding of South Carolina. The state purchased the site of the original settlement at Albemarle Point at a cost of $4.9 million from the owners, who had carefully protected it from suburban development. The site was made a state park and called Charles Towne Landing. Fort Sumter and Fort Moultrie were restored, and both are now open to the public. History became Charleston's leading business.

But the most symbolic event of the Tricentennial Celebration of 1970 did not take place at Charles Towne Landing. It took place at the new Municipal Auditorium when *Porgy* returned home for the first time. The Charleston community — black and white — staged *Porgy and Bess* with a local all-black cast and an integrated audience. Every performance was sold out. The long-overdue performance of *Porgy* reflected the great change that

When Annie Waring, the judge's first wife, died, her six pallbearers were all Warings. When Judge Waring died in 1968, only 12 whites, but more than 200 blacks attended his funeral. And so was buried the distinguished son of a distinguished veteran of the Confederate Army.

had taken place in race relations in Charleston and all over the South between 1941 and 1970.

World War II, like World War I before it, had been a catalyst for change in the black community. On a national level, black leaders began asserting the needs and rights of blacks, beginning with A. Phillip Randolph's proposed march on Washington in 1941. The navy was desegregated during the war, and Harry Truman integrated the army in 1947. In a series of decisions that began in 1944 the Supreme Court gradually recognized the constitutional rights of black citizens.

Judge Waring and "Darkest South Carolina": The Democratic party was closed to blacks in Charleston in the 1940s, and, since nomination in the Democratic primary was tantamount to election, blacks were effectively shut out of the political process. In 1947 Federal District Judge (and eighth-generation Charlestonian) J. Waties Waring held that "South Carolina is the only State which now conducts a primary election solely for whites. . . . I cannot see where the skies will fall if South Carolina is put in the same class with these and other states." The Democratic primary was opened to blacks. The civil rights era had begun in earnest in Charleston.

The Supreme Court may not have given Waties Waring credit for its landmark decision in *Brown v. Board of Education* but civil rights leaders certainly did. According to Tinsley E. Yarbrough in *A Passion for Justice,* Waring encouraged Thurgood Marshall and other NAACP officials "to make a direct assault on the 'separate but equal' doctrine in the public schools." When *Brown* was decided on May 17, 1954, leading civil rights leaders in New York City, including Kenneth Clark, Walter White, and Alan Paton, headed not for Harlem but for Judge Waring's apartment on Fifth Avenue.

Waring was only following precedent, but many federal judges lacked the courage. They preferred to let an appellate court make the tough decisions. Waring continued to defend the rights of blacks. He wrote a dissenting opinion in *Briggs v. Elliott,* one of the nation's first school desegregation cases. Thurgood Marshall, later a Justice of the Supreme Court, came to Charleston to argue the case on behalf of the NAACP in the federal courthouse on Broad Street. The majority opinion for the three judge federal court was written by Judge John J. Parker, the eminent Chief Judge of the United States Court of Appeals. Judge Parker affirmed the legality of segregation in the public schools of South Carolina. Judge Waring wrote a scathing dissent in which he severely criticized the segregation laws. "[S]egregation in education can never produce equality . . . it is an evil that must be eradicated . . . [and] the system of segregation in education adopted and practiced in the State of South Carolina must go and must go now. *Segregation is per se, inequality.*" It was the first pronouncement by a federal judge in the twentieth century that segregation in the public schools was unconstitutional.

Briggs v. Elliott was appealed to the United States Supreme Court where it became one of four companion cases decided under another name by that

Court in 1954. That case was *Brown v. Board of Education*. Waring's dissent was not quoted or relied upon by the Supreme Court because Waring himself had become such a controversial figure and because the tone of his dissent was bitter and critical. Chief Justice Earl Warren wanted the landmark decision to speak softly and calmly to the nation.

Waring came from a long line of Charleston aristocrats. When he was first nominated for a federal judgeship in the 1930s by "Cotton" Ed Smith, his appointment was defeated by northern liberals who thought him too conservative. Roosevelt appointed him in 1941. A former Corporation Counsel of the City of Charleston and a close friend of Senator Burnet Maybank, Waring was the epitome of a Charleston lawyer.

Civil rights demonstration: The city was spared the violence that wounded other Southern cities. Sign in the foreground reads, "Beatles power is young people in concert for peace," a sentiment John Lennon might have liked.

Some Charlestonians contend that Waring began to change in 1945 or 1946 when he became romantically involved with Elizabeth Hoffman, a beautiful lady from up north. The Warings and Mr. and Mrs. Hoffman had enjoyed playing bridge when the Hoffmans visited Charleston. One thing led to another, and shortly Waring and Elizabeth Hoffman were divorced. When they later married each other, Charleston society was scandalized.

Judge and Mrs. Waring were ostracized from Charleston society. She often sat in his courtroom while he presided, and his decisions increasingly favored civil rights. Politicians denounced him, and an effort was made to impeach him. By the 1950s Judge Waring said, "We do not live in darkest Africa. We live in darkest South Carolina." A cross was burned in front of his home at 61 Meeting Street, and rocks were thrown at the windows. U.S. marshals guarded his house. President Truman called him "a very great judge," but it was an opinion not shared by many white Charlestonians. Later the Warings left Charleston, and Judge Waring lived in New York until his death in 1968.

The modern civil rights movement traces its roots back to the 1940s. The National Association for the Advancement of Colored People grew steadily, although membership could prove dangerous. Septima Clark, the distinguished black educator and author, was fired from her job as a schoolteacher in the public schools in 1956 for being an officer in the NAACP. Esau Jenkins of John's Island met in the early years of the movement with Martin Luther King and developed "citizenship schools" for potential black voters on John's Island. Bernice Robinson and Septima Clark further developed the concept of the Citizenship Schools where blacks learned about the Constitution and how to assert their right to vote. Martin Luther King and the Southern Leadership Conference were to spread the idea all over the South in the 1960s. J. Arthur Brown, a successful black realtor, became president of the Charleston chapter of the NAACP in 1955 and membership soared. There were 2,000 members by the end of the 1950s. Charleston's black community mobilized.

Suits were brought to desegregate city facilities. The first integrated facility in South Carolina was the Charleston Municipal Golf Course, opened to both races in 1960. The NAACP, brought suit during Mayor Morrison's administration, but the defense against the action fell to the incoming Gaillard administration.

Palmer Gaillard was the descendant of a long line of stubborn, hardheaded Huguenots. When he was confronted with deciding whether the city of Charleston would resist desegregation, his only question was, "What is the

J. Arthur Brown, one of the leading lights of the Charleston and South Carolina NAACP.

law?" Upon learning that the federal courts would rule against the city's segregation policies, he instructed the city attorneys to conclude the suit, which had been pending for some years, as quickly as possible. This was done, an adverse judgment was received, and the golf course immediately integrated without incident.

There were a multitude of lunch counter sit-ins in Charleston in the 1960s, led by J. Arthur Brown, the Reverend James G. Blake, Marjorie Amos, Herbert Fielding, Esau Jenkins, the Reverend I. D. Newman, the Reverend B. J. Glover, and the Reverend Fred Dawson. Despite efforts of die-hard segregationists to circumvent the law or harass the demonstrators, Mayor Gaillard held firm to a policy of law and order in the streets of Charleston. Protestors were not mistreated. Peaceful demonstrations continued. Arrests were made, and the segregation laws were tested in court. The courts threw them all out. Charleston began to become an integrated city once again — without violence or bloodshed.

The 1960s saw the desegregation of the city's public schools. Charleston was once again chosen by civil rights activists as a major testing ground because of its tradition of peaceful change in the area of race relations. Rivers High School became the first integrated public high school in South Carolina in 1963. Dr. Martin Luther King came to Charleston in 1967 and addressed a crowd at County Hall. He argued against the "Burn, Baby, Burn" philosophy of some black activists and urged Charleston's black community to build the community, not destroy it.

In 1969 a major civil rights confrontation — the Medical University strike — took place in Charleston. The university had become (and remains to this day) the largest single employer in the city. A large percentage of the work force was then (and is now) black, and the protestors sought to have the university recognize their union, bargain with their leaders, promote more blacks, and raise wages from $1.30 per hour. The strike was unusual in that organized labor and the civil rights movement cooperated for the first time. At Emmanuel AME Church, Coretta Scott King and Andrew Young of the Southern Christian Leadership Conference addressed a capacity crowd. The National Guard was called out to keep the peace, but the leaders of the strike, Mary Moultrie and Bill Saunders, saw that no breaches of the peace occurred.

The Hospital strike hit a national chord. "The strike of hospital workers in Charleston, S.C., has become the country's tensest civil rights struggle," the *New York Times* editorialized in the first of three editorials on the subject, and warned of the "dangers of a racial explosion." The *Times* praised the coalition

Septima Poinsette Clark was the daughter of a slave owned by the Poinsette family who late in life became one of Martin Luther King's chief lieutenants in the civil rights movement. "Her extraordinary gifts in teaching," Taylor Branch wrote in *Parting the Waters*, "inspired civil rights leaders to put her in charge of the movement's citizenship schools." These were workshops in which Mrs. Clark turned sharecroppers and other unschooled citizens into potential voters. Branch concluded, "Clark was a saint even to many of the learned critics who predicted she would fail."

behind the strike as "rightly angered by the systematic exploitation public agencies were practicing against underpaid black workers." Martin Luther King had been assassinated the summer before in just such a strike in Memphis, and the city was tense during the months the strike continued. Mayor Gaillard and a new police chief, John F. Conroy, later called "Mr. Cool" for the way he handled the crisis, kept a steady hand on the situation and no one was injured.

The strike lasted 100 days and many protestors went to jail, including the Rev. Ralph Abernathy who described the Charleston County jail as "luxurious." Rev. Abernathy wrote in his memoirs, *And the Walls Came Tumbling Down,* "I remembered the Birmingham jail and considered myself fortunate." Although it ended in a compromise, the strike gave the black community a sense that change was possible, and it alerted the white community to the frustrations of the black worker.

Politically, the black community came into its own in the 1960s. With the passage of the Voting Rights Act of 1965, blacks registered to vote in ever greater numbers. Mayor Gaillard integrated Charleston's City Council in the 1960s by running three black aldermen on his slate. In 1970 Herbert Fielding became the first black to be elected to the General Assembly since the 1880s. Lonnie Hamilton became the first black elected to County Council. James E. Clyburn was nominated in the Democratic primary, but lost in the general election. He went on to become the first Human Affairs Commissioner for the state.

Palmer Gaillard, meanwhile, served as mayor longer than anyone in the city's history — 15 years. He was reelected without opposition in 1963 and 1967, but in 1971 Charleston witnessed another of its award-winning mayoral races.

Despite his moderation in handling the civil rights demonstrations of the 1960s and his appointment of some blacks, by 1971 a majority of the black community was dissatisfied with Gaillard. The issues were no longer segregation and integration, but, rather, economic issues and the role of blacks in city government, among others. The Hospital strike had activated the black community, and so, in 1971, Gaillard faced two opponents, one in the Democratic primary and one in the general election. He barely defeated his opponent William Ackerman, a prominent attorney, in the primary. The election was, like some of the old Grace battles, thrown into the Democratic Party Executive Committee and ultimately into the courts. Gaillard survived the general election, too, and went on to serve one more four-year term. But it was clear, after the 1971 election, that politics would never be the same in Charleston.

A Short History of Charleston

The Americanization of Charleston continued unabated from the 1960s to the 1990s. Changing politics matched the changing landscape. With the opening of Interstate 26 in the 1960s, of the second Cooper River Bridge in 1966, and of the North Ashley River Bridge, Charleston became as suburban a community as any in America. The population of the old peninsula city continued to decline: in 1980 there were approximately the same number of people living on the peninsula as there had been in 1850 — about 40,000. But metropolitan Charleston now includes more than twenty separate government entities and towns. Incorporated towns include Sullivan's Island, the Isle of Palms, and Mt. Pleasant, east of the Cooper River; and North Charleston, Hanahan, Goose Creek, and Summerville, north of Charleston. Unincorporated but growing suburbs include James Island and St. Andrew's Parish west of the Ashley. In 1985 Charleston built a new international airport. The Mark Clark Expressway, Charleston's version of the interstate beltway, opened in 1990.

At the same time that many Charlestonians were leaving the old city for the suburbs and newcomers were filling up yet more suburbs, a group of farsighted preservationists realized that the city had a treasure in her old houses and neighborhoods outside the original historic district.

In 1959 the Historic Charleston Foundation, led by executive director Frances Edmunds, began buying old homes in Ansonborough. The plan was to buy the homes, restore them, and sell them to owners who agreed to protect them. The plan worked, and Ansonborough became a great pioneering success in the preservation movement. Since 1959 hundreds of houses have been restored all over the old city. The foundation is presently trying to save houses in Wraggsborough and Radcliffborough. The Harleston Village area has been restored, too. It was given a boost in 1970 when the College of Charleston became a state college again and millions of dollars were poured into expanding it. Numerous houses were restored, and new buildings were built under the leadership of the college's energetic president, Theodore Stern.

The affluence of the 1960s, 1970s, and 1980s led to even greater changes in the old city: the Gibbes Museum of Art was completely restored, and a modern wing was added; the Market area became a specialty shopping area; the old St. Johns Hotel was demolished, and the Mills House — a replica of the antebellum hotel — was built. Houses were painted and restored, many for the first time in years. In short, old Charleston became something she never had been — clean, new, painted, and preserved. For the first time in her history, her streets were clean. Federal urban development grants (in the pre-Reagan years)

McCrady's Long Room, 2 Unity Alley, where the Society of the Cincinnati entertained President Washington, now houses an exclusive club and Charleston's finest restaurant, Restaurant Million.

It is a little ironic that the Union military assault on Charleston during the Civil War was launched from Hilton Head, which is now the most famous of all South Carolina resorts, and that the Hilton Head type of resort — Kiawah, Seabrook, and Wild Dunes — has finally conquered the city.

The prosperity of the 1980s and early 1990s continued to restore the historic district. Two significant reproduction buildings were built: 134 Meeting Street and 200 Meeting Street. The first, an office building, captures the look of Institute Hall where the Ordinance of Secession was signed, and the second, a bank, imitates the once imposing Charleston Hotel demolished in 1960.

Zulu dancers in Charleston: Every spring the Spoleto Festival USA presents attractions from around the world. In the background, the entrance to the College of Charleston.

and the federal tax laws of the 1970s and 80s had an immense impact on downtown Charleston. Historic buildings became the best tax shelters available and a source of funding for development. As a direct result, much of the historic district was revitalized — in particular King Street and East Bay Street south of Calhoun. Americanization has come to downtown Charleston.

Charleston's economy changed dramatically in the postwar era as well. In 1940, for example, 88.7 percent of the county's retail sales occurred within the city limits. Between 1970 and 1976 that fell to 39.8 percent — a striking comment on the effect of suburban malls. Wholesale activity, traditionally located in the East Bay Street area, also declined, though not as dramatically. Manufacturing activity now centers almost entirely in the North Area. Yet dramatic growth has occurred in other areas, mainly in the growth of the Medical University (4,950 employees in 1977), port industries (5,000 employees in 1977), the Citadel, the College of Charleston, the federal government, public schools, and city and county government. Government workers now account for more than half of Charleston's work force.

The other mainstay of Charleston's economy is tourism, which has increased dramatically since 1970. The number of tourists increased by 60 percent from 1970 to 1976, for example. According to the November 24, 1991 *Post and Courier*, the number of tourists visiting Charleston increased from an estimated 2.1 million in 1980 to 4.7 million in 1990. Horsedrawn carriages increased from 37 in 1984 to 99 in 1991. The resort industry, so elusive to John P. Grace and the Cooper River Bridge Company in the 1930s, has arrived on Kiawah Island, Seabrook Island, and, finally, on the Isle of Palms (Wild Dunes).

Mayor for Modern Times: In 1975, Charleston elected a new mayor, Joseph P. Riley, Jr., a young (32 at the time of his election) but experienced lawyer who had served in the General Assembly. For the first time since Reconstruction the Republican party, resurgent in the city since the Goldwater presidential campaign of 1964, ran a serious candidate for mayor, Nancy Hawk. Riley defeated Mrs. Hawk, who received 30 percent of the vote, and two other contenders in the general election. He received about 51 percent of the vote. He was unopposed for reelection in 1979, 1983, and 1991. He was virtually unopposed in 1987, the Republicans running a token candidate.

Mayor Riley took over in December 1975 in the aftermath of a court-ordered single-member district council plan. The mayor promised in his inaugural address that there would be "more blacks and more women in positions of authority," that his administration would fight crime, seek to annex James Island and the Neck, preserve the historic district, and rejuvenate King Street. He called on his fellow Charlestonians to "join with me and with City Council in a new age of tolerance, harmony and creativity."

The Riley administration has been a whirlwind of activity. The city embarked on numerous development projects, the boldest of which was Charleston Place, a development which originated in the Gaillard administration when city planners determined that a major hotel or convention center on the site would revitalize the King Street retail district. Charleston Place and the Omni Hotel (bounded by King, Beaufain, Meeting and Hasell) was financed through a combination of public and private funding, and was designed to bring conventions to Charleston, rejuvenate the central business district, and focus tourism in the Market area. The project was extremely controversial throughout the 1980s when some preservationists fought the original developer and plan (then called "Charleston Center") in the courts, in government and in the political arena. Mayor Riley finally prevailed in his plan for Charleston Place. The Historic Charleston Foundation and other preservation groups joined him in a compromise plan for the development. The modern King Street-Market Street retail district is essentially a product of the late 1970s and 1980s.

The Riley administration has established housing rehabilitation programs north of Calhoun, rehabilitated Hampton Park, built a new waterfront park on the Cooper River, where the colonial wharves had once been located, utilized federal grants to encourage new construction in the center city, and created agencies to bring jobs to the chronically unemployed. And it has actively sought to bring the black community into the city government. Mayor Riley's best known effort in that regard is Police Chief Reuben Greenberg, undoubtedly the South's (if not the nation's) only Jewish black police chief.

The best-known achievement of Riley's administration has been the Spoleto Festival USA. Twentieth-century Charlestonians had long sought to establish a festival to publicize the city. The Azalea Festival, for example, began in 1934 and featured horse shows, golf tournaments, balls, parades, beauty contests, and even a street crier's contest. The festival fell apart about 1953. All during the period that followed civic leaders debated various proposals.

In the 1970s Gian Carlo Menotti, the founder of the Italian Spoleto

Newsweek called Charleston a "Sleeping Beauty" in reporting on the first Spoleto Festival in 1977 and quoted "Charleston's Cagney-like mayor," Joe Riley, who "sees the Spoleto Festival as a chance to restore the city to its status in the 18th and 19th centuries. . . ."

Festival of Two Worlds, came to Charleston at the instigation of Countess Alicia Paolozzi. Menotti had founded the Italian festival in 1957 and wanted very much to bring it to Charleston. But after many preliminary meetings and conferences with civic leaders, it appeared that the festival was not going to succeed. The two original leaders of the coordinating committee resigned. At that point, Mayor Riley asked Theodore S. Stern, a former president of the College of Charleston (who had successfully presided over the great expansion of that school in the 1970s), to head the effort.

The result was the first Spoleto Festival, USA, held in 1977.

Spoleto brought to Charleston the best in the arts from around the world: the Eliot Feld Ballet, the Westminster Choir, *The Queen of Spades, The Consul,* plays, jazz, films, and lectures. In 1978, it brought Zulu dancers, Ballet's Felix Blaska, *Il Furioso, Vanessa,* a Tennessee Williams play, and more jazz, chamber music, dance, music, crafts, lectures, film, and street theater. "This bill of fare," *Newsweek* said of the 1977 festival, "is like nothing else on the international scene, and Charleston is proud of it." The festival got rave reviews on national television and in the major national newspapers. It had, by the 1980s, become a Charleston institution.

Charleston was discovered by the film and television industry in the 1980s. "North and South," a television production of a popular Civil War novel, was filmed in Charleston, much to the delight of some and annoyance of others. The Citadel refused to allow the filming of Citadel graduate's Pat Conroy's novel *The Lords of Discipline,* which created an intense debate about the Citadel's racial policies. A few years later an actual incident of alleged hazing of a black cadet at the Citadel created a national sensation and had Charlestonians wondering whether life imitates art or vice versa.

Charlestonians began to take a broader look at their history during the Riley years. The black members of City Council articulated a need to recognize prominent figures of the city's African-American past. In 1976 a portrait of Denmark Vesey was hung in the Gaillard Auditorium; in 1985 a portrait of the Reverend Daniel J. Jenkins was hung in City Council Chambers. In 1982 a bronze sculpture of Judge Waties Waring was placed in the corner of City Council Chambers overlooking the Federal Courthouse. The cross-town expressway was named in honor of Septima Clark. In 1988 Charlestonians even celebrated the bicentennial of the ratification of the United States Constitution, that "ordinance" once repealed by a different generation of South Carolinians in Charleston. Playing "Battle Hymn of the Republic," the Fife and Drum Corps of the United States Army Band, resplendent in colonial uni-

It is a little-known fact that Lolita once visited Magnolia Gardens outside of Charleston — in the novel, that is.

Nabokov mentions the Garden's advertisement to the effect that children will "walk starry-eyed" through it, "drinking in beauty that can influence a life." "Not mine," Lolita said. Perhaps she was too young.

A Short History of Charleston

forms, accompanied the membership of the South Carolina General Assembly down Broad Street to the Old Exchange Building to mark the occasion.

One of the most destructive hurricanes in Charleston's history, and one of the most costly hurricanes in America's twentieth century history, hit the city near midnight on September 21, 1989. Hurricane Hugo was a calamity to the Caribbean Islands and to the South Carolina Low Country. The Mayor, Joseph P. Riley, Jr., and County Council Chairman, Linda Lombard, took to the local television airwaves to urge Charlestonians to evacuate the city beginning the night before the hurricane hit. At midnight 24 hours before Hugo swept ashore, the traffic was bumper-to-bumper on Interstate 26 and remained so well into the afternoon of the hurricane. Hundreds of thousands of people left the coast for inland areas.

Hurricane Hugo.

By 10:30 p.m. on September 21st powerful winds battered Charleston; the city was pounded by rain and sheets of water; tides rose. By midnight winds were 130 m.p.h. The eye of the hurricane passed over the city at 11:50 p.m. Eighty percent of the homes at Folly Beach were destroyed. The damage was devastating on Sullivan's Island and the Isle of Palms. Nine people were killed in Charleston County. Nearly every house and building in the city was damaged. The *Wall Street Journal* reported the storm as the costliest in history to the insurance industry. The *New York Times* reported $3.7 billion in losses. "Hugo turned out to be the 10th most intense hurricane of the 137 that have made direct hits on the United States coastline since the turn of the century," the *Times* concluded. Hugo totally destroyed 3,785 homes, according to the *News and Courier*, and 5,815 mobile homes; 486,287 insurance claims were filed.

Massive numbers of trees were knocked down by the storm and the loss changed the look of parts of the city and surrounding areas. Power was out for a month in some places. The National Guard was called in and a curfew put in place.

Gradually the city recovered. The Symphony, conducted by David Stahl, played a special concert. Relief poured in from around the nation and the world, both in volunteers and funds. Insurance companies, some of which went out of business because of Hugo, paid out over $3.2 billion in claims. The 105-year-old Hibernian Mutual went under. Ironically, after a couple of years, the city looked better than it did before Hugo. The hurricane speeded the Americanization of Charleston along.

And what of Charleston's tradition of hedonism? Has it disappeared in the process of Americanization? Not at all. The Charleston ethos lives on, more subdued, perhaps, but alive. Referred to as "The Holy City" by the rest of the state, Charleston is still seen as a hotbed of drinking, partying, socializing, and entertainment. Like their ancestors, Charlestonians still prefer a party to any other activity. Is Spoleto a cultural event for Charlestonians? No. It's a good excuse to get dressed up and go out. Is the Jockey Club dead? Well, yes, it died in 1900, but then the Carolina Yacht Club was established in 1883 and it's still going strong. The country clubs, tennis clubs, golf clubs, yacht clubs, beach resorts, restaurants, and nightclubs have multiplied many times over. There was open gambling in downtown Charleston well into the 1950s, and today the incidence of gambling, prostitution, and striptease joints is still high — outside the city limits. In the 1970s the state of South Carolina gave up and passed a "mini-bottle" law that allows the rest of the state to do what Charlestonians have been doing all along — drinking in bars and restaurants.

The St. Cecilia Society is still giving balls, and Charlestonians still flock to the Dock Street Theater. Spoleto has become "the season," and the music is better than ever. The Greek community sponsors the largest party of all — the annual Greek Festival. And the Hibernian Society still hosts a banquet on St. Patrick's Day.

Josiah Quincy, the Boston Puritan, who visited Charlestown in 1773, would probably be just as outraged today.

Selected Bibliography

There appear to me to be more bad books written about Charleston than just about any subject I know. On the other hand, there are some excellent works. I have listed here the major works on each period; I recommend to the reader all of these. Certain books listed under one period frequently contain material on other periods. The literature on slavery is immense; this selection is a good beginning. I wish to acknowledge my debt to all of the authors and publishers listed.

Colonial Era through the Revolution (and General Works)

Bridenbaugh, Carl, *Cities in the Wilderness: Urban Life in America, 1625-1742.* New York: Capricorn, 1955.

_____, *Cities in Revolt: Urban life in America, 1743-1776.* New York: Oxford University Press, 1955.

_____, *Myths and Realities: Societies of the Colonial South.* New York: Atheneum, 1967.

Coker, P. C. III. *Charleston's Maritime Heritage, 1670-1865.* Charleston: Coker Craft Press, 1987.

Crôvecoeur, J. Hector St. John de. *Letters from an American Farmer.* New York: E. P. Dutton, 1957.

Fraser, Antonia. *Royal Charles: Charles II and the Restoration.* New York: Alfred A. Knopf, 1980.

Fraser, Walter J. *Charleston! Charleston! The History of a Southern City.* Columbia, S.C., University of South Carolina Press, 1989.

Jones, Lewis P. *S.C. — A Synoptic History of Laymen.* Lexington, S. C.: Sandlapper Store, Inc., 1971

Leiding, Harriette K. *Charleston: Historic and Romantic.* Philadelphia: J. B. Lippincott, 1931.

Leland, Isabella G. *Charleston: Crossroads of History.* Woodland Hills, Calif.: Charleston Trident Chamber of Commerce/Windsor Publications 1980.

McCrady, Edward. *The History of South Carolina under the Proprietary Government, 1670-1719.* New York, 1897; New York: Russell & Russell, 1969.

_____, *The History of South Carolina under the Royal Government, 1719-1776.* New York, 1899; New York: Russell & Russell, 1969.

Molloy, Robert. *Charleston: A Gracious Heritage.* New York: D. Appleton-Century, 1947.

Ravenel, (Mrs.) St. Julien. *Charleston: The Place and the People.* New York: Macmillan, 1906.

Rhett, Robert Goodwin. *Charleston: An Epic of Carolina.* Richmond, Va., 1940.

Rogers, George C., Jr. *Charleston in the Age of the Pinckneys.* Norman: University of Oklahoma Press, 1969; Columbia University of South Carolina Press, 1980.

Simons, Albert and Samuel Lapham, Jr. *The Early Architecture of Charleston.* Columbia: University of South Carolina Press, 1927 and 1970.

Sirmans, M. Eugene. "The Colony at Mid-Century," in *Perspectives on South Carolina History,* ed. Ernest M. Lander, Jr., and Robert K. Ackerman. Columbia: University of South Carolina Press, 1973.

Wallace, David Duncan. *South Carolina: A Short History.* Columbia: University of South Carolina Press, 1951.

Walsh, Richard. *Charleston's Sons of Liberty: A Study of the Artisans, 1763-1789.* Columbia: University of South Carolina Press, 1959.

Slavery

Bancroft, Frederic. *Slave Trading in the Old South.* New York: Frederick Ungar Publishing Co., 1931.

Jordan, Winthrop D. *White over Black: American Attitudes toward the Negro, 1550-1812.* Baltimore: Penguin, 1969.

Phillips, Ulrich B. *American Negro Slavery.* Baton Rouge: Louisiana State University Press, 1966; originally pub. in 1918.

Stampp, Kenneth M. *The Peculiar Institution: Slavery in the Ante-Bellum South.* New York: Vintage, 1956.

Wade, Richard C. *Slavery in the Cities: The South, 1820-1860* New York: Oxford University Press, 1964.

Wood, Peter H. *Black Majority: Negroes in Colonial South Carolina from 1670 through the Stono Rebellion.* New York: Alfred A. Knopf, 1974.

The Antebellum Period

Capers, Gerald M. *John C. Calhoun: Opportunist.* Gainesville: University of Florida Press, 1960.

Channing, Steven A. *Crisis of Fear: Secession in South Carolina.* New York: Simon & Schuster, 1970.

Eaton, Clement. *The Growth of Southern Civilization, 1790-1860.* New York: Harper & Row, 1963.

Freehling, William W. *Prelude to Civil War: The Nullification Controversy in South Carolina, 1816-1836.* New York: Harper & Row, 1968.

Hofstadter, Richard. *The American Political Tradition.* New York: Alfred A. Knopf, Inc., 1948

Huger, A. R., and D. E. Huger Smith. *Dwelling Houses of Charleston, South Carolina.* Philadelphia, 1917.

Lerner, Gerda. *The Grimké Sisters from South Carolina.* New York: Schocken, 1971.

O'Brien and Molke-Hansen eds., *Intellectual Life in Antebellum Charleston.* Knoxville: University of Tennessee Press, 1986.

Severens, Kenneth. *Charleston Antebellum Architecture and Civic Destiny.* Knoxville: The University of Tennessee Press, 1988.

Severens, Kenneth. *Southern Architecture.* New York: E. P. Dutton, 1981.

Confederate Charleston

Burton, E. Milby. *The Siege of Charleston, 1861-1865.* Columbia: University of South Carolina Press, 1970.

The Civil War at Charleston. Charleston: Post-Courier, 1966.

Cornish, Dudley Taylor. *The Sable Arm: Negro Troops in the Union Army, 1861-1865.* New York: W. W. Norton, 1966.

Current, Richard N. *Lincoln and the First Shot.* Philadelphia: J. B. Lippincott, 1963.

Potter, David M. *Lincoln and His Party in the Secession Crisis.* 2d ed. New Haven, Conn.: Yale University Press, 1962.

Ramsdell, Charles W. "Lincoln and Fort Sumter," *Journal of Southern History,* III (1937), 259-288.

Sandburg, Carl. *Abraham Lincoln: The War Years,* Volume I. New York: Harcourt, Brace & World, 1936.

Swanberg, W. A. *First Blood: The Story of Fort Sumter.* New York: Charles Scribner's Sons, 1958.

Reconstruction

Ball, William Watts. *The State That Forgot: South Carolina's Surrender to Democracy.* Indianapolis, Ind.: Bobbs-Merrill, 1932.

Simkins, Francis B., and Robert Hilliard Woody. *South Carolina during Reconstruction.* Chapel Hill: University of North Carolina Press, 1932.

Tindall, George Brown. *South Carolina Negroes, 1877-1900.* Baton Rouge: Louisiana State University Press, 1952.

Uya, Okon Edet. *From Slavery to Public Service: Robert Smalls, 1839-1915.* New York: Oxford University Press, 1971.

Williamson, Joel. *After Slavery: The Negro in South Carolina during Reconstruction, 1861-1877.* New York: W. W. Norton, 1965.

More Recent Times

Bass, Jack. *Porgy Comes Home: South Carolina after Three Hundred Years.* Columbia, S. C.: R. L. Bryan Co., 1972.

Cooper, William J. *The Conservative Regime: South Carolina, 1877-1890.* Baltimore, Md.: Johns Hopkins Press, 1968.

Duffy, John Joseph. "Charleston Politics in the Progressive Era," Unpub. diss. University of South Carolina, 1963.

Gaston, Paul M. *The New South Creed.* New York: Alfred A. Knopf, 1970.

Hosmer, Charles B. *Preservation Comes of Age.* Charlottesville: University Press of Virginia, 1981.

Key, V. O., Jr. *Southern Politics.* New York: Vintage, 1949.

Lander, Ernest McPherson, Jr. *A History of South Carolina, 1865-1960.* Columbia: University of South Carolina Press, 1970.

Levkoff, Alice F., Robert Levkoff, and N. S. Whitelaw, *Charleston Come Hell or High Water.* Columbia, S. C.: R. L. Bryan Co., 1976.

Tindall, George B. *The Emergence of the New South, 1913-1945.* Baton Rouge: Louisiana State University Press, 1967.

Vlach, John Michael. *Charleston Blacksmith: The Work of Philip Simmons.* Athens: University of Georgia Press, 1981.

Woodward, C. Vann. *Origins of the New South, 1877-1913.* Baton Rouge: Louisiana State University Press, 1951.

_____, *The Strange Career of Jim Crow,* 2d rev. ed. New York: Oxford University Press, 1966.

Yarbrough, Tinsley E., *A Passion for Justice, J. Waites Waring and Civil Rights,* New York: Oxford University Press, 1987.

Index

A Short History of Charleston